Lincoln the Lawyer

Lincoln
the Lawyer

Brian Dirck

University of Illinois Press

Urbana and Chicago

Library of Congress Cataloging-in-Publication Data

Dirck, Brian R., 1965–
Lincoln the lawyer / Brian Dirck.
p.   cm.
Includes bibliographical references and index.
ISBN-13: 978-0-252-03181-6 (cloth : alk. paper)
ISBN-10: 0-252-03181-4 (cloth : alk. paper)
1. Lincoln, Abraham, 1809–1865—Career in law.
2. Lawyers—Illinois—Biography. 3. Presidents—
United States—Biography.
I. Title.
E457.2.D575   2007
973.7092—dc22 [B]   2006025178

For Nathan and Rachel

Contents

Preface   ix

Acknowledgments   xiii

Introduction   1

1. "Great God Almighty"   9

2. The Brethren   33

3. Promissory Notes   54

4. The Energy Men   76

5. The Show   99

6. Death and the Maidens   120

7. Storytelling   138

8. Grease   154

Conclusion   173

Notes   177

Bibliography and Sources   211

Index   221

Preface

This book examines Abraham Lincoln's law practice from his perspective as much as possible, given the limitations of available source material and the historian's craft. In choosing what to include and what to exclude in the narrative, my guiding question has been: what would Lincoln have seen when he practiced the law?

My main area of interest lies in Lincoln studies and the Civil War era, rather than American legal history. I have accordingly avoided extended forays into arcane legal subjects except when necessary to explain the circumstances of a case or some other facet of Lincoln's career. That said, this study does yield useful dividends for American legal history. There are few modern book-length examinations of the lawyers who lived and practiced in Lincoln's day, and many basic questions about them remain unanswered. What was the day-to-day life of a typical lawyer in Civil War–era America? What did he do? What types of cases did he see, and what was the overall shape of a typical legal practice—not just a prominent case or two, but the hundreds of cases that accumulated in an antebellum lawyer's professional experience over time?

Lincoln offers an opportunity to provide answers because his career is so well documented. This was not always the case. For decades historians only had access to the smattering of random law office correspondence and other papers available in Roy P. Basler's *The Collected Works of Abraham Lincoln,* and the accounts of former colleagues, friends and law partners. Altogether this amounted to several hundred documents; not bad for anyone else, but inadequate for historians trying to get a firm grasp on Lincoln's sprawling practice and the many cases it generated. As recently as 1993, Lincoln scholar Mark Neely rightly lamented that, because of the lack of primary source material, "it is not safe to hazard many conclusions about Lincoln's life as a lawyer."[1]

That changed in 2000 with the advent of the Lincoln Legal Papers Project. The work of forty staff members over a fourteen-year period, the project focused on unearthing every available primary source on Lincoln's law practice, searching eighty-eight courthouses, combing through sixty-one manuscript collections (and the catalogs for several hundred others), and contacting nearly fourteen thousand libraries. Thanks to this Herculean effort, we now have information on over five thousand cases litigated by Lincoln and his law partners, much of it newly discovered. Not satisfied with merely collecting all of this material, the Lincoln Legal Papers staff created a state-of-the-art CD-ROM database, complete with computer facsimile images of the original papers, a comprehensive search engine, and a reference section offering everything from statistical overviews of the practice to photographs of the courthouses within which Lincoln practiced. We can now step back and take a broad look at the entire Lincoln law practice: not just well-known and dramatic cases, but lesser known litigation that may have lacked drama but was nevertheless an integral part of his professional life.

Wherever possible I have tried to bring into the story comparative elements from other attorneys plying their trade in other states and regions during Lincoln's time. I have also analyzed some aspects of Lincoln's practice from the perspective of present-day lawyers. This required caution concerning context: a person practicing the law in, say, South Carolina during the 1840s and 1850s often confronted a different legal environment than Lincoln, and practicing the law today is a different matter than it was in his time. But there are enough common referent points from other lawyers, then and now, to shed some interesting light on Lincoln's practice.

So we can learn a great deal about American lawyers and legal history here. But I must stress that, while this is important, it is a secondary concern. This book's center of gravity is not the law. Nor, strictly speaking, is it the law practice itself—that amorphous collection of cases and clients strung together over many years and connected by Lincoln's presence and little else. My purpose here is not to offer a detailed, blow-by-blow account of each case or client, nor do I wish to use Lincoln's court cases to illuminate the history of contract law, family disputes, civil cases or criminal procedures. Rather, the point is Abraham Lincoln, and what the law did both to and for him.

Something important must have been happening to Lincoln during his days as an attorney. With only a brief respite during his congressional term, he practiced law for a quarter of a century prior to his presidency. Or put another way, he held national elected office for 1981 days, which constituted approximately ten percent of his entire life; he was a licensed, active attorney for 8,552 days, or about 40 percent of his life. Many (if not most) of the people he knew prior to the Civil War were connected in one fashion or another to the Illinois bench and bar.

During the daily encounters with humanity generated by his professional career, Lincoln must have formed basic ideas concerning how human beings interact with one another. The lessons he subsequently learned about human nature and about the communities in which he lived surely carried a weight at least equal to lessons he learned in other walks of life. This is admittedly an assumption, but it seems a reasonable one to make—certainly as valid as the notion that Lincoln formed such ideas while the son of Thomas and Sara, the husband of Mary, the father of his children, the friend of his friends, a politician, an intellectual, a Whig, a Republican, a state representative, a congressman, or a president. Lincoln scholars have drawn broad conclusions about the man and his perceptions of the people around him based on all of these roles.

Yet few have tried to do so with Lincoln the lawyer, despite the fact that the law brought him into contact with a greater variety of people and circumstances than any other role he assumed. Not even his long political career gave him quite the same panorama of humanity, in all its glory. "Passions, deaths, reputations, the incessant and shifting forces of life . . . put the stains of their designs on Lincoln's law practice," wrote poet and Lincoln biographer Carl Sandburg with characteristic flair, "Among his clients were descendants of Cain and Abel, of David and Bathsheba, of prodigal sons, of virgins who brought home oil or came empty-handed."[2]

So what exactly did these multiple, colorful encounters do to Lincoln? What would he have concluded about the ways people form communities, share or divide available resources, negotiate or argue over rights and duties, loan and borrow money, hurt and heal one another? For those conclusions would have in turn influenced the ways in which he dealt with his fellow Americans as a politician and later as president.

These inquiries about Lincoln and the nature of American community are the heart of the matter for me, as a student of Lincoln's life and career. In addition to the contribution this might make to Lincoln scholarship, I wish also to advance a broader research agenda, one for which I laid the foundation in my first book, *Lincoln and Davis: Imagining America*. In that comparative study of the two Civil War presidents, I argued that a fundamental American issue, past and present, is not so much our clashing values, but rather differing perspectives on how much we think we need to know about each others' values—our innermost motives, sentiments and feelings—to form the bonds necessary to create communities. I suggested that Lincoln and Davis offered two very different sets of answers; and in Lincoln's case, I argued that much of his sense of community came from his law practice. In *Lincoln the Lawyer,* I want to broaden and deepen this argument by rooting Lincoln's sense of community firmly in his legal career.

In doing so, I hope to illuminate a side of Lincoln heretofore imperfectly grasped by those who see only Lincoln the railsplitting frontiersman, the savior of the Union, or the Great Emancipator. Those are dominant threads in the multihued tapestry of this extraordinarily complex man. Yet there is another thread, more subtle perhaps, but important—that of Lincoln the lawyer, who spent the better part of a lifetime in the quiet pursuit of a relatively ordinary legal career, a career that nevertheless affected him in ways he probably did not fully understand himself. I will try to suggest how this was so, and in the process argue that the law made a deeper and more important impression on Lincoln the man than we might imagine.

Acknowledgments

The acknowledgments section for every book I publish on Abraham Lincoln or the Civil War may well begin the same way, with an expression of thanks to Philip S. Paludan. Currently the Naomi B. Lynn Distinguished Chair of Lincoln Studies at the University of Illinois–Springfield, Phil is my longtime mentor and friend. He offered invaluable advice on this project, and encouragement for my academic career in general. He is a peerless scholar and teacher. I feel fortunate to know him.

Bill Regier, editor and director of the University of Illinois Press, was patient far above and beyond the call of duty as I worked through the various ups and downs of this book. I hope the end product justifies his support. I am also indebted to managing editor Rebecca Crist, copy editor Anne Rogers, and the staff members and reviewers at the University of Illinois Press who helped see this project through to its conclusion.

Lincoln scholars are an extraordinarily helpful group, and I have often been the grateful recipient of their advice and criticism. Cullom Davis read an early proposal and offered valuable input. Dan Stowell likewise offered useful information and advice in the beginning stages. Thomas Schwartz is always generous with his support, and Michael Burlingame allowed me to tap into his nearly inexhaustible supply of knowledge about all things Lincoln. Dennis Boman, Kevin Gutzman, and Gerald Prokopowicz have been sources of friendly criticism and advice.

In 2003 I was privileged to present a paper at the Lincoln Forum in Springfield, Illinois, where I was able to engage in many a delightful conversation about this project with numerous Lincoln luminaries, including University of Houston law professor Mark Steiner. Mark's own book on the Lincoln law practice was released just as my book was entering the final stages of publication; I was thus unable to draw on Mark's work. However, I strongly suspect that, in the end, our two new studies of Lincoln's practice will complement each other well. During a conference at the National Archives in 2004, I benefited from the input and queries offered by James McPherson, William C. Harris, and Nelson Lankford. Bob Willard invited me to speak before the Lincoln Group in Washington, D.C., and I took advantage of his expertise and the comments offered by the audience.

The staff of the Lincoln Library and Museum in Springfield courteously guided me through their voluminous holdings. Cindy Van Horn of the Lincoln Museum in Fort Wayne, Indiana, has always been quite helpful. The guardians of the Lincoln law office exhibit in Springfield gave me a tour of their facility and patiently answered my questions. I am also the lucky beneficiary of the expert staff at Anderson University's Nicholson Library. Barbara Hoover is an indefatigable source of information. Jill Branscum of the Interlibrary Loan Department is also an indispensable resource; she has always cheerfully met even my most obscure requests for books and other materials.

Various friends and colleagues submitted to my musings about Lincoln and his legal career. Professors Michael Frank, David Murphy, Douglas Nelson, Jaye Rogers, and Joel Shrock, my compatriots in Anderson University's Department of History and Political Science, are all congenial and helpful. Jay Antle and Jim Leiker, both professors of history at Johnson County (Kansas) Community College, offered encouragement and support. Kristine M. McCusker, professor of history at Middle Tennessee State University, has (as always) been a tremendous source of inspiration and friendship. Martha Robinson, professor of history at Clarion University in Clarion, Pennsylvania, helped me understand the essential melancholy of Lincoln and (possibly) rabid bats. Charles Zelden at Nova Southeastern University is a cherished friend whose knowledge of American legal history is vast. He has always been willing to lend an ear and a helping hand, with this and other projects.

Inspiration often comes from places outside academe as well. Glen Thurman often serves as a sounding board and source of eminent wisdom. Paula Maris-Roberts, a fine attorney and colleague, is a wonderful lunch companion, a great conversationalist, and a very good friend. My mother and father never waver in their support; pointing out that they have been indispensable seems a vast understatement. Julie's love is a relatively recent (and wonderful) addition to my life, which she has enriched in ways that are at once immensely powerful and difficult to describe.

Finally, I chose to dedicate this book to my children, Rachel and Nathan. They are old enough to know that daddy writes books, and young enough to be filled with wonder at the very idea of a book. Would that we all kept this quality into adulthood. I hope they do.

Lincoln the Lawyer

Introduction

Sometime during the 1850s Abraham Lincoln wrote down a few thoughts on the subject of being an attorney. They read like the early draft of a speech, perhaps one that Lincoln planned to deliver before a local bar association meeting. The editors of the Lincoln Legal Papers plausibly suggest they were intended for an address he gave at Ohio State and Union Law College. Roy P. Basler, editor of *The Collected Works of Abraham Lincoln,* labeled them "Notes for a Law Lecture," but we do not know where or when, or even if Lincoln used them for any such purpose at all.[1]

His private secretaries John Nicolay and John Hay dated the writing of the notes in July 1850.[2] If so, Lincoln wrote them ten years before his election to the nation's highest political office. The presidency would have seemed very far away in the summer of 1850, for Lincoln had at that point entered the nadir of his political career. Following a brief stint in Congress, during which he distinguished himself chiefly by his unpopular opposition to what became a popular war with Mexico, Lincoln returned home to Springfield unable to secure the nomination of his own party for a second term. Even after he actively campaigned for the victorious Whig presidential candidate Zachary Taylor, he was dismayed to learn how little influence he possessed in the party's upper circles. His numerous patronage requests for friends and political allies were ignored. "You overrate my capacity to serve you," he informed a job-seeking fellow Whig in May 1849, "Not one man recommended by me has yet been appointed to any thing, little or big, except a few who had no opposition."[3]

"From 1849 to 1854, both inclusive, [I] practiced law more assiduously than ever before," he later wrote, and admitted that during this time "I was losing interest in politics."[4] This would later change, but throughout his life Lincoln's up-and-down political career offered a contrast to his rock-solid law practice. By 1850 he had been a member of the Illinois bar for fourteen years, and had been involved—as counsel for the plaintiff, counsel for the defendant, formal and informal partner to a lawyer of record, agent, executor, mediator, administrator, and even presiding judge—in well over two thousand cases. Lincoln knew the practice of law well; in fact, it would not be unreasonable to suggest that, in 1850 at least, he knew more about the law than he did about politics.[5]

Those who have read the "notes for a law lecture" usually focus their attention on the document's final paragraph, in which Lincoln addressed the vexing matter of legal ethics and what he called the "vague popular belief that lawyers are necessarily dishonest." Lincoln found this puzzling, pointing out that Americans who denounced lawyers for their duplicity often entrusted those same lawyers with high public office. Nevertheless, he wanted his fellow attorneys to avoid ethical impropriety. "Resolve to be honest at all events," he admonished, "and if in your own judgment you cannot be an honest lawyer, resolve to be honest without being a lawyer. Choose some other occupation, rather than the one in the choosing of which you do, in advance, consent to be a knave."[6]

This is a reassuring passage, lifting Lincoln above the muck of greedy, grasping barristers that inhabit the national imagination. Americans have an ambivalent attitude toward the legal profession, and Lincoln was a dedicated lawyer who almost exclusively earned his living in the courtroom. The "honest lawyer" passage assuages this somewhat, because it ties Lawyer Lincoln directly to Honest Abe, the man whose integrity has become the stuff of American legend. Numerous Lincoln biographers over the years have used the passage for just this purpose.[7] One who quoted the "honest lawyer" passage opined that those "words should be printed upon card-board and hung in every law office in the land."[8]

Lincoln's admirers have always wanted to find moral lessons in his law practice. "He practiced law like a pioneer," wrote one, "with the pioneer ideas of fairness, of justice, of right dealing." Unencumbered by jargon and soulless precedents, Lincoln was able to employ his superior knowledge of the human soul in the courtroom, his "masculine common sense," and his ideas about "what the law ought to be." He was "a simple-minded country lawyer, who loved the children and who understood human nature as he studied it in the uncouth countrymen of a prairie frontier." His "simplicity, his clearness, his knack of happy illustration and his earnestness [were] the complete armor of his legal battles." Early Lincoln biographer Ida Tarbell believed Lincoln actively sought cases involving miscarriages of justice, and "where he saw injustice he was quick to offer his services to the wronged party."[9]

This perspective holds that the only cases worth our attention in Lincoln's practice are those that offer testimony to his ethics and his ideas concerning universal principles of right and wrong. "He had no patience with any conception of the lawyer's function that did not make him the devoted instrument of justice," claimed one account. Another asserted that Lincoln refused to accept money from clients whom he thought might be on the wrong side of justice, and in one instance returned a fee to a client for whom Lincoln had won his case, on the grounds that, morally speaking, the case should have been lost. Still another tale has Lincoln suddenly discovering in the midst of a trial that there was case law supporting his opponent's position, whereby he told the presiding judge, "I have not been able to find any authority sustaining my side of the case, but I have found several cases directly in point on the other side. I will now give these cases and submit the case."[10]

Here was truly—in fact, unbelievably—"an honest lawyer" who separated himself from the pettifogging legalisms of the courtroom by displaying folksy charm and down-home common sense. The image pervades American popular culture. Henry Fonda's performance in the 1939 film *Young Mr. Lincoln* comes to mind, with Fonda's Lincoln accepting his first law book as barter for food and winning court cases with brilliant backwoods moxie. Or there is Norman Rockwell's 1962 print, "Mr. Lincoln for the Defense," showing Lincoln as an antebellum Atticus Finch, standing in the courtroom with tie and suspenders askew, planting his brawny forearm and fist on a nearby table while he scans a legal brief. The fist redeems the legal paperwork, in a way; it suggests a Lincoln who was not co-opted by the legal profession and its dubious ethics. He is still the frontier hero even as he plots his legal stratagems, a man who has always known what it means to work for a living and who speaks the straightforward truths of American democracy.

There is nothing especially wrong with this version of Abraham Lincoln. He was a fundamentally honest man, and he possessed considerable integrity in and out of the courtroom. He wanted no part of what we would today call "ambulance chasing." "Never stir up litigation," he admonished, "A worse man can scarcely be found who does this. Who can be more nearly a fiend than he who habitually overhauls the register of deeds in search of defects in titles, whereon to stir up strife, and put money in his pocket? A moral tone ought to be infused into the profession which should drive such men out of it." These were words Lincoln himself lived by; he was in no sense a shyster.

But he actually devoted only a small section of the "notes for a law lecture" to the issue of professional ethics. Lincoln spent more time discussing the mundane, everyday realities of a lawyer's trade. "The leading rule for the lawyer, as for the man of every other calling, is diligence," he wrote, "leave nothing for to-morrow which can be done to-day." He suggested that "in business not likely to be litigated,—ordinary collection cases, foreclosures, partitions, and the like,—make all examinations of titles, and note them, and even draft orders and decrees in advance." Lincoln pointed out that "this course has a triple advantage; it avoids omissions and neglect, saves your labor when once done, performs the labor out of court when you have leisure, rather than in court when you have not."

Lincoln also discussed lawyers' fees. "The matter of fees is important, far beyond the mere question of bread and butter involved," he wrote, "Properly attended to, fuller justice is done to both lawyer and client." He admonished lawyers to avoid overcharging for their services, and he also felt it was a good idea to receive only a small part of the total fee in advance. "When fully paid beforehand, you are more than a common mortal if you can feel the same interest in the case, as if something was still in prospect for you, as well as for your client. And when you lack interest in the case the job will very likely lack skill and diligence in the performance."

He sounded a similar pragmatic note on the subject of a lawyer's speaking skills. "Extemporaneous speaking should be practised and cultivated," he advised, for "it is the lawyer's avenue to the public." Not just the voting public, or the public of political parties; Lincoln believed a lawyer's speechmaking abilities were also best utilized within the profession as a way to drum up business: "However able and faithful [a lawyer] may be in other respects, people are slow to bring him business if he cannot make a speech." Lincoln warned his fellow attorneys against the danger of mixing political and legal motives by relying too much on the sort of courtroom oratory that could carry a man into the state house or higher political office at the expense of his court cases. "If any one, upon his rare powers of speaking, shall claim an exemption from the drudgery of the law, his case is a failure in advance."[11]

Judging by the amount of time he devoted in his notes to how a lawyer should do paperwork, research cases, and collect fees, Lincoln believed the work habits a lawyer displayed when he walked into his office every morning were at least as important as the more exalted matters of ethics and the national perception of the profession. For him there was a subtle ethical content in the ordinary nuts-and-bolts features of a law practice. A good lawyer forthrightly faced the law's drudgery without frill or complaint.

Here is a somewhat different permeation of the honest lawyer. "Honest," after all, is a word with multiple meanings. It can mean an individual's moral and ethical capacity, which is how Lincoln himself employed the term in his notes for a law lecture. But it can also suggest a clear-cut, no-frills approach to a subject. Lincoln was an honest lawyer in the ethical sense, but he was also an honest lawyer when he wrote of collection cases, foreclosures, paperwork, and the like— "honest" in the sense of being frank, unapologetic and practical.

It is in this realm of Lincoln's life that we will find the realities of Lincoln's life as an attorney; and it is this Abraham Lincoln that usually escapes our attention, because it seems too routine for this far-from-routine man. Standard accounts of Lincoln's life step from one big event to the next—his election to the Illinois statehouse, his congressional career, his debates with Stephen Douglas, and so on—like rocks on a river. The law practice is merely part of the water beneath, quiet and still and rather dull. Tarbell bluntly observed that "most of his cases were utterly un-interesting," and other Lincoln scholars seem to agree, hardly bothering with them at all and preferring to move on as quickly as possible to bigger and better things.[12]

But those "utterly un-interesting" cases, thousands of them, were the everyday stuff of Lincoln's life—and not just his life as a lawyer. The sheer amount of time he spent with his clients, partners, colleagues, and other courtroom participants met or exceeded the time he spent with family, friends, and political allies. Nor was this time so very dull. Stir it around a bit and peer beneath its placid surface, and the Lincoln law practice yields a surprising surfeit of humanity, of small courtroom stories that run the gamut of behavior and situations. They were relatively inconsequential by themselves, perhaps—a debt collected here, a business partnership dissolved there, an unhappy marriage ended, a bit of chicanery like petty larceny or slander avenged, on behalf of clients whose names and problems mean little today.

Take, for example, a fairly ordinary case, plucked from among the thousands that Lincoln litigated: *Tuthill v. Tuthill,* heard in the Woodford County, Illinois, circuit court in April 1850. Gershom Tuthill retained Lincoln and another attorney, Welcome P. Brown, to represent him when he filed for a divorce from his wife Sophia. Sophia failed to appear in court to contest the matter, and the judge—in this case Lincoln's friend and future campaign manager, David Davis—granted Gershom his wish and dissolved the marriage.

The entire proceeding probably could have been measured in minutes. A single witness appeared, one R. T. Capole. The records do not indicate why he appeared or what he said; but given the circumstances, we can infer that he told the court of the circumstances surrounding Sophia's marital wrongdoings—probably her desertion, and testimony perhaps to Gershom's good character. Thanks to the hard work of the Lincoln Legal Papers staff, we can easily access the paperwork generated by *Tuthill v. Tuthill.* It isn't much: entries in the court clerk and judge's docket books, the court's fee book, and the final decree, recorded in the terse language of a nineteenth-century circuit court: "the Court being satisfied that the Allegations in Said Bill are true it is decreed that the Bonds of Matrimony . . . between said Complainant and said Defendant be henceforth dissolved."[13]

Utterly uninteresting? Perhaps. Cases like *Tuthill v. Tuthill* are of course overshadowed by the truly massive Lincoln accomplishments in other, far weightier areas. But if we really want to understand Lincoln as a whole, in his totality, we would do well to look carefully at all those tiny little legal stories and problems that paraded in and out of his professional life down through the years. There were thousands of people, with thousands of cases. For the most part, we know very little about them. Court officials normally recorded only the bare-bones facts of a case in their docket book, and the various other papers that accompanied a normal case—writs, interrogatories, subpoenas, and the like—reveal little about the litigants themselves.

But this isn't necessarily a handicap; in fact, it is an important clue to the nature of Lincoln's legal career. He knew, or tried to find out, as little about these people as possible. His life as a lawyer dictated distance: from his clients, his colleagues, witnesses and other courtroom participants, and often from the social and economic consequences of the cases he litigated. This was partly a function of his own unique personality, partly a function of the circumstances surrounding such a large and variegated practice, and partly a function of the professional standards for lawyers of his time—such as they were.

This distant, careful Lincoln often gets misplaced in the pioneer lawyer image. In fact, the Norman Rockwell–type Lincoln, and much of the subsequent writing on Lincoln as a lawyer, is founded on precisely the opposite assumption; namely, that Lincoln could somehow penetrate the very depths of the human soul when he got people on a witness stand, or in his law office. This assumption is rooted in research and storytelling that focuses on a relatively few big, famous cases and scattered anecdotes from men and women who observed Lincoln at the bar and who, after the war and after Lincoln's apotheosis as a national hero, wanted to illustrate in his legal career the great man's extraordinary honesty, wisdom, and sagacity.

But we should set this approach to one side. Instead, let's try to get at that other honest lawyer: the one who got up every morning, went to work, and learned—in ways quiet yet profound—about how people interacted with one another in a community, about the realities of their conflicts and abrasions, and about what he should and should not expect from the bumptious sea of humanity that crossed his path. By themselves, the cases mean little in terms of Lincoln's overall development; as a whole, they add up to a quarter-century's worth of lessons at the Illinois bar; lessons about the limits and failings of human behavior, the impossibility of truly plumbing the depths of other peoples' souls, and the need to find ways for communities to function without the perceived necessity of such knowledge.

Lincoln knew the work of a lawyer was drudgery: he said as much. But he never complained or apologized. In him we find no trace of that familiar American archetype, the world-weary attorney-turned-cynic who heaps contempt on "the system" and desperately wishes he could find some other way to make money. Lincoln didn't even tell lawyer jokes, or at least none that have survived in the historical record.

And make no mistake: his legal career was his primary profession. Given an opportunity to identify himself, in a brief autobiography he supplied to the *Dictionary of Congress* in 1848, he wrote, "Profession, a lawyer."[14] Terse, unobtrusive, and direct, it was a totally apt description for this honest lawyer and his career.

Chapter One

"Great God Almighty"

What are you studying?"

Russell Godbey spotted Abraham Lincoln straddling a woodpile one day in the early 1830s, reading a book. It was an odd sight in New Salem—an Illinois village peopled by farmers who by and large weren't avid readers—though maybe not so much for Lincoln. People had grown used to seeing him here and there, propped up and down and around at strange angles, nose buried in a newspaper or book.

Godbey was a stout farmer with a goatee he liked to wear long, a clear, open stare, and a large mouth that turned downward at the ends, the combination of which gave him an almost severely frank countenance—the kind of man who did not mince words and did not like nonsense. In a few years he would make a smart sale of some horses to buy livestock, farmland, and eventually a decent degree of prosperity, settling into a comfortable, balanced life: family of eight (four sons and four daughters), church deacon, state militia captain, a gold watch chain curving out from a slowly increasing paunch. The very picture of respectability was Russell Godbey.

He was a Jackson man—like most people in New Salem—where Lincoln was a Whig. Godbey looked, dressed, and acted the part of a middle-class farmer; he would not have been very distinguishable from a half-dozen other Russell Godbeys in the area. Lincoln, on the other hand, stuck out like a sore thumb, a big one, with his towering height, ill-fitted clothes, and curious mannerisms. Still, Godbey liked Lincoln, who was if nothing else a good storyteller. He had once hired Lincoln to survey some land, and later voted for him despite his Whig politics.[1]

"Abe, what are you studying?"

Lincoln looked up, the clouds of concentration drifting away from his eyes as he brought Godbey into focus. He furrowed his thick eyebrows. His head had been deep into the book, and his answer was uncharacteristically terse. "Studying law."

Godbey could not have been more surprised if Lincoln had told him he was reading up on moonbeams. He could only splutter, "Great God Almighty!"

Lincoln went back to his book.[2]

He never really explained why he wanted to become a lawyer. Perhaps—as with so many other aspects of his professional life—the reasons were so pedestrian that they blended almost unnoticeably into the general background of his life. But the decision itself required effort and diligence, and careful thought. As Godbey's reaction suggests, it was not a natural fit.

People become lawyers for many different reasons. Some want to promote social justice, and decide (rightly or wrongly) that the courtroom is the best place to promote, on the practical level of dispute resolution, high ideals of justice and the greater good. "Where can I work where it will make a difference to society?" is a common question posed to modern-day law school deans. Journalist-turned-law-student Chris Goodrich wrote of a friend at Yale Law School in the late 1980s who, when asked why she was there, answered simply, to "help people."[3]

Others think the law is a good place to feed their competitive spirit, which tends to be highly developed in the legal profession. Courtrooms appeal to some aspiring lawyers as a great place to feed their appetite for (relatively) bloodless forensic combat. Goodrich also remembered a fellow student named Denise, who "liked nothing better than a good argument . . . or a bad argument, so long as her position was winning." Recalling his days growing up in tiny Kinsman, Ohio, renowned early-twentieth-century lawyer Clarence Darrow noted that the local tinsmith doubled as justice of the peace and wrote, "I never missed a chance to go over to his shop when a case was on trial. I enjoyed the way the pettifoggers abused each other."[4]

Still others just need a good job. The law "affords fewer prospects of making great estates," Daniel Webster observed, "but more certainty of earning a comfortable living." The law offers a generally lucrative and accessible path to middle- and upper-class comforts for people who might not otherwise bring to their pursuit of happiness anything more than a sharp mind. It was "a means to a livelihood," early-twentieth-century lawyer and poet Archibald MacLeish explained, though he also admitted that "it was a very exciting intellectual discipline." "Law has always meant brains, money, security, and respect," observed one recent law student.[5]

Those who in Lincoln's day contemplated the law as a possible occupation faced somewhat different circumstances. In an age when reform was so tightly wound around religious people and institutions, the profession seems to have attracted relatively few genuine social reformers. Its competitive aspects were appealing to those with high political ambitions: Lincoln's longtime rival Stephen Douglas, for example, who used his relatively brief stint at the bar to propel himself into the state attorney general's seat in 1834, a judgeship, and eventually the U.S. Senate.[6]

Antebellum men could also look upon the bar as a good place to earn money and a respectable living. This was more than just a paycheck; it was an identity within which was bound up much of what it meant to be a man. In Lincoln's father's day, manhood had been a function of farming and agriculture, occupations where the lines between work, home, and family were so blurry as to be almost irrelevant. But by Lincoln's time, the relatively new concept of a profession—a lawyer, a doctor, a minister—involved separating one's way of earning a living from domestic life, and investing the workplace with an extraordinary amount of prestige and importance. "In what condition is a man placed, who has no regular calling or profession?" asked a commentator in 1852, "Certainly without any definite object or aim. He must either give himself up to indolence and ease, or else employ himself about many things and no one thing in particular."[7] Young men knew they were crossing a line into full-blown manhood when they received whatever training was necessary to ply their profession. Future president Rutherford B. Hayes described the start of his legal studies as "enter[ing] the portals of the profession in which is locked up the passport which is to conduct me to all I am destined to receive in life."[8]

What about Lincoln?

If a desire to promote some abstract sense of justice was a motivating factor in Lincoln's pursuit of a legal career, there is no record of the fact. In his "notes for a law lecture," Lincoln mentioned diligence, thrift, industry, and personal honesty as necessary character traits for a good lawyer, but he did not argue for a lawyer's place as an agent of the good society. Lincoln did place moral truth and its pursuit at the center of his political philosophy, speaking of the "moral lights around us" and "the light of reason and the love of liberty in this American people." But as an attorney Lincoln gave no indication that he felt it was his duty to nurture the moral lights in a courtroom.[9]

He did have a competitive nature, as witnessed by his love of wrestling and games: everything from chess to handball.[10] His competitiveness and his legal studies functioned in close proximity to one another, timewise. One neighbor recalled that during that winter of 1831–32, Lincoln "read in the mornings and Evenings—would play at various games."[11] But no one around him seems to have thought him an overly fierce competitor, and no one remarked upon a manifestation in him of a win-at-all-costs mentality. Possibly he came to enjoy the forensic warfare of the courtroom, but he never actually said so; and there is no suggestion that this was decisive in bringing him to the profession in the first place.

Did he pursue the law because he wanted "brains, money, security, and respect"? This comes closer to the mark. In 1832 he was twenty-three years old, and he certainly needed a steady job, for he had already sampled quite a few others—postman, store clerk, land surveyor, raftsman and riverboat worker, and manual laborer of various types—which had combined to lift him just above the edge of poverty. Or, as he put it, all those odd jobs had merely "procured bread, and kept soul and body together." If he ever wanted to become more than the village jack-of-all-trades, he had to find a respectable, steady occupation.[12]

But there were other routes to respectability besides the law for a healthy white man like Lincoln, routes that were less risky and fit better with his pedigree. Farming was the preferred occupation of his neighbors. In terms of accessibility and social approval, it was probably the easiest option. Given his background—"I was raised to farm work"—and lack of education, Lincoln stood a better chance of growing up to be Russell Godbey than he did John Marshall, or even Stephen Douglas. In doing so he might have better availed himself of his family's slim resources. Lincoln's father Thomas was a farmer and a carpenter. Their strained relationship aside, he could probably have obtained sufficient training in woodwork from Thomas to supplement a farming income. It was a common enough arrangement in his day.[13]

The law was, comparatively speaking, a much riskier venture. It was easy to become a lawyer in the 1830s; a little too easy. Lawyers were "as plentiful as blackberries," and Americans routinely complained that the nation had too many of them. "A town that can't support one lawyer can always support two," went a popular joke. More than one lawyer-to-be wondered if some profession with a bit more security might not be in order. Daniel Webster temporarily interrupted his legal studies in 1802 to take up school teaching and pay the bills for his ailing father's household, and during the interlude wondered if it might not be a better idea to remain a teacher, where he was guaranteed at least a steady (if modest) living. "What shall I do?" he wrote a friend, "Shall I say 'Yes, Gentlemen,' and sit down here to spend my days in a kind of comfortable privacy, or shall I relinquish these prospects, and enter into a profession [the law] . . . where my living must be squeezed from penury (for rich folks seldom go to law)?"[14]

Lincoln had no viable alternative like teaching should he falter at his studies, fail his bar exam, prove unable to establish a good partnership, or drum up business. Other American attorneys usually came to the profession with an alternative ready at hand should the law prove a disappointment. Boston's Jeremiah Gridley ran a newspaper while studying for the bar and, like Webster, possessed experience as a schoolteacher. Edward Hatch might have fallen back on his early career as a blacksmith had his legal career proven a failure. Others could move from lawyering to more lucrative fields when the opportunity arose. Illinois attorney Lyle Smith gave up his practice not long after he started because of a fortune reaped in land speculation. Southerner Angus Patterson was able to take over the practice of an older lawyer who was slowly making the transition to cotton planter. Lincoln's future secretary of state William Seward gladly gave up his law practice to start a new career in land development.[15]

In contrast, Lincoln did not have much in the way of viable alternatives. If the law had proven to be a disappointment, he might possibly have returned to the hand-to-mouth odd jobs he managed to pick up here and there in New Salem. He would have probably gotten by well enough, but it was not an encouraging prospect for anyone who wanted to do more than merely "keep body and soul together."

Lincoln might have told himself that his education offered a reasonable security blanket—if he had any. Most other neophyte lawyers possessed the rudiments of a liberal education to help them along. John

Belton O'Neal, for example, briefly attended college before he tried his hand at a legal career. Johnson Hagood was described as a "self-made man" by contemporaries, and he resembled Lincoln in his path to the law—he came from a poor family and once worked as a general store clerk—but even Hagood had gotten some exposure to the classics and what might be called a light liberal education. Although there was no formal professional standard for a prelaw education, most American attorneys agreed that no young man should seek entrance to the bar without a few years of intellectual preparation or, better yet, a college degree. But Lincoln had nothing. He himself later wrote that he hesitated before beginning his legal studies because, as he put it, he "rather thought he could not succeed at that without a better education."[16]

He also lacked the family connections that sometimes guided a beginning attorney. Ebenezer Hoar read law in his father's office in Concord, Massachusetts, before being admitted to the bar in 1839; Thomas Coffin Amory of Boston read for the exam in his uncle's office, as did John Holley of Wayne County, New York, and Roswell Field, who would someday act as Dred Scott's lawyer. An elder family member could also steer a young man clear of the bar if it seemed like a poor choice. Future Confederate president Jefferson Davis was dissuaded by his older brother Joseph—a rich Mississippi lawyer and planter— from a legal career, and chose to attend West Point instead.[17]

Lincoln was in many respects a cautious man. "He was Slow to form his Opinions [and] he was deliberate," according to a friend. At some point he would have carefully weighed the possible risks and rewards involved in a legal career—and there were substantial risks.[18] On the other hand, there were aspects of his life prior to 1832 that, taken together, pushed him in the general direction of the bar. The law may not have been an inevitable fit for this lanky, semieducated farm boy—but Godbey's "Great God Almighty!" reaction wasn't quite fair, either.

Lincoln knew courtrooms at an early age. His father spent a fair amount of time serving on juries, filing deeds, and attending sheriff's sales in Kentucky. Thomas also found himself embroiled in legal disputes involving the title to his land. The state was notorious for its inaccurate land surveys and bad record keeping, and Thomas was taken to court in a variety of lawsuits stemming from conflicting claims to his property. He was sued for an unpaid debt in 1813, and he was subjected to legal action by a carpentry customer who sued Thomas for the "unworkman like manner" in which he prepared some lumber. The case was later dismissed. Even as a child, Lincoln was surely aware of his father's ongoing legal issues; he might have accompanied Thomas to one of his court appearances.[19]

After the family relocated across the Ohio River into an area of southern Indiana known as Pigeon Creek, Lincoln lived about fifteen miles from three different courthouses in Warrick, Spencer, and Perry counties. At various times he found his way into these courts and watched their proceedings from the galleries along with other spectators.[20] He loved a good speech, and courtrooms were a great place to hear an oratorical performance. Frontier Americans enjoyed "court day," described by one contemporary as a combination of "bustle, business, energy, hilarity, novelty, irony, sarcasm, excitement and eloquence." Trial arguments in such circumstances were one of the best forms of entertainment around. "The people came hundreds of miles to see the judges and hear the lawyers 'plead,' as they called it," remembered one Indiana attorney.[21]

When he arrived in New Salem, Lincoln continued his courtroom hobby, attending the proceedings of a village justice named Bowling Green. Green was very fat—"weighing I should think not far from 300 pounds," according to one account. He was also a slob, especially for a judge, presiding over his little legal fiefdom in shirt and trousers, "the latter supported by one tow linnen suspender." Like Lincoln, Justice Green was given to jokes and funny stories, and the two men struck up a friendship. Some in New Salem later suggested that Green acted as an elder father figure and mentor for Lincoln. Lincoln was also said to have argued cases before Green's court, "as there were no Attorneys nearer than Springfield."[22]

Watching (and perhaps participating) in these legal proceedings, Lincoln would have observed the need for close and careful reading, and for competent speechmaking, at the bar. He was good at both. "Lincoln was a great talker [and] a good reader," remembered his cousin, Dennis Hanks. To some of the hardscrabble farmers who were his neighbors, those habits smelled of idleness. "Abe was awful lazy," recalled a farmer, "he worked for me [but] was always reading and thinking—[and I] used to get mad at him." The law was the only profession within his reach where reading and talking were not the mark of laziness, but of merit—that, and politics.[23]

Law made sense in that way, as well, for the legal profession fed

Lincoln's political ambitions. Lawyers, politics, and democracy went hand in hand in Jacksonian America. "It is a fact well known," wrote an antebellum observer, "that the most important offices and public trusts under our government, have been conferred for the most part on members of the Legal Profession."[24] Five years before Lincoln was licensed to practice law, Alexis de Tocqueville famously noted in *Democracy in America* "the authority [Americans] have entrusted to members of the legal profession, and the influence that these individuals exercise in the government." Lincoln himself would later marvel at the "extent confidence and honors are reposed in and conferred upon lawyers by the people."[25] If competitiveness was not one of his marked traits, ambition certainly was; and the law was a surer path upward, and led to higher ground, than farming or some other trade.

So there were both sound reasons and disturbing caveats in Lincoln's decision to pursue a career in the law. It was in retrospect a wise choice—but it was not inevitable. Other possibilities clouded his mental horizon, even as he worked his way through his makeshift legal library. He thought of becoming a blacksmith, for example, and he worried that his "experiment" at becoming lawyer might end in failure even if he passed the bar exam.[26]

But eventually he crossed the threshold from being New Salem's jack-of-all-trades to a focused student of the law. Precisely when or how this occurred is difficult to say. More than likely there wasn't a particular moment. He plugged away at the books, occasionally beset by doubts but persistent nevertheless. At some point his mental scales tipped decisively in favor of the law. At some point it seemed, if not a certain proposition, at least a plausible one—in his own head, anyway, if not perhaps for neighbors like Russell Godbey.

The first law book Lincoln picked up in pursuing his legal career— the book he was in all likelihood reading on that woodpile—was Sir William Blackstone's *Commentaries on the Laws of England,* what historian Daniel Boorstin called the "do-it-yourself guide to becoming a lawyer." Nearly every would-be American attorney started with the *Commentaries,* reading and rereading and memorizing it one chapter at a time. "It was pretty dry work and pretty hard work," remembered one lawyer, "if it had been set to music I think I could have sung it." Angus Patterson of South Carolina read Blackstone to prepare for the bar. Future lawyer (and governor) William Plumer of New Hampshire "read the whole of *Blackstone,* rapidly through . . . and then went over it a second time, with a view to its more thorough comprehension." Albert Pike read only the first volume of Blackstone, but this was enough to get him admitted to the Arkansas bar in 1834. And Blackstone sat on the bookshelves of the famous as well as the obscure. Thomas Jefferson recommended it as required reading for any American lawyer, despite the fact that he hated the *Commentaries'* conservative defense of the British legal system. James Kent, widely considered to be the leading legal scholar of Lincoln's day, claimed he "owed his reputation to the fact that, when studying law . . . he had but one book, Blackstone's *Commentaries,* but that one book he mastered."[27]

The *Commentaries* were all about logic and order. The point was often not so much the actual legal rules and concepts it contained, but also the habits of thought Blackstone imposed on Lincoln and other law students. "In studying Blackstone's 'Commentaries,' the object should be twofold—legal information and mental discipline," noted Rutherford B. Hayes, "and success in the attainment of one of these ends implies success in the other."[28] A lecturer at Oxford University in the 1750s, Sir William's avowed purpose in writing the *Commentaries* was to make of the law a rational thing, "to be cultivated, methodized, and explained."[29] Thumbing through its pages, Lincoln found in the *Commentaries* carefully delineated rules for everybody from kings to commoners, and how they might go about buying, selling, marrying, giving birth, dying, divorcing, voting . . . engaging in nearly any imaginable form of human behavior.

Lincoln read more than Blackstone, although it is difficult to discern just what he read and when. We can, however, hazard a few guesses. He studied Joseph Chitty's *A Treatise on Pleading, and Parties to Actions, with Second and Third Volumes, Containing Precedents of Pleadings, and an Appendix of Forms,* or Chitty's *Pleadings,* as nearly everyone called it. Chitty was a workbook designed to teach attorneys the differences between the various types of remedies they would seek in court for different clients and their needs. There was a different remedy for every type of lawsuit—assumpsit, debt, covenant, detinue, case, trover, replevin, trespass, and ejectment—each with its own wording that had to be followed with utmost precision, lest it be tossed out of court. Lincoln had to know when to file a writ of trespass, and when to file a writ of trespass on the case (Chitty devoted most of chapter two to this matter), and how to word each one accordingly. Victory or defeat could often hinge on the correct phraseology. "The action of trespass only lies for injuries committed with force," Chitty explained in a typical passage, and "the words *contra pacem* should uniformly accompany the allegation of the injury." Chitty's *Pleadings* was packed with such observations and advice, all written in an erudite prose that managed to be both spare and dense at the same time. Lincoln would have found Chitty a real chore to read. Yet it was information that was absolutely vital for any attorney.[30]

He also picked up a copy of Joseph Story's treatise on *Equity Jurisprudence,* though he must have done so some time after he read Blackstone (Story's book was published in 1835). Equity was one of the more arcane concepts Lincoln confronted in his studies. A branch of the English legal system with roots in the medieval era, equity law was a complex set of legal rules based on general principles of justice and fairness—"equity," in other words—as opposed to the common law's more precedent-oriented approach. "In the most general sense, we are accustomed to call that Equity, which, in human transactions, is founded in natural justice, in honesty and right," Story wrote. Over time, the English system had developed common law and equity as two separate sections of the law, each with its own distinct guidelines and rules; common-law courts, for example, could only require payment of money as a legal remedy, whereas equity courts possessed a wide variety of remedies.[31]

The distinction between equity and common law was transferred, more or less, into the American legal system, albeit with local variations and exceptions. Most American courts possessed some version of equity jurisprudence that required lawyers like Lincoln to become familiar with both the general philosophy of equity and its unique forms of pleading and argument. Story's writings on the subject were meant to do just that. Lincoln would have found in Story's *Commentaries on Equity Jurisprudence* a detailed history and explanation of the English and American equity law systems. Story also explained the differences in equity among actual, positive, and constructive fraud; the equity remedies for accidents, mistakes, and errors (including, for example, the well-known maxim *ignorantia legis neminem excusal,* or, as Story put it, "ignorance of the law will not furnish an excuse for any person"); as well as the equity rules for dower rights, business partnerships, securities, property boundaries, and rent.[32]

Lincoln also read the *Revised Statutes of Illinois,* and he was able to look at the four volumes of James Kent's widely read *Commentar-*

ies on American Law, published between 1826 and 1830. There were also lesser known works that Lincoln would have found useful: Nathan Dane's *General Abridgement and Digest of American Law,* or perhaps Zepheniah Swift's older *Digest of the Laws of Evidence in Civil and Criminal Cases* and *Treatise on Bills of Exchange and Promissory Notes.* The latter would have been especially valuable, given the large numbers of cases he would eventually handle involving debt collection.[33]

Although books were affording Lincoln an entrance portal into the law, he obtained other, more practical experience as well. James and Nancy Cox asked him to write the deed for their sale of 175 acres to Matthew Marsh and Charles J. Clark. He did the same thing for Isaac and Jane Colson when they sold forty acres of Sangamon County land to Matthew Young, as well as Jesse and Christina Baker's sale of 120 acres to James Eastep. And there were other legal tasks available. In December 1835, Lincoln dug through the records of the state land auditor's office at Vandalia to retrieve the sales history of some real estate for Thomas Nance. When Alexander Ferguson decided to sell his ferry in New Salem to Alexander Trent, he had Lincoln draw up the bill of sale.[34] Modern lawyers call this "boilerplate" work, in which they use readily available forms to dot the i's and cross the t's of simple business transactions. Lincoln would not have found earning a few cents, a meal, or maybe just a pat on the back by doing "boilerplate" particularly taxing.[35]

Lincoln also acquired the same sort of little courtroom experiences available to everyone else in his neighborhood. While living in New Salem, he was called in Justice Green's court to serve as a character witness for a man named Peter Lukins. Lincoln wasn't much help. "He is called Lying Peat [*sic*] Lukins," Lincoln declared. He served on several juries, and in 1832 he was called to serve as a witness for John Close, Jr., who sued to collect money owed him by John Ritter. Two years later he became peripherally involved in an ugly incident concerning an accusation of attempted rape leveled against three men by a woman named Sally Marshall. Lincoln, along with several others, signed documents guaranteeing that one of the defendants, Thomas Edwards, would appear in court (the state's district attorney later dropped the matter).[36]

Lincoln spent nearly four years this way, reading and picking up odd jobs here and there to make ends meet while he made his slow climb toward the bar. Four years was a long time—longer than most law students in his day. Texas attorney William Pitt Ballinger, for example, took a little less than three years to complete his studies in his uncle's Galveston office, and this included a brief stint of military service during the Mexican War. Lincoln's future secretary of treasury Salmon Chase studied for about two years in a Washington, D.C., law office. During his examination, the judge in charge suggested he study one more year, but eventually relented and admitted him to the bar. Generally speaking, two to three years worth of study was the norm.[37]

Some of Lincoln's delay can be ascribed to his intellect. He was intelligent but not quick, and "Slow to form his Opinions." He was blessed with excellent memory skills but took a while to absorb and keep information, particularly of the dense, technical sort found between the covers of law books. People saw him copying whole sections of books to jog his memory along. Lincoln "always seemed to be doing Something Coolly and Slowly so," noted a friend. He was well aware of this trait in himself. "I am slow to learn and slow to forget," he said, "my mind is like a piece of steel, very hard to scratch anything on it and almost impossible after you get it there to rub it out."[38]

It took time and mental elbow grease to do all the scratching required of a law student; and life intruded, as well. In April 1832, coming out of his first winter's worth of slogging through Blackstone, Lincoln volunteered to serve in the state militia during the Black Hawk War, earning him little military experience—"I had a good many bloody struggles with the musquetoes," he joked—but many new acquaintances among his fellow militiamen, including his future law partner, Stephen Logan. Lincoln also had his political career to look after. "When the Legislature met, the law books were dropped, but were taken up again at the end of the session," he later wrote. No doubt the law books were sometimes dropped for other reasons, as well.[39]

But they were always picked up again, and it was Lincoln, by himself, who did the dropping and the picking up. This was most unusual. The vast majority of law students in his time studied under the tutelage of somebody: a relative, friend, or an older attorney who for whatever reason had taken an interest in apprenticing someone into the profession. James Edward Henry of South Carolina, for example, was given law books, room, and board by an elder attorney while completing his studies. Robert Crittenden of Kentucky studied under his older brother, John J. Crittenden, before moving to Arkansas. Robert H. Adams, a Virginian, pursued a Lincolnian route to the bar by studying alone, but the feat was so remarkable that a colleague called him a "rare original genius" and observed that it was truly amazing Adams could create a decent career for himself "unfriended and undirected."[40]

This is not to say that Lincoln studied entirely in a vacuum. He made frequent visits to Springfield, twenty miles away, where he met lawyers plying their trade or, like himself, serving in the state legislature. By 1836 he was a regular visitor to John Stuart's law office, located on the second floor of Hoffman's Row, a line of two-story brick buildings located a block away from the main square. It wasn't much of an office: mismatched chairs, a table, and a bookshelf, likely permeated with the smell of tobacco and piles of musty papers. But it was well located—right over the county courthouse on the first floor, and in the middle of what was becoming a bustling business and government district in Springfield.[41]

At some point in 1836 Lincoln felt prepared enough to try formally entering their company by taking the bar exam. Unfortunately, there is no record of who administered the exam, what sort of test it was, or how comfortably Lincoln passed it. Lincoln himself contributed to this blank spot. In an 1859 campaign autobiography, he did not specifically mention passing an exam, skipping in his narrative from the period in which he studied the law to his next political milestone, election to Congress, in 1846. In a second, longer autobiography written during the presidential campaign of 1860, Lincoln did not mention a test, either, writing only that "in the autumn of 1836 he obtained a law license."[42]

We do know that it was an oral, not written exam (no state required a written test to become a lawyer until Massachusetts did so in 1855), administered by a lawyer or judge appointed to the task by the court.[43] In fact, the laws of Illinois in 1836 did not require any test for lawyers, beyond certification from a county court that the person in question possessed "moral character." This was done for Lincoln on March 24, when the clerk of the Sangamon County circuit court, William Butler, squeezed into the docket book—between *Blankenship v. McGenty* and a probate case for James D. Henry, deceased—a single sentence indicating the court's certification that Abraham Lincoln was "a man of good moral character."[44]

The proceeding has a quaint, old-school quality, especially from the perspective of modern times. The idea of giving a man who had read a few books and answered a few questions the imprimatur of "professional attorney" seems absurd. It was so even to Lincoln's contemporaries. As one antebellum humorist quipped, "a shed for an office procured, the next thing [for an aspiring attorney] was a license; and this a Circuit court Judge was authorized to grant . . . in a manner which shall ever inspire gratitude—he asking not a single legal question; an eloquent silence which can never be appreciated except by those who are unable to stand an examination." Another jokester penned a story about a judge examining a prospective lawyer with a few pertinent questions, thus prompting the following exchange:

> "Now, are you aware of the duty you owe me?" [the judge]
> "Perfectly."
> "Describe it."
> "It is to invite you to drink."
> "But suppose I decline?"
> [Candidate scratching his head]—"There is no instance of the kind on record in the books. I cannot answer the question."
> "You are right . . . let's take the drinks, and I will sign your certificate."[45]

But even if Lincoln was tested in a formal way, this did not matter as much as we might think. What did matter, what pushed Lincoln across the threshold of the legal profession, was not a modern-style piece of paper, a license he could frame and hang on his wall, backed by a professional legal hierarchy. It was, rather, the informal approval of other lawyers—not lawyers organized as a vast profession, but rather lawyers as individuals, who met Lincoln face-to-face and oriented their judgments according to their own lights. Godbey's "Great God Almighty!" reaction to Lincoln's law aspirations was amusing; if real lawyers reacted to Lincoln in the same way, that wouldn't be funny at all.

From this point of view, Lincoln's certification as a "man of good moral character" was not a trivial matter. It was a serious sizing up of the man by other men who saw this certification as a way to guard their profession's reputation. "Before an applicant is admitted to the Profession, he is required to procure a properly authenticated certificate from the County Court, that he is a man of 'probity, integrity, and good moral character,'" lawyer W. H. Ward proudly pointed out, "Thus jealous is the Legal Profession of its own honor, and the obligations of moral principle."[46] But certification of Lincoln's moral character was just the beginning. Before he could become a full-fledged lawyer, Lincoln had to find a way to actually earn a living in the courtroom.

Modern lawyers have a wide range of options available to them when they reach this point. A few enter academe, serving as law professors in what are generally thought of as prestigious positions. Others become public service professionals, working for government regulatory agencies. Still others are hired as consultants in business and industry, employing their legal expertise in deciphering government regulations or finding ways for their companies to avoid lawsuits. Some begin climbing the demanding but lucrative career ladder in a large urban legal firm, advancing from associate to partner while handling increasingly large and complex cases for ever-larger retainers and fees. At the other end of the spectrum are attorneys who (for far less money than their Wall Street counterparts) take advocacy tasks for the poor and underprivileged, employed by organizations that represent disadvantaged segments of society. Again, the vast professional structure of modern law comes to their aid, providing the scaffolding by which new lawyers can build their particular futures.[47]

Almost none of these options was available to Lincoln. Since there were very few law schools, there was practically no such thing as a law professorate. The government regulatory agencies that employ many modern lawyers did not exist. Most antebellum businesses were too simple in structure to hire lawyers as consultants or in-house counsel; there wasn't enough litigation or regulation to justify the expense. Big law firms that could offer an easily identifiable, self-contained career path were few and far between, and there were no legal advocacy organizations for the poor. Occasionally an attorney could find an interesting little niche: a Louisiana lawyer named Carlton, for example, earned a living translating civil law treatises from Spanish to English; New York lawyer Peter van Schaack opened a small law school after blindness made it impossible for him to practice. But such strategies were more the exception than the rule.[48]

Most lawyers in Lincoln's day were left to their own devices. This usually meant trying to create from scratch a general legal practice. Some rookie lawyers went at it completely alone; but this was hard. A safer option was finding a partner, someone who had some connections. If he had read for the bar exam in an established law office and was fortunate enough to have established a good relationship with his mentor, a new lawyer might be able to slide into an already established practice, one he had likely observed firsthand while poring over books or doing clerk duties. Or perhaps he had made some connections in the legal community while running errands or doing boilerplate work. Or he had a school friend or family member ready at hand who was also an attorney and would be willing to help.[49]

Up to this point Lincoln had always been short on partners, in multiple senses of the word. He had made his way through life knowing nearly everyone but enjoying a partnership-style collaboration with no one. Now, however, luck and his militia service with John Stuart during the Black Hawk War intervened.

Stuart was an established Springfield lawyer, but politics was his first love. A Southerner from the prominent Todd family of Kentucky, he was tall and handsome, his manners polished almost to the point of excess—he liked to greet people with a sweeping, low bow—and he moved fluidly in Springfield's high society. Stuart wanted to "network," and he wanted to become a Southern-style gentleman of affairs in Illinois.[50]

By 1837 he had decided to part company with his first partner, Henry Dummer. Dummer was a hardworking Yankee from Maine who at first hadn't thought much of Lincoln when he came by to borrow books and pursue his unlikely law career. "He was an uncouth looking lad," Dummer later remembered, with an "insane love in telling dirty and Smutty stories." Still, Dummer had to admit, "what [Lincoln] did say he said it strongly—Sharply."[51]

It is hard to tell just why Dummer and Stuart parted ways. Maybe Dummer had concluded there were greener pastures than Springfield in which to pursue his practice. But it is also likely he quit the partnership because of Stuart's preoccupation with politics at the expense of the firm's business.[52]

Whatever the reasons, it was a decision that probably did not involve much rancor or ill-feeling. "Partnership" in the antebellum bar connoted a relationship that was quite a bit more casual than today's more ordered professional and business enterprise. Law partners in Lincoln's day could be close—they could be family members, in fact— or they could be little more than acquaintances who shared an office and divided the firm's earnings. There were no binding rules for how partners conducted themselves. It was not uncommon for a lawyer to have multiple partnerships, advertising in one town as a partner with one of that town's barristers, and functioning in a similar fashion in another part of the state.[53]

Lincoln jumped at the chance to partner with John Stuart, and with good reason. He could avoid those difficult first months of a newly minted lawyer's professional life, stepping right into an established office with a clientele and cases readily at hand. Politically it was not a bad idea, either. He and Stuart had become allies in the statehouse as part of the Whig faction known as the "Long Nine" (because of their members' unusual height), and Stuart was well connected with many of the same people whom Lincoln would depend on to secure his political future in the party. Sharing an office with Stuart also meant sharing his contacts and remaining privy to the political news and information that floated around Stuart's presence. Stuart's motives are a bit more difficult to fathom. In the end he was probably motivated, as was nearly always the case, by politics. Lincoln was becoming a man of some influence among Springfield's Whigs. He was not a political powerhouse, but he was a useful contact for an ambitious man like Stuart.[54]

The new firm of Stuart and Lincoln advertised their existence in the *Sangamon Journal* on April 15, 1837. Lincoln's first known case as a licensed attorney came three months later, when he represented David Wooldridge in the Sangamon County circuit court over a dispute involving Wooldridge's failure to pay James P. Hawthorn for breaking the sod on thirty-eight acres of farmland, and also for failing to honor an agreement whereby Hawthorn could use part of the land to raise crops. The parties eventually reached a settlement out of court.[55]

The judge in *Hawthorne v. Wooldridge* was thirty-seven-year-old Stephen Logan, a Kentucky-born member of the Springfield legal community. Like Stuart, Logan brought a formidable array of qualifications to the bar, having studied in the office of his uncle, a judge, at the relatively young age of seventeen. He built a solid reputation in his home state before moving to Springfield, where in 1835 he achieved a judgeship in his own right.

When Lincoln appeared before Judge Logan, he saw a mixture of intellectual precision, Scotch irascibility, and backwoodsy etiquette. The judge must have been something of a terror to younger members of the bar. He had a well-deserved reputation as a grouch, "snappy, irritable [and] fighting like a game fowl." He was also an exacting taskmaster, insisting that every writ and decree adhere to strict standards

of wording and punctuation. On the other hand, he checked the lawyers' homework while surrounded by piles of white pine shingles and
a gunnysack full of shavings, for he was an inveterate whittler. Logan
was also surpassingly ugly, a smallish, wizened little man whom some
likened to a gnome. In the charitable words of a fellow lawyer, Logan
"discarded the ornamentations of dress" and was handicapped by the
fact that "nature had not given in his appearance any indication of
his talent." Temperament and pine shavings aside, quite a few people
regarded him as possessing the sharpest legal mind in the state.[56]

The firm of Stuart and Lincoln lasted the same length of time as
Stuart and Dummer—about four years. During that period, Stuart's
political fortunes waxed strong. In 1838 he performed the relatively
rare feat of besting Stephen Douglas in a state election, beating the
"Little Giant" for a congressional seat by a mere thirty-six votes out
of thirty-six thousand cast. Two years later Stuart was reelected; he
would serve in Washington, D.C. until 1843. He had become one of the
leading members of the state's Whig party, a twice-elected congressman and a politician to be reckoned with. His heart and head were in
Congress, not the office on Hoffman's Row.[57]

In the meantime, Lincoln learned on the job. Stuart was not even
in the state most of the time. The firm did have cases—quite a few of
them, in fact. Lincoln handled contract disputes, debt collection, partnership dissolution, probate, assault and battery, larceny—just about
anything a general practice could throw at him. Ensconced in their
little office, slouched on a buffalo robe chair and sometimes sleeping
in a bed stuck over in one corner, Lincoln found himself puzzling over
unfamiliar areas of the law, often as alone as when he puzzled his way
through Blackstone on a New Salem woodpile.[58]

Even when he wasn't distracted by politics, Stuart was indifferent to
the detail work of the law, and this rubbed off on Lincoln, who while
partnered with Stuart was sometimes inexcusably sloppy. "We have
been in a great state of confusion here ever since the receipt of your
letter," he wrote to a fellow lawyer named Levi Davis in March 1838.
Davis had inquired about a land title case involving Lincoln and Stuart,
and one of Davis's clients. Lincoln could only reply that "we beg your
pardon for our neglect in this business; if it had been important to you
or your client we would have done better." Given that Davis was a leading member of the Springfield bar—was the state auditor, in fact—this
must have been an embarrassment for everyone involved.[59]

He also had not shed his bumpkin image. When Stuart sent Lincoln to represent the firm in a case involving an Englishman named John W. Baddeley, Baddeley thought Lincoln looked like "a country rustic on his visit to the circus" and found another lawyer.[60] Incidents like this cost the firm—which wasn't earning a great deal of money in the first place. Five- and ten-dollar retainers were the rule, and in one case their client paid part of his fee by furnishing a fifteen-dollar coat to Stuart.[61]

Lincoln hit a low point during the winter of 1840–41, suffering bouts of nervous depression (what physicians of the era called "hypochondriasis") that left him for a time unable to attend to his affairs in the legislature and in the practice.[62] His problems stemmed from a variety of sources—difficulties with his courtship of Stuart's cousin Mary Todd chief among them—but some of his depression may also have been caused by professional frustrations. When he and Stuart corresponded they focused almost exclusively on politics—when they corresponded at all. "I have had no letter from you since you left [for Washington, D.C.]," he complained to his partner in January 1841.[63] In April they agreed to dissolve their partnership.

At this point, good fortune again smiled on Lincoln. Just as Stuart bowed out, Logan stepped in. During the four years that had elapsed since Lincoln tried his first case in Logan's courtroom, the judge had resigned his position on the bench (he found the pay inadequate) and reentered private practice. He partnered for a while with Edward Baker, Lincoln's good friend (Lincoln named his second son in honor of Baker) and another ambitious Whig lawyer. But Logan came to feel that Baker was too careless with money. Logan "was industrious and very thrifty," to the point of miserliness, traits that—combined with his steely-eyed legal mind and stern personality—likely made him a difficult man with which to share an office.[64]

Nevertheless, many a lawyer would have tolerated Logan's foibles to become his partner. He was a former judge with political influence, and he already possessed an extensive practice. Stuart enjoyed virtually his pick of the Springfield bar—and yet he chose Lincoln. Some wondered why. Four years into his career, Lincoln had proven competent but not spectacular. There were better attorneys in Springfield, men with more education and more experience.

But Logan had seen a lot of Lincoln in four years. He tried numerous cases in Logan's courtroom before Logan resigned, and after the judge returned to the bar they appeared on opposite sides a number of times.[65] They also acted as cocounsel in a high-profile 1838 case, *People v. Truett,* in which they defended Henry Truett, accused of murdering a local doctor and minister named Jacob Early over a political dispute (the two men were rivals in the Democratic Party). Senior counsel Logan thought enough of Lincoln's speaking abilities that he allowed him to deliver the closing argument to the jury. Lincoln gave what Logan praised as a "strong and sensible speech." The jury found Truett not guilty by reason of self-defense.[66]

Logan settled on Lincoln largely because of Lincoln's speaking abilities. "Both he and Baker were exceedingly useful to me in getting the goodwill of juries," he wrote. Logan wanted a partner whose speaking abilities could complement his research and reasoning talents. Logan had the technical expertise in the law that Lincoln lacked; Lincoln was a more appealing and winsome trial lawyer. It was a sound foundation for partnership.[67]

On a practical level, their firm was quite successful. Logan and Lincoln lasted roughly the same amount of time as Stuart and Lincoln, but tried more cases in a wider variety of venues. With Logan, Lincoln saw more appellate cases in the state supreme court and the U.S. federal court. He also earned more money, enough to feed a growing family and settle into a comfortable home within easy walking distance of their office. Lincoln had to be pleased; he was not a rich man, but he was earning a steady, consistent living.

Some saw Lincoln's partnership with Logan as his rather belated opportunity to read for the law under the guidance of a teacher in the traditional manner, as perhaps he should have done before he was granted a license. There may be something to this, though hard evidence is lacking.[68] Logan did correct many (though by no means all) of Lincoln's slipshod office habits. He cleaned up the wording in Lincoln's briefs, and he offered an example to Lincoln of the value of prudence and preparation. But he does not seem to have been patronizing in his efforts, and on the whole he admired Lincoln's work ethic and tenacity. His "knowledge of the law was very small when I took him in," Logan recalled, but "he would work hard and learn all there was in a case he had in hand. . . . He would get a case and try to know all there was connected with it; and in that way before he left this country he got to be quite a formidable lawyer."[69]

Lincoln seems to have valued Logan's advice. He apparently deferred to Logan's judgment as the senior partner, allowing him to draft the firm's pleadings. Logan could be a prickly fellow, so perhaps Lincoln learned how to "handle" his partner, though again the historical record is silent on this point. Whatever the case may be, Lincoln admired Logan's legal skills, telling fellow attorney Usher Linder that he hoped to someday become as good a lawyer as his partner.[70]

Given its prosperity and the partners' cordial relations, Logan and Lincoln might have continued for a long time. But in 1844 Logan told Lincoln that he wanted to form a new partnership with his son David. "So we talked the matter over and dissolved the partnership amicably and in friendship," Logan remembered. By then, Logan had gotten to know Lincoln well, and he shrewdly observed that "Lincoln was perhaps by that time quite willing to begin on his own account." Always the junior partner, Lincoln by 1844 had seven years' experience in the courtroom, many friends and contacts, and the self-confidence of a man who no longer worried about whether he could make a go of it as a lawyer. Logan sensed that Lincoln had outgrown his junior partner status. The next time he would place his name at the top of the shingle.[71]

Stuart and Logan gave Lincoln a good set of guidelines on how to select a law partner. First rule: choose someone whose skills complement, rather than duplicate, your own. Lincoln did not need someone who was connected politically, or whose chief skill lay in persuading a jury. He could handle those matters himself. Second rule: choose someone whose strengths cover your weaknesses, and vice versa. Lincoln was aware of his own lack of formal education, and knew that, however hard he might work, deep legal research and the finer points of drafting pleadings and writs would likely never be his strongest suit. Third rule: personal regard and close friendship is nice, but not necessary. And if a senior partnership is what you want, pick somebody new to the profession who doesn't mind being the junior partner.[72] Contemplating this, Lincoln would have only needed to look across the room, where sat twenty-six-year-old William Henry Herndon: "Billy," to most people.

Herndon had just completed his studies for entrance to the bar in the Logan and Lincoln office. According to Billy, Lincoln ran up to him breathlessly one morning in 1844, "and with more or less agitation [told] me he had determined to sever the partnership with Logan." Herndon claimed to have seen this coming, but he did not foresee Lincoln's offer of a partnership. "I confess I was surprised," he wrote,

"I was young in the practice and painfully aware of my want of ability and experience." This did not matter to Lincoln, who "remarked in his earnest, honest way, 'Billy I can trust you, if you can trust me.'" Herndon recalled that Lincoln was forever after loyal to him. When other lawyers tried to undermine him by playing up Herndon's weaknesses, Lincoln would reply, "'I know my own business, I reckon. I know Billy Herndon better than anybody, and even if what you say is true I intend to stick by him."[73]

It is a typical Herndon tale: dramatic, suspect in the details (dissolution of the partnership was Logan's idea), sentimental and a little overwrought, and most of all placing Billy in a favored position in Lincoln's heart. During their twenty-one-year partnership, Herndon thought he knew Abraham Lincoln better than any other man. "I believe we understood one another perfectly," he declared.[74] They did have in common the fact that they were both born in Kentucky (like half the Springfield bar, it seems) and shared an affinity for Whig politics.

But there the similarities ended. Herndon was raised in a comfortable middle-class household in Springfield and briefly attended Illinois College in Jacksonville. He left after only one year and returned home, where a temporary falling out over politics with his father caused him to take a room and a clerking job with Springfield general store owner (and Lincoln's close friend) Joshua Speed. While at Speed's, Billy developed a reputation as a good conversationalist and a passionate political buff. He also developed an interest in the law, and in 1842 went to work at Logan and Lincoln, clerking and studying Blackstone and company for the bar exam.[75]

Herndon had his share of faults. He had a loose-cannon quality that could make him unpopular when he spoke his mind, which was often and on nearly every subject. He was also an alcoholic. But he was sober most of the time, and as a rule he was hardworking, a talented legal researcher and draftsman. They were comfortable together, finding between them an eccentric sort of compatibility, like dancers swirling to different routines while somehow missing each other's toes. Throughout his life, Lincoln avoided partners when he could, preferring glancing ricochets with the many to deeper penetrations with the few—or the one. But when he had to create a partnership—with Herndon, with Mary, and later with men like William Seward, Edwin Stanton, and Ulysses S. Grant—he had a knack for forging relationships whose surface peculiarities raised eyebrows but that worked on some sort of subterranean, partly undetectable level. And so it was with William Herndon.[76]

Lincoln seems to have felt a deeper sense of personal attachment to Billy than either Stuart or Logan. He once bailed Herndon out of a jail after a drinking spree, and he tolerated Herndon's various eccentricities without complaint. Herndon "admitted that his conduct frequently was an embarrassment to Lincoln," according to Herndon's friend Jesse Weik. But, Billy added, "I must insist that in his treatment of me Mr. Lincoln was the most generous, forbearing, and charitable man I ever knew."[77]

But Lincoln always kept a distance from his partner. Easygoing he may have been, but he wanted the junior/senior partner status preserved, and this necessarily limited the intimacy of their relationship. Lincoln drew up most of the firm's important pleadings, and he decided how fees would be divided. "If any one paid money to him which belonged to the firm, on arriving at the office he divided it with me," Herndon wrote. "If I was not there, he would wrap up my share in a piece of paper and place it in my drawer." Herndon had no complaints on this score, as Lincoln was generous to a fault. Still, Lincoln was the one who did the dividing. He called his partner "Billy," while Herndon always stuck to "Mr. Lincoln."[78]

John Stuart and Stephen Logan might well have nodded in recognition of this rather distant Abraham Lincoln. They of course encountered Lincoln in different circumstances, as a new lawyer and junior partner, and their partnerships lasted for considerably shorter periods than Herndon's two decades. Still, the silent spaces in their postwar testimonies about Lincoln speak volumes: Stuart never really suggested that he enjoyed a close friendship or knowledge of Lincoln's heart. Logan claimed even less. In his more honest moments, Herndon admitted that he didn't quite know what Lincoln thought of him; and in his truly honest moments, Herndon confessed that he wasn't too sure what to make of Lincoln, either. "Even after my long and intimate acquaintance with Mr. Lincoln I never fully knew and understood him," he admitted. Lincoln "never revealed himself entirely to one man . . . even those who with him through long years of hard study and under constantly varying circumstances can hardly say they knew him through and through."[79]

But they did know his professional identity; he was a bona fide attorney, with all the baggage—good or bad—that the label carried.

Even Russell Godbey eventually came around. "One time Abe and I were on the North Side of the [Sangamon?] River," he recalled, when they came upon a man and a horse whose harness lines had become hopelessly tangled. I "halloed to Abe, 'Abe do come here and See these thing[s]. A Philadelphia lawyer Can't undo them. You are an [Illinois] one and may do it." According to Godbey, Lincoln "looked at them Some time—Studied them . . . and undid them." The farmer admitted, "this Cut a Knot I Couldn't."[80]

Chapter Two

The Brethren

In many ways, Lincoln enjoyed less camaraderie with his partners than he did with the Illinois bar in general. It was a large brotherhood. Springfield was home to eleven other lawyers when Lincoln first entered the profession. Most of the surrounding communities, if they were of any size or substance at all, sported at least one or two attorneys. Illinois was not unusual. Nationwide, the number of lawyers had increased dramatically since the Revolution, serving the needs of a growing populace and a booming commercial economy.[1]

They stood out, these men. Their little rectangles of advertising space in the hometown newspaper were accompanied by other advertisers who created, bought, or sold tangible things. Logan and Lincoln's August 1841 advertisement in the *Sangamon Journal,* for example, appeared near Ethan T. Cabiness's ad for his service as a portrait painter and a box for John F. Rague, "architect and Builder—manufacturer of Stucco Work." Lincoln and Herndon's ad in the 1850 *Illinois Daily Journal* lay beside that of Mr. C. C. Phelps, "manufacturer of a large assortment of chairs" (complete with a little woodcut engraving of a chair); Lowery, Lamb and Company's ad for "Hollow Ware"—sugar kettles, lard kettles, "odd lids," and skillets; and other ads for a Springfield lumber company, rope factory, leatherworks, and carpet maker.[2]

This was pre–service industry America, where most people produced, bought, and sold things and defined themselves by the quality and quantity of those things: chairs, hollow ware, carpets, or more often the crops they dug out of the ground. White men, most of them farmers, knew who they were when they picked up, say, an ear of corn, shook the dirt off it, and saw healthy yellow kernels staring back at them.

What stared back at Lincoln when he shook the dirt off his law practice and tried to get at what he contributed to society? What exactly did a lawyer create? Farmers had their crops, and merchants had the goods they bought and sold. Mill owners had their mills and what they ground, cattlemen their cows and the milk and beef they produced, raftsmen their rafts and the cargoes they carried. Even other professionals could point to something tangible. Ministers had the souls they saved, the reformed drunkard here, the baptism there. Doctors displayed their medicine and instruments. They could exhibit healed wounds, delivered babies, and saved lives. But lawyers?

They made words, and lots of them. Words written in books like Blackstone's *Commentaries* got Lincoln and his fellow lawyers into the law, and once there they found themselves awash in a sea of words—in casebooks, docket books, pleadings, interrogatories, court orders, and writs. There were also spoken words: negotiations between lawyers and their clients, trial arguments between lawyers and before judges, cross-examinations of witnesses, opening and closing arguments to juries. Attorneys differentiated among themselves based on what they could or could not do with words. An attorney could earn the respect of his peers with well-crafted pleadings and finely honed writs and interrogatories; and he could gain the respect of those outside the bar with a good jury argument or courtroom speech.

Jacksonian America was fascinated by oratory. Debate societies sprang up in nearly every major American town; Lincoln made his first major speech before the Springfield Young Men's Lyceum in 1838 on "The Perpetuation of Our Political Institutions." "In the great journal of things happening under the sun, we, the American People, find our account running, under date of the nineteenth century of the Christian era," began Lincoln's speech, "We find ourselves in the peaceful possession, of the fairest portion of the earth, as regards extent of territory, fertility of soil, and salubrity of climate."[3] The Gettysburg Address it was not; but flowery oratory was considered high entertainment in 1838, and a speech-making attorney could ride that skill into the statehouse or higher. Many did so, Lincoln included.

But for every admiring gaze directed at lawyers who could invoke "the great journal of things happening under the sun," there was also a scowl, a shaken head, a muttered disdain. "A common man goes to a lawyer as a supernatural being, possessed as by inspiration, all knowledge of matters of law," noted one early-nineteenth-century observer, "the ignorant have nearly the same idea of a lawyer as of a conjuror." The magic of words could all too easily seem like sorcery to those who were innately suspicious of well-heeled attorneys, men who failed to produce anything tangible, who seemed to earn their pay by preying on the misfortunes of those who did "work for a living." Some of those farmers, merchants, mill owners, and raftsmen lost the things they produced because of words, in trials where the other side's lawyer could write a better pleading or give a better speech.[4]

Quite a few of Lincoln's neighbors wanted to dispense with lawyers altogether, and they acted on the impulse. Throughout the early nineteenth century, a movement was under way, successful to a greater or lesser degree in various parts of the country, to demystify the law by taking it away from its common-law roots and writing rules out in simple language that was accessible to any layman. Several states tried to create informal associations that could settle disputes among their members without going to trial, or by making it possible for anyone to plead a case in a courtroom. For a while, Lincoln's former home state of Indiana abolished all requirements for admission to the state bar; to practice law, a Hoosier needed only to be a registered voter and possess the ubiquitous "good moral character."[5]

Lawyers banded together in the face of such threats. They needed to convince their skeptical neighbors that their command of the law's words was unique and indispensable to the proper functioning of society. Much of a lawyer's professional identity consisted of this careful guardianship of their own particular wordcraft.

But they did not do so in the modern sense of creating a national organization. There was no American Bar Association, or any real attempt to organize and regulate lawyers nationally. Even on the state and local level, lawyers created little in the way of a formal professional structure. Few states possessed an organized, statewide bar association, and those that did often only exacerbated feelings among their neighbors that something sinister was afoot in the profession when they gathered behind closed doors.[6]

Some attorneys created small county- and township-level associations, organized around the men who practiced in a particular court or district. These were often little more than gentleman's clubs, whose members could comfortably drink, smoke, and converse in the company of other lawyers. "All insensibly, court and bar, grow quite smutty," groused one Massachusetts attorney after attending such a meeting. Other associations took up more dignified tasks. The attorneys who worked in Peoria, McLean, Sangamon, and Tazewell counties created a bar association in 1845 that met and passed a resolution that they "most fittingly deplore[d] the death of William H. Wilmet, Esq., late of this court." In 1859 a meeting of the Springfield bar, complaining about the "great accumulation of business, and the consequent vexatious delays, and oppressive expense attending litigation in Sangamon County, imperatively require at least a diversion of a portion of the criminal and civil business from that Court, and the establishment of a Common Pleas Court." The association also wanted to find a way to regulate lawyers' fees, and appointed committees to look into all these matters.[7]

From such humble beginnings would the ABA and other organizations eventually grow, but not until well after the Civil War. Before that time, associations drafted resolutions, proposed bills, and mourned their dead. They tried to address nagging problems like caseloads and fees. Given the high percentage of lawyers who served in state legislatures, a bar association could influence the drafting of bills that related to the profession. But such influence would be informal and sporadic. Associations possessed no teeth, no sanctioning power that could make lawyers toe the line and obey their edicts; nor could they make themselves final arbiters of who did and did not enter the profession.[8]

If Lincoln were a modern lawyer, we would imagine him entering the legal profession as if he were opening the door to some vast professional edifice, its framework made up of interlocking sets of law schools, examination boards, bar associations, committees, rules, and regulations nearly ad infinitum. But antebellum lawyers erected no such scaffolding. Lincoln's experiences among other members of the bar is more akin to his moving within a loose association of men arranged around physical spaces, spaces that they used to separate themselves from the rest of society and establish their status as professionals necessary to the orderly functioning of society.

The space closest to Lincoln in time and proximity was his law office; or rather, law offices, for he had several during his career. While partnered with Stuart and for a while with Logan he remained on Hoffman's Row. In 1843 Logan and Lincoln moved to the Tinsley building, a choice spot on Springfield's town square and within a short walking distance of the state capitol. Lincoln and Herndon put out their shingle in the Tinsley building until 1852, when they moved to a place across the square on its northwest side, near Fifth Street. There they remained until Lincoln's departure for Washington, D.C. in 1861.[9]

Lincoln's offices were utilitarian to a fault, with nothing resembling a décor. Walking into his Tinsley building office, Lincoln would have first laid eyes on a long pine table that dominated the center of the room, capped by another, shorter table at the top in a "T" shape. The tables were marred by little slashes made by someone with a pen knife, which is perhaps why they were covered in a worn green baize cloth. Scattered about the room were a stove for heat, a rocking chair, several cane-bottom chairs, and a couch that just accommodated the senior partner's lanky frame when he lay out upon it to read. A secretary with pigeonholes stood to one side, and two sets of bookshelves held the firm's library, estimated by some to have been as large as two hundred volumes (a testament to Herndon; Lincoln was not much of a book collector). There were the usual suspects: Blackstone, Chitty, Story, treatises on contracts and international and commercial law, as well as statute books from Illinois. Along with these basic tools of the trade were other odds and ends: case reports on the British Court of Exchequer, a couple of New York state statute volumes, a book on medical jurisprudence, another on poisons (picked up perhaps by Lincoln when he defended a man named Theodore Anderson, accused of killing his brother with strychnine in 1856), a couple of congressional reports dating from Lincoln's brief term as a representative, and some literary bric-a-brac (a copy of *Don Juan,* Byron, some Shakespeare). Maybe they were arranged in some kind of order, but it is easier to imagine the books packed willy-nilly, some upside down, others with the spine facing the wrong way, pieces of paper jutting out from the tops where Lincoln or Herndon wanted to mark something they had found.[10]

Antebellum law offices erred on the seedy side, but the Lincoln and Herndon office was such an epic mess that even other lawyers were taken aback. The room was "apparently innocent of water and the scrub-man since creation's dawn," according to one. It had windows that might have afforded a decent amount of light had the panes been clean (they were not), or had they been opened, which was likely not very often, since they opened over the roof of a stable. There was no carpet, and the dark hardwood floor was, like everything else, covered with a thick patina of dust and dirt. One youth who studied for the bar under Lincoln and Herndon claimed to have found plants from a half-open bag of bean seeds sprouting in a dirt-encrusted corner. The table was nearly always covered with papers, inkwells, books—the detritus of the lawyer's world of words. An overstuffed envelope bore a label in Lincoln's hand: "When you can't find it anywhere else look in this."[11]

Utilitarian and organized just barely enough to function, Lincoln's office was a man's space, as antebellum America understood men. Victorian-era conventions surrounded manhood with values of stout, aggressive simplicity, of linear, unadorned frankness. Professional men were supposed to create an aura of focused, powerful industry, a straight-to-the-point ethos that took little heed of a table pocked with knife marks, dust, or bean seeds. Women worried about such things. The culture of the time called for the middle-class white woman to surround her world with laced domesticity, according to an easier, statelier pace than the frenetic business world of men.[12]

Lincoln received an education in these male/female contrasts every morning. He awoke in a bedroom adorned with soft colors and richly patterned wallpaper. He shaved before a proper mirror finished in rich walnut. After breakfast and on his way to the front door, he passed the "sitting room" on his left and the "front parlor" on his right, both tidy spaces with large fireplaces and windows flanked by heavy draperies, a comfortable leather chair, and a mirror. The door that he opened had a brass nameplate, "A. Lincoln," affixed to its front. It was Mary's world, her workplace: respectable, domestic, and well-tended, "just such a dwelling as a majority of the well-to-do residents of these free Western towns occupy," according to a New York visitor.[13]

Mary worked every bit as hard as a man to maintain her home, but society told her to paper over the sweat, grease, and effort with a façade of "feminine" softness. Her husband operated under no such restraints. When he arrived at the office, Lincoln stepped into the much different world dominated and designed by men, a world characterized by an almost rude frankness and an utter indifference to appearance. There was a touch of masculine bravado in his cheerful disdain for order. "Do you see that spot over there?" Lincoln asked a prospective clerk, pointing to a black blotch on the office wall. The firm had hosted two other law students, Lincoln explained. "Well, one of these young men got so enthusiastic in his pursuit of legal lore that he fired an inkstand at the other one's head."[14]

Lincoln's office was a place where he was able to relax in ways that were difficult for him at home. Mary sometimes upbraided him for his sloppiness, for answering the door in his shirtsleeves ("wait a moment and I'll trot out the womenfolk for you," he once told some visitors, to Mary's horror), for strewing papers and books out on the floor, and for reading while propped against an upturned chair. But in his office he could rest reasonably sure that his reading and thinking routines would arouse no criticism—or at least not overly so. "Lincoln never read any other way but aloud," Herndon groused, "This habit used to annoy me beyond the point of endurance." Nevertheless, Billy tolerated his partner's eccentricities, of which there were many. "Lincoln's favorite position when unraveling some knotty law point was to stretch both of his legs at full length upon a chair in front of him," wrote Herndon, and "in this position, with books on the table near by and in his lap, he worked up his case." Others noted his more general thinking habits. "He would pick up a book and run rapidly over the pages, pausing here and there," remembered a clerk, "at the end of an hour—never, as I remember, more than two or three hours—he would close the book, stretch himself out on the office lounge, and with hands under his head, and eyes shut, he would digest the mental food he had just taken."[15]

But if Lincoln enjoyed his office as a place to digest mental food, he also found it to be a limiting space. He was easily distracted there—in fact, he often got bored. He "detested the mechanical work of the office," and would drop the law books for storytelling and jokes at any opportunity. Milton Hay, a lawyer whose office was next door, disparaged him as "an old poke easy." According to Herndon, he and Lincoln would discuss nearly anything other than the law at length in the office: the nature of God (albeit Lincoln did not much like metaphysics), the nature of humanity, psychology, democracy, and, of course, politics. "Billy, what is the meaning of 'antithesis'?" he suddenly asked Herndon one day, ushering in a long talk on this and other subjects.[16]

But it does not seem to have become a place for extended bull sessions with the boys, along the lines of the general store counters and cracker barrels where Lincoln had once held forth as a clerk. The office was the place where Lincoln interacted with his partners, his clients, and the occasional law student who prepared for entrance to the Illinois bar. Accounts of Lincoln in his office describe him reading alone and conversing with Billy; they rarely describe Lincoln talking to groups of other lawyers in the office. He often seemed bent on fitting his storytelling and joke skills—which were better suited for a group of men rather than a one-on-one conversation—to the ambience of his office. "I have heard him relate the same story three times within as many hours to persons who came in at different periods, and every time he laughed as heartily and enjoyed it as if it were a new story," Herndon wrote.[17]

The office compelled him to engage in repeated conversations with individuals: clients, his partner, and others. Lincoln was more comfortable holding forth before an audience. "On many topics he was not a good conversationalist," Herndon noted, "putting it a little strongly, he was not even polite. If present with others, or participating in a conversation, he was rather abrupt, and in his anxiety to say something apt or illustrate the subject under discussion, would burst in with a story." Billy related his partner's behavior in the office when confronted by someone with whom he did not particularly want to converse. "Lincoln would do most of the talking, swinging around what he suspected was the vital point, but never nearing it, interlarding his answers with a seemingly endless supply of stories and jokes." The person in question would be buried in a deluge of stories, and only later, upon "blowing away the froth of Lincoln's humorous narratives he would find nothing substantial left."[18]

Lawyers in Lincoln's day had a term, "office lawyer," and it was not a compliment. It denoted a paper-pusher who preferred to bury himself in the dry minutiae of law books rather than going out the door into the wide world to practice law. Real lawyers, real men, tried their mettle before the jury and the gallery, before the world at large.[19] Lincoln knew this. He was ambitious, and he knew his ambitions could be answered to only a limited extent in his office. The office was not a very good proving ground—but the courtroom was.

"Courtroom" was an elastic idea in Lincoln's day. Litigating cases in counties all over central Illinois, he saw halls of justice that were barely worthy of the name. Before it was replaced with a decent brick structure in 1849, DeWitt County's courthouse could have been mistaken for a fur-trading post; it was crudely constructed of pine clapboards with no adornment. At the other end of the spectrum, the Sangamon County courthouse—his home field, so to speak—was a stately structure of Greek revival columns and decorous white marble.[20]

The law office was a preeminently masculine space, and the courtroom was, as well. Ladies were allowed, of course; they showed up as trial participants—witnesses, litigants—and spectators in the gallery. But in nearly every case, courtrooms, even the crude ones, physically separated spectators and casual participants from the all-male bench and bar. The more sophisticated courts provided a physical boundary: Logan County's courthouse in Mount Pulaski, Illinois, had a sweeping semicircular rail separating the jury box and lawyer's area from the rest of the room. Others, such as the courthouse in Postville, Illinois, separated participants from audience merely by the spacing of the furniture.[21]

Lawyers who crossed that space entered what the profession conceptualized as a man's proving ground. Here, the brethren judged themselves according to the loose set of values that characterized a trial lawyer. They valued forthrightness, that same straight-ahead, no-frills attitude that stripped their offices of pretense. Attorney Stephen D. Miller, for example, won praise from his fellows for his courtroom pragmatism: "Nothing of fancy entered into his speeches." It was one thing to make ornate speeches at lyceums and on the stump; but it was quite another to try to bury a jury with lots of "fancy" that did not also include a solid, forthright argument. "When unadorned, adorned the most," went a motto among lawyers.[22]

They also valued the force of intellect required to make a good argument, the power of oratory necessary to sway a jury, or the more hazily defined but palpable ability to impose one's will on a case. Lawyers admired other lawyers for taking bold risks to win a judgment. Perhaps most of all, they valued a good forensic show. Southern lawyer Henry S. Foote remarked with glowing terms on a case he once witnessed involving "several lawyers of standing" and a jury of "singularly good-looking men," who altogether put on a display of forensic combat that, in Foote's opinion, was an "intellectual treat."[23]

At the same time, however, lawyers valued discretion, a professional version of good manners whereby attorneys would fight their fights at trial, using every skill available to them, but in such a way as to respect and value their opponent's abilities and honor. William D. Martin and James Louis Petigru of South Carolina, for example, were both intense courtroom rivals and close friends. Other attorneys admired that they could argue "opposite sides of every litigated case, without the slightest interruption to their friendship." Lawyers by and large wanted this sort of courtroom camaraderie, and lamented its occasional absence. "As to the habit of *abusing and vilifying* the opposite party, and of accusing honest witnesses of *perjury,* of which it is lamentably true that lawyers are all too often guilty," wrote an antebellum attorney, "so far as the Profession is concerned . . . neither is required in the discharge of professional duty."[24]

A degree of bombast during a trial was tolerable, but lawyers also valued quiet meticulousness in the pursuit of victory. "Accuracy and diligence are much more necessary to a Lawyer, than great comprehension of mind, or brilliancy of talents," Daniel Webster argued, for the lawyer's "business is to refine, define, and split hairs. . . . A man can never gallop over the fields of Law on Pegasus, nor fly across them on the wing of oratory. If he would stand on terra firma he must descend."[25]

Such lessons most attorneys took to heart; and they earned praise from one another to the degree that this was so. Illinois lawyer Samuel D. Lockwood garnered admiration for his low-key but effective trial persona. "He pursued the even and noiseless tenor of his way," noted a fellow attorney, "making no enemies, but a host of friends." Memphis attorney Henry T. Ellet was admired for his extraordinary courtesy and civil attitude toward other members of the bar. On the other hand, lawyers who went over the top at trial could earn their colleagues' displeasure. William Lomax was thus criticized by his fellows for "a total want of tact in the conduct of a case." Leman Church of Connecticut likewise pursued courtroom combat to an unseemly extreme; "he wanted to fight, no matter whether for right or wrong," noted one colleague with disdain. New York's Thomas Sherwood rubbed his brethren the wrong way with what one described as his "rather irritating way of taunting his opponents."[26]

Where juries were concerned, lawyers liked directness and logic, like that of Keating Lewis Simon, who was praised for his "logical and manly" jury speeches. The profession as a whole liked passion, but more often they admired a lawyer's ability to control that passion, to turn it on and off when necessary and play to the emotions of the jurors. Lincoln's friend and fellow lawyer Usher Linder described with evident respect the manipulative skills of an attorney named John Rowan who, during a case involving a civil suit for damages "for the seduction of an accomplished and beautiful girl," recited lines from the poem, "The Vicar of Wakefield": "When lovely woman stoops to folly . . . No art can soothe her melancholy."[27]

Attorneys have always had to strike a series of balances in the courtroom: countering the need to win with the need to maintain collegiality with the rest of the bar, countering the need for passion with the need for self-discipline, and balancing emotion with emotional manipulation. Given the constantly shifting nature of the profession, with partnerships dissolving and reforming, lawyers ascending to and descending from the bench, and clients calling on multiple attorneys to perform tasks related to different pieces of litigation, a lawyer could not know whether an adversary in the courtroom today might not become co-counsel tomorrow, or perhaps even the judge hearing a case. Overly aggressive or offensive behavior was not a good career move, on a variety of levels.

Lincoln knew how to strike these balances, possessing what one observer called "courtroom finesse to an extraordinary degree." He had a reputation as a tenacious litigator, one who knew how to employ a technicality or pitch an argument to get what he needed. People underestimated him at their peril. "He was wise as a serpent in the trial of a cause," fellow lawyer Leonard Swett noted, then added ruefully, "I have got too many scars from his blows to certify that he was harmless as a dove. . . . Any man who took Lincoln for a simple minded man would very soon wake [up] with his back in a ditch."[28]

But Lincoln was also unfailingly polite during a trial, his desire to win tempered by a good sense of professional courtesy. "He never misstated evidence," observed one colleague, "but stated clearly and fairly and squarely his opponent's case." He knew how to properly dilute the pursuit of a trial victory with comradeship, even when others at the bar did not. Henry C. Whitney recalled a case he tried in which he was opposed by Lincoln and another lawyer named Oliver L. Davis. "O.L. was a dirty fellow and he informed me that they were going to bea[t] me *awfully,*" Whitney related, so "I got alarmed and went to Lincoln about it." Lincoln "reassured me—said it was like any other lawsuit—they might be beat or I might but not to worry." Whitney breathed a sigh of relief. Nevertheless, when the time for the trial came, "Lincoln bore down on me harder than anyone." Whitney saw this not as an instance of Lincoln's duplicity, but rather a commendable example of his professional ability to be at once ruthless and amicable. "Lincoln was very adroit in managing a case," he wrote.[29]

Even allowing for the usual leavening of Lincoln mythmaking, these testimonials ring true; they fit Lincoln's general demeanor in other areas of his life. He was an essentially passive man, more liable to search for a way around than through a problem. He valued collegiality—not just with other lawyers, but also with politicians of all stripes.[30]

But there were limits to the conviviality possible in a courtroom. The setting in which Lincoln was most comfortable—a group of men trading stories and repartee—could function only to a limited degree in a courtroom where, however much they wished to paper over the fact, competing lawyers were trying to beat each other and score a win. Lincoln never cared for direct confrontation, and one suspects that, on a private level, he sometimes had a difficult time "bearing down" on a colleague or a neighbor to win a case. For a genuine sense of comradeship, of the broad but not deep sort he valued, Lincoln transitioned into the widest space of all, and the one that gave him the most satisfaction and enjoyment: the circuit.

Circuit riding was not unique to Illinois. Many American states at one time or another relied on lawyers like Lincoln to join with other lawyers and itinerant judges and travel through an area, stopping at county seats and litigating cases in short order for whomever it was necessary to do so. In a lightly taxed nation with a shortage of public funds necessary to pay judges' salaries, it made sense to appoint one judge to oversee courts in several different places rather than pay for the maintenance of a judge at each location.[31] It also made sense for attorneys to follow in the judge's wake. They found the circuit system to be a necessary companion to their office practice. Unless that office was located in a large urban area, a lawyer could not hope to earn a steady, acceptable living only from whatever cases happened to appear on his doorstep. Rather than waiting for lawsuits to come to him, a lawyer was well advised to go looking for lawsuits.[32]

When Lincoln went looking for business on the circuit, he did so with a sort of picturesque pragmatism, in which he had whittled away any unnecessary encumbrances like they were the chips on one of Logan's pine sticks. He could not carry many books—Blackstone and Chitty, perhaps, plus whatever he happened to be reading for entertainment—or much paperwork. He stuffed the lot into a green carpetbag, which was also home for his extra changes of underwear. Over his usual dark suit and vest he draped a blue cloak he had picked up while in Congress, and sometimes a shawl. His hat was "innocent of a nap," and he toted a faded green umbrella—with "A. Lincoln" sewn in white cotton into the fabric—that had a broken handle and was kept folded by a piece of string. His circuit attire was like his office: basic, unadorned to the point of sloppiness, and pared down to the essentials necessary to do the job at hand. "He might have passed for an ordinary farmer," noted one observer.[33]

Lincoln plied his trade in the Eighth Judicial Circuit of Illinois, a large portion of central Illinois including at various times Sangamon and sixteen other counties. It was known as the "mud circuit" because of its awful roads and rural conditions. Even the county seats were, in the words of one lawyer, "located at small and primitive villages." Lawyers and judges could spend as much as three weeks in one of these places, tending to whatever litigation came their way.[34]

The Eighth was not unique; circuit life in general for an American lawyer was difficult. Usher Linder, who rode Illinois' Fourteenth Circuit (comprising over a dozen counties), wrote about putting up in farmer's cabin while in the Wayne County seat of Fairfield, where he ate meals consisting of "fat meat, corn bread and coffee, made from parched buckwheat." The roads were bad there, as well, "and in many places impassable for carriages [so that] the judges and all the lawyers traveled on horseback." Other states had circuits with similar problems. When South Carolinian William Nibs rode circuit, he felt compelled to stuff his saddlebags so full of papers that they stuck out "straight as a log." This did not keep the papers safe. Nibs once forded a river deep enough to soak all his belongings, and colleagues spied him on the far shore drying his clothes, books, and papers in the afternoon sun.[35]

Lawyers were often unsure whether they loved or hated this "unsteady, nomadic life." On the one hand, riding circuit was a hard way to earn a dollar, "going in vehicles over dirt roads, sometimes good— sometimes dirty, and not infrequently quite muddy." The accommodations were shoddy and the food was bad, with the travelers putting up in "homely farm-houses and village inns" and compelled to "sleep two to a bed, and eight in a room." On the other hand, they brought a sense of bravado to the circuit, an idea that men could prove themselves by enduring all of this and earning a living. Younger attorneys were advised to go out on the road instead of "lounging about their own Court-Houses. . . . They would learn more law [on the circuit], and get more practice in a year, than they [otherwise would] in ten." Here the trappings of the "office lawyer" fell away. Circuit lawyers lived on their wits, without the safety net of precedents and case law to back them in their reasoning. "Each county, of course, had a somewhat different population, and a somewhat different class of business," Whitney observed. "Each recurring week brought with it a new and different class of clients to treat with—new and diverse juries to entertain, cajole or convince; new and different conditions of chaos, to bring order from."[36]

When he first entered the bar, Lincoln did not travel very much, perhaps because he was newly married, or because he could not afford the expense. "The first trip he made around the circuit after he commenced the practice of law, I had a horse, Saddle, and bridle, and he had none," recalled a friend, "I let him have mine. I think he must have been careless as the Saddle skinned the horse's back." As his career matured, Lincoln expanded his circuit riding, especially after he partnered with Herndon. Springfield and Sangamon County were always his primary source for business, but especially in the mid-1850s, after he returned from Congress and recommitted himself to his practice, he saw a lot of circuit litigation. In faraway Vermilion County alone (which bordered Indiana), he litigated 152 extant cases.[37]

Lincoln became heavily committed to the circuit. He was the only one among his peers who rode it in its entirety and during the whole term. This sometimes meant that he was away from Springfield for three months at a time. Others attended part of the courts' sessions (two or three, depending on the county) or focused their efforts in a few areas. When he moved from the Fourteenth to the Eighth Circuit, for example, Usher Linder only practiced in Vermilion, Edgar, Shelby, and occasionally Champaign counties.[38]

But Lincoln stayed, and according to everyone who knew him, he loved every minute of it. "He never complained of the food, bed, or lodgings," recalled a friend. "If every other fellow grumbled at the bill-of-fare which greeted us at many of the dingy taverns . . . Lincoln said nothing." Herndon thought that Lincoln was somehow in his element on the mud circuit, a place where he and the other lawyers could find "relaxation from all the irksome toil that fell to their lot."[39]

Lincoln had sound business reasons for riding the entire circuit. Although his partnerships with Stuart, Logan, and Herndon generated most of their business in the Springfield/Sangamon County area, around 40 percent of their cases came from elsewhere in the Eighth Circuit. Lincoln and Herndon in particular made a steady living from circuit cases, most of which Lincoln litigated. He earned good money on the mud circuit—good enough to compensate for the crowded beds and bad food. The circuit was also very useful for his political

career. He made many contacts among clients and courtroom spectators, and also among the lawyers and jurists who were often active
members of the Whig and later Republican parties.[40]

There were rumors that Lincoln's circuit practice was the product
of more than politics or business. His friend David Davis claimed that
Lincoln spent so much time on the road in an attempt to escape what
had become an unhappy marriage. Most of the other lawyers on circuit
tried to return to their homes on Saturday evenings, to "see their family and friends," Davis wrote. But "Lincoln would refuse to go home—It
seemed to me that he was domestically unhappy."[41]

From this source originated a longstanding myth about Lincoln's
law practice: that he endured the long hours and bad conditions because he was running away from Mary and her unstable temperament.
"Lincoln's true home at that time was the circuit, with its freedom
from domestic strife," wrote one historian. "An uncongenial home life
was responsible for this reluctance to return to his family when the
opportunity presented itself," argued another.[42]

Lincoln's marriage may or may not have been inordinately troubled;
historians still hotly debate the issue. But any direct connection between Lincoln's domestic and circuit life is dubious, based on thin and
suspect evidence. The chief culprit here was not so much David Davis,
but Herndon. Billy believed the Lincoln marriage was a stormy and difficult union; he claimed to have often found Lincoln asleep on the office
couch when he arrived in the morning, at which point he knew "that
a breeze had sprung up over the domestic sea, and that the waters
were troubled."[43] When he received David Davis's speculations about
Lincoln's "domestic unhappiness" in an 1866 letter, Herndon altered
Davis's words to read "it seemed to *us all* that he was domestically
unhappy," implying that this was the consensus judgment of the entire
bar.[44]

But those observers who thought that Lincoln's circuit activities
were evidence of an unhappy home life missed the point that, in going
out on the road, he was spending less time not only in his house, but
also his office. Herndon usually did not accompany Lincoln; he stayed
in Springfield and tended to the paperwork in much the same way that
Mary stayed home and tended to the household chores. Billy would
no doubt have been offended by the suggestion that perhaps Lincoln
was avoiding both him and Mary; that he liked the bar, collectively,
more than both his partners, domestic and professional.

Certainly the circuit offered interesting company. A dozen or so Springfield lawyers rode the Eighth at one time or another, as well as lawyers from other towns who joined the traveling legal retinue when it came to their area. There was Ward Hill Lamon, a garrulous young Virginian who moved to Danville in 1837. He was introduced to Lincoln by John Stuart and became one of Lincoln's primary associates when he litigated Vermilion County cases. "We rode the circuit together, traveling by buggy in the dry seasons and horse-back in bad weather," Lamon recalled. Lincoln was at first suspicious of Lamon's Virginia roots. "You Virginians shed barrels of perspiration while standing off at a distance and superintending the work the slaves do for you," he told Lamon. "It is different with us. Here it is every fellow for himself, or he doesn't get there." Lamon reassured Lincoln that he disliked slavery, "and from that hour we were friends," particularly when Lincoln discovered that Lamon could very nearly match him joke for joke.[45]

There was also Leonard Swett—he who spoke of the scars Lincoln had inflicted on him in various courtroom battles—who served in the Mexican War and read law in Maine before moving to Illinois. Educated and meticulous, he came to feel as if he understood Lincoln's intellectual qualities as a lawyer better than anyone. Whereas Lamon tended to see in Lincoln a sociable road buddy, Swett saw an effective legal mind, someone whose powers of logic were considerable and who was able to convey his reasoning to a jury with singular skill. Lincoln's "mode and force of argument was in stating how he had reasoned upon the subject and how he had come to his conclusion, rather than original reasoning to the hearer, and as the mind of [the] listener, followed in the groove of his mind, his conclusions were adopted," Swett believed.[46]

Lamon and Swett flattered themselves that they came to intimately know Lincoln while traveling with him on the circuit. So did Henry Whitney, an Urbana lawyer who was twenty-three when he met Lincoln in 1854. Whitney fancied himself an armchair philosopher and psychologist, so that when the subject of Lincoln's moodiness arose, he thought he knew the reason: Lincoln's mother "was in constant trepidation and frequent affrights . . . while she was pregnant [with Lincoln] and these affrights and trepidations made a maternal *ante natal* impression on our hero; that was the most of it. [Lincoln's] melancholy was stamped on him while in the period of gestation. [I]t was part of his nature and could no more be shaken off than he could part with his brains." For good measure, Whitney added "[John] Stuart told me his liver did not secrete bile—that [Lincoln] had no natural evacuation of bowels etc."[47]

Most of the other lawyers on the Eighth circuit did not presume to understand Lincoln's bodily functions. Moving in and around him as traveling companions, co-counsel, opposing counsel, clerks, and judges were a variety of other, more obscure men. Daniel Wolsey Voorhees was known as "The Tall Sycamore of the Wabash" because of his height; he lived in Terre Haute, Indiana, and sometimes crossed into Illinois to do business on the Eighth. Asahel Gridley was a failed Bloomington merchant who turned to the law when his store went under; Lincoln may have met him during the Black Hawk War, when they both served in the state militia. Theophilus Lyle Dickey was likewise a ruined land speculator from Macomb and later Rushville, who parlayed his law career into an eventual judgeship. Albert Bledsoe was yet another southern expatriate from Kentucky; he abandoned a ministry in the Episcopal Church to practice law. Benjamin S. Prettyman brought expertise as a land surveyor to his cases at the bar. George Lawrence brought his drinking habits, which did not seem to affect his pool game; David B. Campbell brought his violin, which he played while traveling the Eighth.[48]

Presiding over this crew, in numerous formal and informal ways, was David Davis—circuit court judge, prankster, and raconteur, source of gossip about the Lincoln marriage for Herndon, a hail-fellow-well-met to some, an insufferable autocrat to others. He was a bear of a man, weighing nearly three hundred pounds and requiring a two-horse buggy to make his way about. People remembered him as a natty dresser, a picky eater, acquisitive to the edge of greedy, and given to snap judgments: a large—very large—bundle of extreme impulses, some appealing, others less so.[49]

Lawyers on his good side saw in him a boon companion, hospitable and always ready with a story or joke. When the circuit court came to his home town of Bloomington, he hosted lavish dinners for the traveling legal retinue. On the road he led them like a circus ringmaster. "We had no hesitation in stopping at a farmhouse and ordering them to kill and cook a chicken for dinner," wrote Whitney (one suspects the imperious Davis did the "ordering"). When they arrived in Danville, "Lamon would have whiskey in his office for the drinking ones, and those who indulged in petty gambling would get by themselves and play till late in the night. Lincoln, Davis, and a few local wits would spend the evening in Davis's room, talking politics, wisdom, and fun." Swett once entered Davis's hotel room to find him and Lincoln "dressed for bed, engaged in a lively battle with pillows, tossing them at each other's heads," a battle that left the portly judge so fatigued he "leaned against the foot of the bed and puffed like a lizard."[50]

The image of a jolly fat man swinging pillows faded quickly away in the courtroom, however. Davis ruled from the bench like a king. He required lawyers to observe all the niceties of courtroom protocol, deferring to his judgments without question. Those who did not do so suffered, as did their clients. Swett once incurred his wrath and found himself consistently on the losing end of Davis's judgments. Asahel Gridley made the mistake of crossing Davis, who had interrupted Gridley's jury summation by sneering, "You don't call that law, you are talking to the jury, do you?" Gridley rather recklessly told him to mind his own business, after which Davis replied that "I'll instruct the jury directly; and then we'll see who rules this court."[51]

Gridley was probably not invited to Davis's evening bull sessions. The judge presided over the social life of the Eighth Circuit with much the same authority he wielded in court, and with nearly the same power to make or break men. "The feelings were those of great fraternity," noted Whitney, "and if we desired to restrict our circle it was no trouble for Davis to freeze out any disagreeable persons." Just what Davis did to "freeze out" people is not clear; he may have done something relatively mild (refusing to invite a lawyer to his dinner parties) or he might have gone so far as to rule against a "disagreeable person" in court. The judge was capable of such behavior.[52]

All of which highlights the very fluid relationship between the men on the circuit. In Danville, for example, they stayed at McCormick's house, a local hotel where "jurors counsel prisoners and everybody all ate at a long table." Davis, Lincoln, Swett, Whitney—these men could easily don or slough off the ordinary conventions of legal propriety, deferring to judicial dignity and the boundary between bench and bar in one setting and at one particular moment, and then gleefully blurring those same boundaries the next. And Lincoln knew how to play these angles. "While several of us lawyers were together, including Judge Davis, Lincoln suddenly asked a novel question of court practice, addressed to no one particularly," Whitney recalled, "to which the Judge . . . replied, stating what he understood the practice should be." Lincoln laughed. "'I asked that question, hoping that you would

answer,'" he said with satisfaction. "'I have that very question to present to the court in the morning, and I am glad to find out that the court
is on my side.'"[53]

It is hard to say what is more striking here: that Lincoln could go
fishing for a courtroom stratagem like this, or that he could tell Davis
to his face what he was doing. The lines were blurred further still
when Davis put Lincoln on the bench in his absence. Lincoln served as
judge in over three hundred cases while Davis left the circuit, often to
attend personal business. No one seems to have found this objection-
able or unusual.[54]

The common denominator, the foundation that bound the circuit
together, was not their roles as men who represented the plaintiff, men
who represented the defendant, or men who sat in judgment over a
trial, for those roles were malleable; rather, it was their status as men
who had tested one another by various professional and masculine
standards and found one another acceptable. They shared hotel rooms,
food, beds, and fires. They watched out for one another, in a variety
of ways, great and small. One circuit lawyer, for example, had a habit
of getting overwrought during his jury summations, during which "his
coat tails would fly apart and disclose a white expanse" of exposed
underwear. The other attorneys took up a collection to buy the man a
patch to cover his pants. When they came to Lincoln, he smiled and,
with his penchant for wordplay, joked, "I can't contribute anything to
the end in view."[55]

Lincoln was as peculiar on the circuit as he had been in New Salem
and elsewhere. He dressed like a farmer but read books on geometry
and poetry. He told witty stories and yet could successfully prose-
cute a dry or boringly technical case. He was by turns fun-loving and
moody, a fact several people noted. Jonathan Birch, a fellow lawyer,
witnessed Lincoln holding forth in the court clerk's office, surrounded
by other lawyers and telling some story. "His eyes would sparkle with
fun," Birch remembered, "and when he had reached the point in his
narrative which invariably evoked the laughter of the crowd, nobody's
enjoyment was greater than his." An hour later, however, Birch would
see Lincoln in the clerk's office or some other place, seated on a chair
with the back leaned against the wall, "his hat tipped slightly forward
as if to shield his face; his eyes no longer sparkling with fun or merriment, but sad and downcast and his hands clasped around his knees."
Birch thought him "the very picture of dejection and gloom. Thus

absorbed have I seen him sit for hours at a time defying the interruption of even his closest friends. . . . It was a strange picture."[56]

But on the circuit, his peculiarities fit. No one ever suggested he was one of the "disagreeable persons" whom Davis and others should freeze out. His stories and jokes and, more important, his skills as a lawyer helped him fit in. Most of all, perhaps, Lincoln met the professional standards of manliness, and this despite the fact that he did not drink, gamble, or otherwise perform according to wider cultural conventions of the day. He was direct and unpretentious in his professional demeanor, he was both aggressive and courteous in his pursuit of courtroom victory, and he obviously enjoyed the fraternity of other men.

Lincoln's masculinity on the circuit was defined by his status as a "character." All these lawyers and judges wanted to see themselves as "characters." After Lincoln's death they rushed their circuit memories of the dead president into print, and their approaches—their storytelling plots—were all the same: the circuit bonhomie of Lincoln and his merry band of odd fellows, and he the oddest of them all. As such, he could interact with and then disengage from the men around him almost at will. The circumstances of the circuit practically demanded that it be so, for the same men who one evening shared a bed could the next day find themselves fiercely opposing one another on opposite sides of a trial. In this company, Lincoln found himself among men who would listen to his stories and jokes without necessarily expecting to plumb the depths of his inner soul, as a wife at home or a partner in the office.

Davis, Swett, Whitney, and others could indulge theories about Lincoln's character, marriage, birth, bowels, and whatnot—but in their more honest moments they knew that, in the end, all they got from Lincoln himself were surfaces. Whitney found Lincoln secretive, and Swett thought he was manipulative and coolly calculating, writing that Lincoln "used every force to the best possible advantage . . . he never wasted anything. . . . He would be just as kind and generous as his judgment would let him be—no more." As for Davis, the judge noted that "Lincoln was a peculiar man; he never asked my advice on any question." Whitney agreed. "I think Davis had no influence on Lincoln," he declared.[57]

Victorian conventions of male friendship were romanticized, emphasizing the need to find some sort of soul-baring place. But Lincoln's circuit brethren do not seem to have ever really tried to do this with

Lincoln. The conventions of their own profession taught them to tack back and forth between comrade and opponent, and even lawyer and judge, making it expedient not to inquire too closely into the hearts and motives of their fellow barristers. Lincoln's own personality taught them this, too. Rather than trying to penetrate the outer layer of Lincoln's stories, jokes, and so forth to get underneath them and excavate the real Lincoln, the hidden Lincoln, they accepted the oddities as essentially being Lincoln. Perhaps on occasion they got a glimpse—Lincoln brooding by himself—but only on occasion, and only a glimpse. There is not in any of the circuit anecdotes a suggestion that Lincoln understood he was being watched, that he let them see his deeper self, whatever that self was. On this level, they accepted him, and he accepted them. No circuit anecdote records Lincoln brushing a colleague away, getting annoyed or irritated because a fellow lawyer had gotten too chummy or had some unreasonable expectation of deep friendship, or anything of that sort.

Lincoln was at his best and most comfortable on the circuit; more so than in his office or the pressure cooker of a courtroom. This was true to the extent that, when he was offered a lucrative Chicago partnership in 1852, he turned it down. He begged off by claiming that "the close application required of him and the confinement in the office . . . would soon kill him." Herndon then remembered him adding that "he preferred going around on the circuit, and even if he earned smaller fees he felt much happier."[58]

Chapter Three

Promissory Notes

L incoln could not always be so indifferent to what he earned. Three years before he was licensed as an attorney, he was desperate for money. He was an insolvent debtor facing financial ruin.

In 1833 a New Salem man named William Berry persuaded Lincoln to enter a business partnership with him and purchase the remains of a failed local general store. Berry was convinced it could be turned into a successful business, once the Sangamon River became a highway for deep-draft vessels. The two men bought the place, which was owned by William Greene. They also purchased what was left of another store that had been wrecked by local vandals. Like nearly everyone else in New Salem, they did not have much cash, so they floated the enterprise with money borrowed from friends and neighbors, including the $300 bond required of Illinois tavernkeepers.[1] They thought they had the makings of a successful business. But others weren't so sure. When Greene came home late at night after the deal was done and woke his father to tell him that he had unloaded the store at a profit, his father was so happy that he got his wife up to fix their son a "*fust rate* supper."[2]

Greene's father was a better businessman than Lincoln or Berry. The Sangamon River was not navigable enough to produce much new business, and Berry made matters worse by his drinking and generally incompetent management. Lincoln soon found himself leaning on his elbows at the counter, reading books while surrounded by piles of unsold tea, sugar, coffee, tools, clothes, and other goods. When the store "winked out" (as Lincoln later put it), the partners were in dire straits, owing a large amount of money with little means of making good on their debts.

Repayment would not be a simple matter. By the time the store died, the various IOUs used to support it had circulated through the neighborhood and changed hands several times. Two creditors had sold their $52.36 note to a third man named William Watkins, and Watkins sued Berry and Lincoln for payment. The judge predictably ruled in Watkins's favor. Lincoln and Berry appealed the ruling to the circuit court, where they again lost and found themselves in debt for a total of $57.86.[3]

This was only the beginning. A year later, Lincoln was hauled into court again, this time over a $379 note he, Berry, and Green signed for Reuben Radford. Radford had earlier sold this note to Peter VanBergen, a Springfield land speculator, farmer, and moneylender. A lot of men in the community loaned other men money, but VanBergen was one of the few who solicited such business in the *Sangamon Journal*.[4] He was also one of the very few who openly attached his name to the fact; others preferred a discreet, anonymous little advertisement indicating "money to loan in small parcels," that directed interested parties to contact the *Journal's* editor for more information.[5]

A man like VanBergen would not lightly forego repayment of a debt; he sued Green, Berry, and Lincoln. Berry, whom Lincoln later characterized as a "shiftless soul," consummated his uselessness in the matter by dying, while Greene scraped together enough cash to get the amount reduced to $154. This was not enough to satisfy VanBergen, who brought the matter back into court. To pay the rest of the note, the sheriff seized Lincoln's horse, saddle, and surveying equipment. Even then, the horse and other paraphernalia brought only $81, leaving a substantial sum still unpaid. "Mr. L[incoln] was then very much discouraged," remembered a neighbor.[6]

He had good reason to be, for by the time the dust settled he was deep in debt, to the tune of nearly twelve hundred dollars, and unable to pursue his primary occupation of land surveyor. The problem was partially solved when a friend bought Lincoln's surveying equipment at auction and returned it all to him. But he spent years paying off what he called his "national debt." He was not entirely free until sometime in 1847 or 1848—more than a decade after he had first embarked on the sorry little venture.[7]

Lincoln had other options. He might have pleaded an inability to pay and let the whole matter be decided by the courts. Or he might have packed up and left. His ties to Illinois were not yet so strong that relocation was an unthinkable option, and it would have made tracking him down that much more difficult. Many other Americans chose the better part of valor in the face of debilitating debt.[8] But Lincoln did not, apparently from a sense of moral obligation as much as anything else. He achieved some emotional distance in that he did not seem to take the actions of his creditors personally. He did surveying work for VanBergen not long after the general store mess, and eventually represented him in several court cases.[9] But Lincoln felt his obligation to repay his creditors on a deep-seated and personal level. For their part, his neighbors had sized up his character and found it sufficient to warrant a loan.

This was important because, in the American business world of the 1830s, reputation still mattered. The economy was cash-poor and built largely on credit, and credit was extended or withheld as much on the basis of a potential debtor's character as anything else.[10] People liked Lincoln, he seemed forthright and sincere, and so they opened their wallets for him. "I believed he was thoroughly honest," one of his backers said, "and that impression was so strong in me I accepted his note in payment of the whole. He had no money, but I would have advanced him still more had he asked for it."[11]

In Lincoln's grandfather's day, debt was a matter of personal character. Eighteenth-century creditors assessed a potential loan based on whether the borrower was "sober," "honest," "thrifty," or "prudent." Money obligations had more to do with gentility than any cold calculation of interest, investment, or even whether the money might be repaid. "Nothing is more common, both here and in Europe, than for men of honor to contract debts without intending to repay," noted one observer. Excessive business debt was tied directly to images of "slavery," with the baggage that term carried. A "slave" to business debt was more than just a loser in the game of business; he was a morally dubious dependent on his creditor "master."[12]

But credit and debt became increasingly commercialized during the early nineteenth century, as better roads, steamboats, canals, and railroads bound Americans together in distances measured by the hundreds of miles rather than across the wheat field or down the country road. The resulting business transactions were necessarily less face-to-face and less dependent on the vagaries of character studies and neighborly good will. Debts that were once incurred between gentlemen of honor were now more impersonal, morally neutral transactions. The hard judgments that law and society directed against people who borrowed money beyond their means lessened somewhat, as debtor's prisons began to disappear and state legislatures passed laws awarding bankruptcy relief to downtrodden borrowers.[13]

But a hint of morality continued to surround commercial transactions, and many Americans still argued that bad businessmen who overextended themselves should be censured by the community. An 1850 editorial in the *Illinois State Journal* railed against what it saw as the harmful local habit of excusing an otherwise good person's bad business practices. "It is the duty of the community to rebuke and repress these pernicious glosses, making the truth heard and felt that inordinate expenditure is knavery and crime. No man has a moral right thus to lavish on his own appetites money, which he has not earned, and does not really need." In the *Journal's* opinion, a little social ostracism would do a world of economic good. "If public opinion were right on this subject, if a man living beyond his means . . . were subjected to the reprehension he deserves, this evil would be instantly checked and ultimately eradicated."[14]

Some people still went to jail when they could not pay their bills. In 1830, New York had ten thousand people in debtor's prison; ten years later in Massachusetts, over a thousand debtors languished behind bars.[15] Americans no longer habitually called debt "slavery," but they did describe debtors as having been "embarrassed," a term carrying overtones of shame.[16] Ministers decried a credit system that encouraged avarice and recklessness, and there were numerous books, pamphlets, and editorials, written by religious-minded reformers like Henry Ward Beecher, or concerned capitalists like Philadelphia merchant John Sargeant, that urged debtors facing ruin to engage in "a fair disclosure, a full surrender, and equitable distribution." Antebellum Americans had not yet shed older notions that sentiment and conscience should govern business transactions.[17]

Lincoln would become a lawyer at just the time when the American market economy was a half-born animal, breeching between the old notions of custom, honor, and tradition and a new, impersonal commercial order. The legal system acted as midwife, providing the rules for transactions between creditors and debtors, entrepreneurs and investors, moneylenders like VanBergen and hopeful young men-on-the-make like Lincoln—thousands of business deals, taking place in a sprawling, unruly new market economy in which everybody wanted to participate but nobody fully understood. As a general store operator, Lincoln received a painful lesson in the dangers of overextending his credit lines; as a lawyer he would be expected to understand the ins and outs of credit and debt from both sides of the equation. Sometimes he would be expected to help creditor clients get their money back; on other occasions, he would have to protect debtors who had gotten themselves in over their heads, much as he had once done with his own "national debt."

He performed these tasks with at best rudimentary professional help. Blackstone's *Commentaries* observed that paper credit was a form of "transaction now introduced into all sorts of civil life," and in a brief section near the end of the second volume, he laid out the rules governing relations between creditors and debtors: a three-day grace period after the repayment date, the requirement of a signature "under or on the back of the bill" when it was assigned to a third party, and so on. If the rules were properly observed, according to Blackstone, the IOU was "now a contract . . . grounded on an acknowledgement that the drawer [debtor] has effects in his hands, or at least credit sufficient to warrant the payment." If this were not so, Blackstone wrote, then it should be presumed that bankruptcy laws and other remedies were designed to ward off a total calamity befalling otherwise honest men who may have had a run of bad luck. "Trade cannot be carried on without mutual credit on both sides," he wrote, and the laws should protect those afflicted by "accidental calamities, as by the loss of a ship on tempest, the failure of brother traders, or by the non-payment of persons out of trade." But the law ought never to protect reckless or incompetent businessmen. "If a gentleman, or one in a liberal profession, at the time of contracting his debts, has a sufficient fund to pay them, the delay of payment is a species of dishonesty," Blackstone admonished, "and if, at such time, he has no sufficient fund, the dishonesty and injustice is the greater." Here Blackstone's own upper-class biases and conservative bent shone through, as he asserted that "no one shall be capable of being made a bankrupt, but only a *trader;* nor capable of receiving the full benefit of the statutes, but only an *industrious* trader."[18]

This was all well and good, and must have sounded straightforward enough to Lincoln as he read the *Commentaries* in the roads and fields around New Salem—read it even as he was buried in the litigation caused by his general store enterprise, in fact. But almost immediately complications and ambiguities likely arose in his mind. Was he, Abraham Lincoln of the failed business and the "national debt," lacking in Blackstonian industry and honor? And where did a man like Peter VanBergen—who advertised his willingness to loan money, sued to collect unpaid debts, and then later blithely employed one such debtor as his attorney to collect other debts—where would a VanBergen fit into Blackstone's scheme? The *Commentaries* offered a good guide to the structure of credit and debt: grace periods, endorsements, and the like. But it said little of value concerning the human relationships that were wound around that structure, beyond pious advice about thrift and gentlemanly values that were of limited practical use on the Illinois frontier.

The promissory note was an apt symbol for this netherworld of moral and commercial, personal and impersonal debt. It was more than an eighteenth-century handshake between gentlemen, but it was also less than the notarized, legally proscribed and formalized paperwork governing borrowing and loans that would emerge later in the century. Blackstone called it "a plain and direct engagement in writing, to pay a sum specified at the time therein limited to a person therein named." In less technical terms, the promissory note was a small square of paper upon which was written the hopes of aspiring (maybe even slightly desperate) entrepreneurs like Lincoln, Berry, and Greene. It was a chance taken on the honor of a man like Lincoln by other men like VanBergen, who stood ready to collect should calamity ensue, regardless of the circumstances, with an "its-just-business" shrug of the shoulders. It was a crude form of currency that worked reasonably well in a new town like New Salem.[19]

Lincoln practiced law in a veritable shower of these little notes. They rained down on him, year in and year out, for his entire twenty-five-year practice. While it would be a mistake to assign any modern notion of specialty to an antebellum general practitioner like Lincoln, creditor/debtor litigation was the dominant motif of his professional life. Insofar as Lincoln specialized in any area of the law, he was a debt-collection attorney.[20]

The raw numbers are revealing. Of the four thousand or so extant cases in which Lincoln was an attorney of record, over twenty-five hundred involved some form of debt litigation.[21] In 1837—his first full year as a lawyer—he was involved in ninety-one cases, sixty-five of which entailed some form of debt collection. Five years later, Lincoln was involved in 219 cases, 175 of which likewise involved debt collection—nearly 80 percent.[22] In 1842, many of the nondebt cases were handled by Logan only, whereas Lincoln handled nearly all debt litigation that made its way to the firm.[23] There were relatively few cases during 1842 in which Lincoln was the lone representative of Lincoln and Logan that did not involve debt collection issues.[24] In fact, Logan himself retained Lincoln twice in 1842 as his attorney to recover debts, from John Wilbourn for a $239 note, and then a man named Littleton Gardner for another debt of about the same amount. Lincoln won the Wilbourn case for his partner; Logan later dismissed the case against Gardner.[25]

As the senior member of Logan and Lincoln, Logan seemed disposed to leave debt collection to his junior partner, unless the case was inordinately complex or involved an appeal to the Illinois Supreme Court.[26] When Lincoln soloed that year, it usually involved relatively simple debt litigation. In November 1842, for example, Lincoln appeared in the Christian County courthouse to represent the interests of Alexander Ralston. Three years previously, Ralston had given a $100 promissory note to a man named John Gilbert, and Gilbert in turn gave the note to Henry Hardin. When Hardin tried to collect on the note with Ralston the latter refused to pay, claiming that the note had expired and moreover that he had already made good on the debt by giving various dry goods to Gilbert as part of their new business partnership. The court apparently did not accept this explanation—perhaps Gilbert disputed this, or maybe Ralston didn't properly document his little business labyrinth—and awarded Hardin $143 to cover the note and (presumably) other costs.[27]

Most of Lincoln's debt cases were such straightforward, bread-and-butter lawsuits. In April 1857, John N. Grant employed Lincoln to sue for collection of a promissory note for over $200 from Allen Combs, who failed to appear in the Sangamon County circuit court to defend himself. The judge awarded the amount of the note and damages to Lincoln's client.[28] Three years earlier, Lincoln appeared in the McLean County court on behalf of Asahel Woodworth, who sued Jesse Cox for failing to pay a debt; that court awarded Woodworth $110.48.[29] In July 1839, Lincoln represented James Bell, a dry goods merchant and Springfield entrepreneur who had been given a promissory note for $150 by Garrett Elkin, a local doctor who did double duty as Sangamon County's sheriff. Elkin gave Lincoln the power to "confess judgment"—that is, to admit the debt was valid in court—whereupon the court awarded Bell $159 in damages.[30]

And so it went, an endless stream of notes, literally thousands of them, during Lincoln's professional career. They provided good, steady work. Debt cases that only involved collection on a promissory note earned Lincoln anywhere from $5 to $50, depending on the circumstances: the number and amount of the notes, perhaps the distance Lincoln had to travel (Sangamon County court cases usually cost his client about $10), and possibly whether the case involved a jury trial or an appeal.[31] Not a lot of cash, to be sure, but the volume made up for the low return. Lincoln looked on debt collection as his foundation, his guaranteed source of cash year in and year out, around which he could pack other litigation that might be more lucrative but less reliable. Murder trials, divorces, and the like were relatively infrequent—but there was always another note.

He was more likely to represent the plaintiff than the debtor—much more so. Lincoln was the defendant's attorney in 713 debt-related cases during his career; he represented the plaintiff in such cases more than 1300 times.[32] It might be tempting to read into this a political or class bias on Lincoln's part. Scholars have long debated the role attorneys played in creating America's commercial economy. Some suggest that lawyers like Lincoln were the "shock troops of capitalism," acting as the witting tools of the rich and using the law in various ways to create massive inequities in Jacksonian America. Lincoln was always an outspoken advocate of commercial development, so it might be argued that he harbored an ingrained sympathy for the creditor class of capitalists, as opposed to their often hapless debtor victims.[33]

But this would be simplistic, and not very accurate. There was no clearly identifiable line separating a "creditor" from a "debtor." Many people were both at the same time, borrowing and loaning money in the same breath. Lincoln sometimes represented the same client as debtor and as creditor in different cases. John Billington, for example, hired Lincoln to collect on three $500 notes from James Mattlen, who borrowed the money to buy a flour and sawmill operation in Waynesville, Illinois; two years later, Billington was himself sued in a Sangamon County court by Henry Cannon, and this time Lincoln acted as Cannon's attorney.[34] Far from connecting Lincoln to an oppressive "capitalist class," Lincoln's debt-collection practice suggests that the very idea of such a class was problematic in antebellum America's fluid economic environment, particularly on the Illinois frontier.[35]

Approached by a creditor like Bell, Lincoln would have thumbed through his dog-eared copy of Chitty's *Pleadings* and found the normal form for debt proceedings, the writ of assumpsit. This particular writ was an ancient legal tool with roots in the fourteenth century. Assumpsit is a Latin term, meaning literally "he promised." If Lincoln were the attorney for the creditor, he would have filled out a writ that presumed a legally binding promise of repayment had not been kept. There was also a "writ of debt," but assumpsit was more useful and potentially more lucrative. An action of debt tried to recover only the amount of the note, whereas an action of assumpsit could require that amount and damages.[36]

Lincoln had other alternatives besides writs of debt and assumpsit, depending on a given creditor's circumstances. In 1842, Archibald Goddin hired Lincoln to help him foreclose a mortgage on Braddock Richmond, which involved Lincoln in a *scire facias* proceeding, another common-law form that was designed to help a creditor recover money owed on an agreement (in this case, a mortgage) that was over a year old.[37] In 1856, John Hart retained Lincoln to collect from William Dean money owed him from a variety of circumstances: two promissory notes, a $4 rental fee for the use of Hart's horses, $9 for board, and another $25 for various expenses. Dean lived out of state, but Lincoln found that he owned property in Illinois and subsequently pursued writs of attachment so the court could seize Dean's property and sell it as a way of satisfying his client's demands. Before the court could follow through on this, however, Hart and Dean apparently reached some sort of mutually agreeable arrangement, and Hart dropped the suit.[38] In 1837, Lincoln and Stuart represented the interests of Nicholas Bryan, who sued Thomas P. Smith for $31 worth of rock that Smith had failed to provide. Since the case involved more than a promissory note, Lincoln and Stuart filed a motion of "trespass on the case upon promises," which accused Smith of "contriving and fraudulently intending craftily and subtly to deceive and defraud" Bryan by failing to either provide the rock or return Bryan's money. Smith's financial situation was dire—court records indicated at least a half dozen other lawsuits from various creditors directed against him for various debts.

Strapped for cash, he failed to appear in the Sangamon County circuit court, which in turn seized a lot he owned in Springfield, the proceeds of which were used to repay Lincoln and Stuart's client, and several others.[39]

Writs of trespass on the case upon promises, scire facias proceedings, attachments, the omnipresent writs of assumpsit—they were like arrows in Lincoln's quiver, each with a slightly different length and shape, and each best suited for hitting different targets. Lincoln's experience and training as an attorney required him to assess the "targets" and then choose which "arrow" was best suited to strike its mark.

If he represented the debtor, he faced an entirely different set of problems. Now the question was how he might go about fashioning a convincing defense against a creditor who likely possessed some sort of written record that Lincoln's client had made a financial commitment.[40] Lincoln had a few options. He could counter that the debt in question had already been paid, as in the 1851 case *Alexander v. Parrish.* That particular case turned out well—the plaintiff, Milton Alexander, decided to drop the matter, and the suit was dismissed.[41] He could argue that the note had expired, if it had a specified date.[42] He could make the case for a "set off," pointing out that the defendant had incurred other expenses during a given business transaction that should be taken into account when assessing the amount of a debt.[43] Or Lincoln could argue on more narrowly technical grounds, as in 1838, when he got a debt dismissed in the Tazewell County circuit court for lack of jurisdiction.[44]

He could also try to persuade his client that a formal declaration of bankruptcy was the best strategy. But bankruptcy normally wasn't a viable solution. There was no bankruptcy legislation for most of Lincoln's lifetime, despite the fact that the U.S. Constitution explicitly authorized its creation. The subject was politically sensitive. Many ordinary people viewed bankruptcy legislation not as a way to protect those who were down on their luck, but as a means by which creditors could further dun debtors. Commerce-minded Whigs like Lincoln tended to favor bankruptcy laws as a way to encourage entrepreneurship and reasonable risk-taking, but Democrats dominated the presidency and Congress for much of the period, so little was accomplished.[45]

A Whiggish Congress finally passed a bankruptcy bill in 1841, and soon thereafter Lincoln (no doubt along with many other members of the American bar) was swamped with clients looking for a fresh start. Prior to 1842, Lincoln had been involved in only seven cases on the federal level.[46] Now he frequently found himself in the U.S. district courtroom petitioning the justices for discharges of debt under the new law. Lincoln litigated seventy-three such cases in seventeen months, nineteen alone during the month of October 1842. The proceedings were perfunctory and highly routinized. In one of those October cases, for example, he petitioned the court for bankruptcy relief on behalf of Henry A. Craw, who owned only a thirty-nine-acre plot of land and $60 worth of assets, but who owed a whopping $14,000 worth of debts. The court granted Craw's bankruptcy petition.[47]

Under pressure from the sort of disappointed people who lost thousands of dollars to men like Craw, Congress quickly repealed the act.[48] Lincoln's bankruptcy litigation bonanza was subsequently short-lived; he brought his last known bankruptcy petition before the court in June 1843.[49] It likely wasn't much of a moneymaker for him, anyway, since a bankrupt client was by definition unable to afford much in the way of lawyer's fees. Bankruptcy was so unusual that Lincoln didn't quite know what his fee for a discharge petition should be, confessing to a colleague that "I can not say there is any custom on the subject." One bankruptcy client, James Gambrell, could only pay Lincoln with a $20 promissory note for some firewood. For a man like Lincoln who spent so much of his time chasing down these little pieces of paper, it was a dubious reward, at best.[50]

On the whole, Lincoln's odds of success as a debtor's lawyer were not high. Taking the debt cases for a typical year, 1853, he could claim a victory—in the sense that his client was neither compelled to pay the debt or reach an out-of-court settlement—in only three of the twenty-nine cases in which he represented the defendant. In 1856 his odds were no better; of thirty-six such cases, he was again successful in only three. Two years later, Lincoln represented the interests of only thirteen debtor defendants, and they all lost or settled out of court. "There was no ground upon which to stand the case off," he informed one client.[51]

But how would Lincoln have defined "success" in this context? Most of his debtor clients had to know that, once they ended up before a judge facing their own signature on a valid promissory note, their options were very limited. If the debtor in question was himself owed money by another person, maybe he just needed time. Retaining Lincoln to fend off a hopeless case may have been just that; a stopgap, and a relatively cheap one at that: give Lincoln a few dollars to slow down collection long enough to dun someone else for the money. From this point of view, a lost case could have still been a "success" in the sense that it allowed a debtor to get his affairs in order. Lincoln was like a finger stuck in the dike, a finger that could not stay forever but might stay long enough to ward off the worst effects of the inevitable flood of debt.

In 1856, for example, Lincoln represented William J. Allen, a twenty-seven-year-old fellow lawyer from Marion, Illinois, who had been elected to the state legislature and would later serve as a U.S. circuit court judge. Allen was a man of means and social status. But he was unable to make good on two notes, totaling over $1200, that he had given to George W. McCollom. McCollom hauled Allen into court and convinced the judge to attach some of Allen's property. Lincoln apparently persuaded his client and McCollom to reach a settlement whereby Allen would pay back the notes, with interest, provided McCollom stayed the execution for nine months; perhaps just the time Allen needed to scrape together the money.[52]

But for every William Allen who used Lincoln as a stopgap, there were many others who were drowning and flailing about fruitlessly for a life preserver. In 1847 he represented Jesse Griffin from De Witt County, who had previously been ordered by the local justice of the peace to repay a $71.67 promissory note to John Ayers for some furniture. When the sheriff tried to execute the judgment by selling Griffin's property, he reported that Griffin had no assets. But Ayers got wind of the news that Griffin had just bought a house and a plot of land in Waynesville, Illinois—paying more than $100 in the process—and then tried to hide the transaction by deeding the lot to his six-year-old son, Josiah. Ayers filed a new suit in the De Witt circuit court, claiming fraud. Griffin hired Lincoln, who in court was greeted with the fact that his client had been foolish enough to purchase the Waynesville lot from none other than the justice of the peace who had ordered repayment of the promissory note in the first place, thus making the little subterfuge with his six year old an embarrassing debacle. The circuit court naturally seized the Waynesville lot and sold it to satisfy the debt.[53]

Lincoln's debt collection put him in touch with many people who had absolutely no means of satisfying their creditors. In 1837 Lincoln and Logan sent a promissory note owed by Thomas D. Potts to Galena, Illinois for collection, only to be informed that the note could not be paid because Potts was "worth nothing." Many other debtors simply disappeared—Braddock Richmond, for example, who was sued by Lincoln client Archibald Goddin in a foreclosure case but then failed to appear in the Tazewell County circuit court. The judge peremptorily ruled for Goddin, but to what end? Richmond was probably never seen in the area again. There were no professional collection agencies that specialized in tracking down delinquent debtors, and the notoriously thin law enforcement authorities could spare little time for such pursuits.[54]

People like Richmond could perhaps be forgiven for fleeing, because a stationary debtor who chose to remain at home faced attachments and sheriff's sales, with little recourse or relief. Sometimes, when presented with the *fait accompli* of a court proceeding by the creditor to get the money in question, a client would give Lincoln the power to "confess judgment" in court. The judge then had to decide whether the confession would be allowed (it usually was), at which point court officers sifted through the debtor's assets looking for a means of repayment. In November 1840, a Springfield merchant named David Spear allowed Lincoln to confess judgment on a debt of $110 owed by him to William D. Barrett. The confession proceeding handed over to the court a town lot in Springfield, which Barrett then purchased at a county auction for $111.75, thus satisfying the debt. Sometimes the power to confess judgment was written directly into a business arrangement. In 1846 Aaron Cosby secured a $466 debt with the firm of Atwood, Cole, and Crane on the promise that, should he fail to pay the note, Lincoln as his attorney would automatically confess judgment, probably at the insistence of his creditors, who harbored doubts about Cosby's ability to repay the loan. They must have known what they were doing, for Cosby did fail to pay his debt and Lincoln dutifully confessed judgment.[55]

Lincoln would not have been required to do a great deal of creative thinking for cases like Cosby's and Spear's. Indeed, debt collection in general did not demand extraordinary aptitude on his part—filling in of blank spaces on a writ of assumpsit required little in the way of lawyerly imagination or skill. Relatively few debt-collection cases involved a jury trial, or even the calling of witnesses. In 1850, for example, Lincoln litigated forty-two debt-collection cases: the usual mix of promissory notes, disputes between business partners and neighboring farmers, and so forth. Of those forty-two cases, only eight involved witness or deponent testimony, and only four resulted in a jury trial.[56]

Of course, debt matters could become complicated—Ralston's claim of having already paid his debt to Gilbert, for example—and debt collection was often embedded within other transactions and forms of litigation: probate, breach of contract, business partnerships, divorce, and child support payments.[57] Debt and mechanics' liens were also a fairly common mix; Lincoln litigated cases involving contractors who were sued by builders for failing to construct houses, parts of houses (porches, windows, doorframes, and the like), shops, railroads, sawmills, distilleries, flour mills, bridges, hotels, barns, and the local Sangamon County jail.[58]

Debtors and creditors alike tried to avoid trials: debtors for obvious reasons, but creditors also wanted to steer clear of actual litigation, preferring instead to use the threat of a lawsuit as a stick to force voluntary repayment. H. T. McHenry placed advertisements in the local Springfield paper asking "my friends to pay up some old scores" or risk "an unpleasant alternative." Other ads urged debtors to "Look at This!," "read and reflect," or admonished that "a stitch in time saves nine." Most creditors preferred to "save nine" by staying out of a courtroom and keeping the fees involved in hiring an attorney; and who really wanted to play the part of Simon Legree before a gallery of his neighbors by hauling another neighbor into court?[59]

Lincoln understood this. He frequently counseled his clients to attempt an arrangement out of court whereby all parties might reach a degree of satisfaction. "The payee of the note did write me that he had written [Luther S.] Allard on the subject of the note in your hands," Lincoln wrote to R. S. Thomas in 1854, and "if the letter does . . . agree to take $110 and my fee, settle the matter that way." In his notes for a law lecture, Lincoln made this philosophy explicit. "Discourage litigation," he advised other attorneys. "Persuade your neighbors to compromise whenever you can. Point out to them how the nominal winner is often a real loser—in fees, expenses, and waste of time." Lincoln practiced what he preached, managing to facilitate a negotiated settlement in a little over 380 of his debt-related cases.[60]

When clients did not pursue what Lincoln thought to be a reasonable settlement, he could grow annoyed. In 1859 he took a case for Peter Ambos, the treasurer of the Columbus Machine Manufacturing Company, who wanted to collect on five promissory notes owed to the company by James Barret. The amount of money involved was large, more than $10,000, and Lincoln tried to work with Barret—whom he described as "an honest and honorable man"—to sell some of his assets and satisfy Ambos by making payments on the debt without the necessity of a trial. "My impression is that the whole of the money cannot be got very soon, anyway, but that it all will be ultimately collected, and that it could be got faster by turning in every little parcel we can, than by trying to force it through by the law in a lump." But Ambos pursued Barret unmercifully for the entire amount. He put pressure on Lincoln, too, even suggesting at one point that Lincoln had failed to file some paperwork properly, thus delaying the case still further. Irritated, Lincoln finally suggested that Ambos get another lawyer. "I would now very gladly surrender the charge of the case to anyone you would designate, without charging anything for the much trouble I have already had," he wrote. Ambos did not take Lincoln up on the offer, who left the litigation in Herndon's hands as he departed for the White House—with some relief for, as he confessed, the Ambos lawsuit "has been a somewhat disagreeable matter to me."[61]

Debt collection could be frustrating, but more often than not it was just tedious. It might earn a living, but was otherwise little more than a stepping-stone to bigger and better things. Mississippi attorney Alexander G. McNutt, for example, was a struggling Vicksburg lawyer who was about to go broke until a local merchant threw all of his debt-collection business McNutt's way, enabling him to pull himself up by his bootstraps and establish a decent practice, along with a political career that eventually placed him in the governor's chair.[62]

Lawyers like McNutt who specialized in collection services (and there were some who did so) chose an avenue of the legal profession that called more for solid than flashy. Nashville collection attorney Godfrey Fogg, Sr. was described by a contemporary as having "conspicuously evinced all the qualities needful to success in that branch of his chosen profession." These included industry, "soundness and vigor of intellect," and "an adequate fund of legal erudition." It did not, however, include excellent speaking skills—"Mr. Fogg possessed few of the graces of oratory"—because debt cases were usually not entertaining fare for the citizens populating a courtroom gallery.[63]

But a debt-collection practice that on the surface looked boringly straightforward actually placed lawyers on ambivalent ground concerning how far they should go to collect a debt. A lawyer might do little more than file a writ, get the court to recognize the debt's validity, and then allow the local sheriff to worry about finding the debtor and seizing his assets. On the other hand, some attorneys thoroughly searched out debtor assets, tracking down leads in other counties and leading sheriffs to the whereabouts of land and other property owned by delinquent debtors.

Debt-collection lawyers had to be careful. They needed to be diligent enough that clients felt they received their money's worth, but a perceived excess of zeal might be construed by their neighbors as hard-edged and mean. On the cash-poor, credit-rich Illinois frontier many of Lincoln's neighbors owed someone else money; promissory notes resided in a lot of pockets. Watching him assist the court in seizing someone's else's land, home, cattle, cash, and other property surely led some to think, "there but for the grace of God . . .".

Lawyers did not yet have the level of professionalization necessary to collectively insulate themselves from the wagging fingers of neighbors who wondered how they could be so heartless. Plenty of people thought the whole affair was cruel and undemocratic. "We should not see men snapped and snarled at as dogs," groused one critic, "we should not see lawyers demanding five percent for delivering a creditor his money which has been paid him, for recovering it, and which he has long detained and employed to his private purposes."[64] Lawyers themselves did not know where to stand on these issues. There was "a certain class of cold-blooded collecting attorneys," sniffed one lawyer, "who were known to put in exercise all the harsher expedients known to the law" in representing their creditor clients. This smacked of a questionable opportunism. Following an economic downturn in Mississippi during the 1820s, according to Henry S. Foote, "it was really almost like the letting loose of an avalanche from some lofty Alpine height. Attorneys came in great numbers almost by every stagecoach."[65] They did so because it was easier to dun strangers than friends. "The business of *collection* fell into the hands of attorneys who had not long been resident in the distressed and bankrupt community," Foote wrote. Local lawyers were squeamish about collecting from anxious neighbors, "persons long known to them by multiple acts of civility and kindness."[66]

Lincoln was no stranger to central Illinois. He knew a lot of people. Many of them were his friends. They were voters, and they were potential customers. He could not afford to alienate either neighborhood debtors who might see him as a ruthless sort, or neighborhood creditors who might think twice about hiring him if he seemed to be a less-than-industrious collector.

The only real solution was distance. As he went about tracking down debtors, or trying to protect debtors from the results of their own business errors, Lincoln needed to cultivate an I'm-just-doing-my-job attitude, and this in an era before there was a sophisticated structure to the bar that afforded a ready-made professional identity.

The process probably began during the initial interview. Imagine Lincoln and his client meeting in his office. They would be seated across the beat-up table with all the penknife marks, the noise of the traffic from Springfield's downtown streets filtering through the window from below. Lincoln sweeps away the clutter of the place, maybe tossing a few newspapers in the corner before settling down. Maybe Billy is there, maybe not. It is not hard to see him avoiding such things, research being his strong suit. So maybe he excuses himself and ambles across the square to dig through the law library in the statehouse, or buries himself in a book on the couch.

Does Lincoln take notes? Possibly. He would want to write down somewhere at least the barebones information of names, dates, and money amounts. Knowing Lincoln, he grabs whatever paper is near at hand. This is an era before the ubiquitous modern legal pad (which was not invented until 1886), and Lincoln is famously sloppy in administrative matters, so he likely somewhere has a pile of nondescript sheets of foolscap or whatever: a "debt-collection" stack, maybe, or his version of a "to do" file. Or maybe the notes get stuffed inside that stovepipe hat.

Much of what he has to say does not have to be written down; the litigator of countless debt cases, Lincoln has a mental checklist ready at hand. If the client is a creditor, he asks some basic questions about the transaction: Who owes you the money? How much? When was the note due? Maybe he wants the client to produce the note, to verify its existence and whether it meets the basic requirements of legal authenticity: names, amounts, signatures, and due dates. Who was the original signee, and how many times has it changed hands? Do you know anything about the debtor's financial situation?

If the client is a debtor, Lincoln pulls out of his head a different checklist. How much do you owe? Who has the note? Maybe Lincoln quietly sizes up the client seated across the table: his clothing, his demeanor, whether he has an air of real desperation about him. Can you come up with the money? Do you have any assets you can sell? Any land? Livestock? What about your house? He probably has some way of suggesting, in a roundabout and tactful way, that it would be best not to try hiding anything from the court.

Perhaps Lincoln is just a bit more animated, a bit more cheerful when the client is a creditor. He likes entrepreneurs, and politically he is an economic development–type Whig who is naturally drawn to men who have money and loan it out as a way of spurring new investments and business. On the other hand, perhaps he assumes a slight air of sympathy with a debtor: echoes of the Berry store and his national debt.

Modern lawyers call this the creation of a "legal self." They are taught that the initial interview with any client is a crucial moment at which they need to establish a persona appropriate to the situation at hand. A divorce lawyer, for example, must often steer the client away from the inevitable anger and resentment of such a proceeding, and so tries to strike a balance between compassion and a coolly rational, unemotional appraisal of the case. Nearly all lawyers need to cultivate their "insider status," the idea in the client's head that they need the lawyer's expertise and skills if they are to receive their just rewards. And nearly all lawyers, whatever their specialty, seem to feel the need to emphasize the head over the heart—that is, to set the client's feelings of anger, pride, revenge, and the like aside and focus on the more prosaic matters of what can be proven and what cannot, and what the law will or will not allow.[67]

Lincoln's "legal self" for debt collection pointed towards the need to emphasize routine, as a way of establishing a proper personal detachment from the proceeding itself. Of course, it helped that many of these business transactions truly were routine, involving exchanges that called forth no particular feelings from anyone concerned: Asa Harrison sued William Greer for failing to refund money on delivery of some hogs; Robert Purvance sued William Carothers for payment of five promissory notes, worth $85 each; George Blane sued Thomas Bainbridge for a $114 debt over the boarding of a couple of farmhands—the cases line up, one after the other, in an assembly-line manner.[68]

But there were other debt cases that surely weren't so routine, cases involving personal tragedy, loss, and difficulty. In 1858, Elisha Crane rented a wheatfield from Frank Thompson, and promised to give Thompson a third of the crop as payment. But the wheat crop was wrecked in a hailstorm and further depleted by rust, so that Crane, despairing of getting any crop at all, decided not to harvest what little was left. Thompson hired Lincoln and sued Crane for the rent; Lincoln won the case and got Thompson $45.

The court documents do not by themselves convey much more than the outcome of a typical case, one of hundreds like it in the records of Illinois' judicial system and Abraham Lincoln's sprawling debt-collection practice. But there were human elements involved. The sharecropping arrangement itself suggests that Elisha Crane was not a man of means, so perhaps he cursed his sour luck with more anxiety than usual as hail banged down on his crop. Maybe he appealed to Frank Thompson for more time, another rental arrangement, some Christian charity—anything. Perhaps Thompson was sympathetic but himself in need of money to meet his own needs. Or maybe not; maybe Thompson was callous and entirely oblivious to Crane's difficulties.[69]

We will never know all the layers of personal and social meaning that lay beneath the surface of *Thompson v. Crane* and countless other such cases. But Lincoln would surely have known at least some of this; he could not afford to get too involved in the fact that many debtors had families who needed the money and would suffer because of a debt's collection, or the fact that many debtors knew him personally, or were connected to him in any number of ways. People he collected money for—or collected money from—later sat on juries in other cases Lincoln litigated, or attended political rallies where Lincoln spoke, or ran into him on the streets of Springfield.

On those occasions when personal considerations arose, Lincoln backed off. In the Barret case, he realized that his characterization of Barret as an "honest and honorable man," his attempts to mediate a payment arrangement on the debt, and his personal exertions in trying to help Barret find ways to pay his debts, might appear to some as if he had allowed a friendship to compromise his professionalism. In a letter to one of the litigants, Lincoln therefore took pains to point out that "there are no special personal relations between Barret and myself. We are personal friends in a general way—no business transactions between us—not akin, and opposed on politics."[70]

Lincoln was usually able to muster the necessary distance to litigate collection cases involving people who in other contexts he knew well. In 1853, he and Herndon represented James Shields, with whom he had nearly fought a duel several years before, to recover the proceeds of an $1,100 note. He also litigated two collection cases involving his famous political rival Stephen Douglas (even though Lincoln never seems to have represented Douglas himself), and he represented Joshua Speed—perhaps his closest friend and confidant—in a variety of business matters. In 1844, Lincoln was even willing to act as an attorney for several men who sued Speed in a complicated debt/foreclosure case.[71]

His relationship with Speed offers a telling illustration of Lincoln's professional ethic of distance. Before the war Joshua Speed was the only man with whom Lincoln could be described as sharing an intimate friendship. They shared room and board in Speed's Springfield general store when Lincoln came to town to begin his law practice, and they shared advice on life, politics, marriage, and women. "You well know that I do not feel my own sorrows much more keenly than I do yours," read a typical exchange from Lincoln to Speed during the winter of 1842, when both young men were at or near the doorstep to matrimony, with all its attendant anxieties. "I hope and believe, that your present anxiety and distress about *her* [Speed's fiancé, Fanny Henning] health and *her* life, must and will forever banish these horid [*sic*] doubts, which I know you sometimes felt, as to the truth of your affection for her." Lincoln wrote of such matters to no one else, and revealed to no one else but Speed his own fears and worries about his relationship with Mary, and women generally. Here was a rare thing indeed for Abraham Lincoln: a trusted, personal confidant. "You know my desire to befriend you is everlasting—that I will never cease, while I know how to do any thing," he wrote Speed.[72]

If there was ever a person with whom Lincoln might have mixed business and friendship, it would have been Speed. But the tone of intimacy vanished when Speed became a client. The sections of his letters to Speed dealing with various collection matters sounded much like any other business correspondence, and he carefully delineated the sections of their letters dealing with business and pleasure. "Yours of the 9th. Inst. is duly received, which I do not meet as a 'bore,' but as a most welcome visiter [*sic*]," he wrote to Speed in May 1843, "I will answer the business part of it first." Lincoln could also grow stiff and even rather annoyed with his old friend when he believed Speed was not quite able to understand the litigation Lincoln pursued in his behalf. "It may be that you do not precisely understand the nature and result of the suit against you and Bell's estate," Lincoln wrote, "It is a chancery suit, and has been brought to a final decree, in which, you are treated as a nominal party only. . . . So far, you are not injured; because you are released from the debt. . . . I should be much pleased to see [you?] here again; but I must, in candour, say I do not perceive how your personal presence would do any good in the business matter."[73]

As his practice matured, Lincoln saw fewer debt cases than earlier in his career. In 1845, he litigated fifty-six debt-related cases, which was 67 percent of his total for that year. Five years later, he litigated forty-two debt cases out of seventy-three, and in 1857, fifty-two of the ninety-one cases in which Lincoln appeared as an attorney of record involved debt collection of some kind. In other words, collection constituted somewhere around 50 to 60 percent of his practice; not quite as much as it once did.[74]

But debt was still a substantial presence in his practice. It was also a type of litigation he preferred to handle himself. In 1845 Herndon was the sole attorney of record on only three debt cases, and even twelve years later, when presumably a busy Lincoln would have entrusted such matters to his junior partner, Herndon went solo on only fourteen debt cases. During 1860, the final full year of his practice, Lincoln was still an attorney of record in sixty-two debt cases.[75]

His debt-collection practice seems rather like all those penknife marks on his office table—a collection of tiny little gouges, of no real interest to anyone other than the litigants themselves. Not historians, who can find little storytelling or analytical meat on their desiccated bones; not society as a whole, which witnessed far too many debt transactions to count during the volatile early years of the Market Revolution; and probably not to Lincoln himself, who needed the work but who surely saw the endless stream of assumpsit writs and perfunctory collection judgments as rather like the white noise of his professional life—a background buzz of little cases.

He kept at debt collection past the point where it was a necessary part of his practice. By the mid-1850s he had enough lucrative cases in other areas that he could probably have foregone the smaller promissory note cases that were vital in his early days as a lawyer. But small-scale debt litigation remained, all the way to the end of his law career, so that one wonders whether it is indicative of some deep insecurities in Lincoln, an unwillingness to let go of five-dollar debt cases because, small though they were, they represented steadiness for a man who grew up poor and experienced his share of instability.

Whatever the case may be, from his own experience as a debtor and his "national debt," and also from years of watching just how damaging excessive debt could be, Lincoln carried at least one trait away from his debt practice: he rarely borrowed money.[76] He never bought into another pig in a poke like the Berry store; in fact, he seldom invested money in any business enterprise. He even avoided the era's favorite hobby of land speculation. Throughout his life, Lincoln was "frugal to excess," according to one colleague. Herndon observed that Lincoln had "no avarice of the get" but he did have "the avarice of the keep."[77]

By "the keep" Herndon meant financial prudence, to an excessive degree (at least according to Billy). But we could read a bit deeper and see in this value of personal prudence about money a more professionally driven discretion about the sorts of questions he should ask about the characters of the hundreds of debtors and creditors whom his practice paraded before him. He could not really ask Blackstone's questions about whether or not the creditor was industrious enough to deserve the money, or whether the system favored dissolute debtors. Eighteenth-century notions about gentlemanly honor and debts contracted in the shadow of one's character were becoming increasingly obsolete, and for a lawyer like Lincoln, got in the way. Ironically, the same man who was once loaned money on the basis of his own honesty and rectitude would as a lawyer come to see that such things did not matter so much, not from the perspective of a debt-collection lawyer. All that really mattered, in the end, were the notes.

Chapter Four

The Energy Men

J ames Frazier Reed came to Lincoln about a note sometime
in the early winter of 1845–46. Lincoln and Herndon's law
office was at that time located in the Tinsley Building, near
Springfield's busy central square. Getting to the office,
Reed would have dodged people, wagons, horses, oxen, and maybe
some pigs or a few stray dogs. If there had been any recent rain at all,
he would also have picked his way through the water left standing
in the wheel ruts that crisscrossed the town's packed-dirt thorough-
fares. At his back was the state capitol building, still unfinished, put
there at least in part because Springfield's mud roads hooked into a
county road system that, for all it lacked in ambience, gave legislators
decent access to the town; and so Springfield thrived.[1]

The bustle fit Reed well. Born in Ireland, he was older than Lincoln—
forty six—but he had the drive of a man half his age. Reed was involved
in a variety of projects: lead mining, a general store, manufacturing,
farming, real estate, and railroad speculation. His cabinet furniture shop
became the nucleus of a small town named after him, Jamestown, on
the Sangamon River just east of Springfield. He was yet another veteran
of the Black Hawk War, and he was the U.S. pension agent for Springfield.

There were those who took Reed for snobbish, but that wasn't quite
right. He dressed well and rode fine horses, but he was more high-
handed than high-and-mighty. Reed felt the pressures of a growing
family—he had four children under his roof, along with a sturdy but
somewhat difficult wife, who suffered from constant migraine head-

aches—and the pressures of the need to get ahead, and he reacted with straightforward boldness. He seemed to be untroubled by doubt.[2]

When he made his way up the stairs of the Tinsley building to Lincoln and Herndon's office in the winter of 1846, Reed had gotten himself overextended. He had borrowed close to $1,000 from another Springfield man named William Butler, and Butler called him on the note. Reed couldn't pay, so Butler sued him in the Sangamon circuit court. Reed retained Lincoln and gave him the power to confess judgment. The court ruled in Butler's favor. All in a day's work for Lincoln.[3]

It was routine for Reed, too, because he made a habit of living on the edge. In 1842 the circuit court sold some of his land to satisfy a $45 debt, and a year later he was successfully sued by a man named Maurice Doyle for a $516 note. William Butler brought three other suits against him for promissory notes and a mortgage foreclosure. Reed was also unable to pay the laborers he hired to haul rock and wood for a railroad bridge he and Reuben Bradford contracted to build. Lincoln represented Reed in many of these proceedings, as well as several others. The Irishman was a steady source of business.[4]

Reed was an American archetype, the very picture of that restless vigor described by Alexis de Tocqueville in his 1831 classic *Democracy in America*. Touring parts of New England, the South and the West, Tocqueville saw many versions of James Reed: driven men of humble birth who reached out in all directions at once trying to prosper and become a winner in the American game. Tocqueville shook his head at them, thinking their eyes were bigger than their stomachs. "Their taste for large fortunes persists, though large fortunes are rare," he wrote, "and on every side we trace the ravages of inordinate and unsuccessful ambition kindled in hearts which it consumes in secret and in vain."

He was not sure he liked this aspect of American life. It often smacked of a small, grasping quality that he found repugnant. On the other hand, Tocqueville thought the frank style and straightforward manners of these same Americans was bracing. "There are many little attentions that an American does not care about," he noted, because "he thinks they are not due to him, or he presumes that they are not known to be due. He therefore either does not perceive a rudeness or he forgives it; his manners become less courteous, and his character more plain and masculine."[5]

Americans stripped away the manners and the "many little attentions," and what was left was energy, raw and unembellished. Tocqueville saw it everywhere around him: people pushing, shoving, dodging, and colliding into one another because their efforts pressed out rather than up. American energy was flat and broad, and actually rather monotonous. "The love of wealth mainly drives them into business and manufactures," he wrote, and "they cannot prosper without strictly regular habits and a long routine of petty uniform acts. The stronger the passion is, the more regular are these habits and the more uniform are these acts."[6]

Springfield crackled with this kind of energy. There was Robert Allen of Greensburg, Kentucky; the same age as Reed, he made a comfortable fortune in real estate speculation, farming, mercantile sales, and a stagecoach service that carried passengers and mail to and from Springfield. Amos Cutler was a harness maker and tanner who sold real estate on the side. Jacob Bunn was a native of New Jersey who ran a grocery, bought and sold land, and eventually became a banker. David Spear prospered as a dry-goods merchant, land speculator, and stockholder in railroads and banks; he owned $80,000 worth of land by 1860.[7]

Lincoln knew them well. Bunn employed him often as a debt collector, as did Robert Allen. Lincoln also signed the petition recommending Allen's appointment as a U.S. marshal, and his widow retained Lincoln to settle the debts accrued against Allen's estate after he died in 1854. Lincoln acted as an arbitrator for the dissolution of a business partnership between David and Isaac Spear, who owned a general store—located in a building once owned by James Reed. Springfield's entrepreneurs crisscrossed one another like those ruts in the mud street. They appeared at Lincoln's law office door—as they did for other attorneys in the area—because their "long routines of petty and uniform acts" often involved extensive debt and risk.[8]

Lincoln usually showed up when their frenetic pursuit of wealth had gone too far. This meant a deluge of promissory notes, of course, as they loaned money and then sought a return on a delinquent debt, or borrowed money they could not repay. But there were other circumstances in which Lincoln helped ease their pain.

As he did with David and Isaac Spear, Lincoln was sometimes called upon to help settle accounts when partnerships ended. In the Spear case, their partnership in the general store had been long (eighteen years) and apparently prosperous; during the negotiations, they agreed to divide several thousand dollars worth of real estate and merchandise. Other partners could not or would not settle their differences out of court. Peter VanBergen— who had loaned Lincoln money for his failed New Salem general store and then sued Lincoln when the store collapsed—entered into a land-speculation partnership with William Singleton, in which VanBergen would supply the capital for Singleton to buy and sell plots of land at a profit. Singleton bought over a thousand acres of land, but Van Bergen was unhappy with his partner's accounting for his investment and hired Lincoln and Herndon to dissolve the partnership and recover almost a thousand dollars of his money. Singleton responded that VanBergen actually owed him over $5,000 for the expenses he accrued while managing their land. Their disputes were never resolved, and after several years, the Sangamon County Circuit Court removed the case from its docket.[9]

Partnership dissolutions could be difficult, requiring Lincoln to pick his way around all sorts of relationships while trying to successfully disentangle the partners in question. When gold fever struck Springfield during the 1849 California rush, five local men—Lewis and Hayden Keeling, H. C. St. Clair, John Robinson, and the appropriately named Gold Butler—formed a partnership to travel to California and equally divide whatever money or land they earned. Butler in turn divided his share with another man, Robert C. Arnold, and then died during the westward trip. Butler's estate administrator and Arnold hired Lincoln and Herndon, asserting that the other partners had made a considerable profit on their California adventure but had shared none of the proceeds with Butler or Arnold. Lewis Keeling's attorney argued that Butler had never really been a legitimate partner in the scheme in the first place. Keeling eventually settled the matter for $200, and the court formally dissolved whatever arrangement had once existed between the men.[10]

Some of these affairs were far-flung across time as well as space, as was evident in the 1846 case of *Hawks v. Lands.* Matthew Hawks was another man-on-the-make who came to Illinois from Kentucky planning originally to take up farming but instead invested his money in a dry-goods firm. He partnered with Samuel Lands, but in 1841 Lands decided to drop out of the business, agreeing to give Hawks the firm's assets as long as Hawks also paid the firm's debts. This included a $500 note Lands owed the firm of Rockhill and Company, a note that for some reason Hawks felt he should not pay. Lands felt otherwise and sued Hawks, winning a judgment in the McLean County circuit court on a technicality (Hawks had not filed his paperwork in time). The court ruled that Hawks had to pay up, to the tune of $419.43.

That was no small sum, especially for a striver like Matthew Hawks. The dry-goods store had proven to be a constant struggle, with too much competition and too few profits. Hawks decided instead to try different pursuits: flaxseed oil (used in medicines as a laxative and an expectorant), wool production, and cloth dressing. A good American-style entrepreneur, he tried to do all three at the same time, growing some of the flax himself while loaning out bushels of seed to area farmers (who would in turn sell back to him the product he made into oil), and also operating three wool-carding machines to create and dress cloth. He set up distribution lines in Chicago and St. Louis, slowly building his little flax and wool empire.

But there was still that pesky debt from the dry-goods store, and in 1846 he hired Lincoln to do something about it. Appealing the case to the state supreme court, Lincoln argued that the judge in the case five years previously had incorrectly denied Hawks a continuance to address his paperwork problems, that the court accepted some papers that were wrongly numbered, and that the judge had improperly refused to accept a $1,200 "set off" against the original store debt that would have paid the Lands's note. None of this helped; Hawks lost his case. He would later abandon the flax-oil project, concentrating instead on wool carding, and then turning to an entirely different line—managing a hotel.[11]

Go-getters like Matthew Hawks could step on a lot of toes when their projects ran into trouble. In 1855, Lincoln was hired by Eliphalet Knight to sue the heirs of Washington Carter, his deceased partner in a business that bought and sold livestock and speculated in land and farming. At issue was a 615–acre plot of land. Lincoln brought Knight's interests to the Vermilion County circuit court, and the judge appointed a three-man commission to divide the land; the commissioners eventually gave Knight half the parcel, awarded dower rights to Carter's widow, and split the rest among three minor heirs. By the time the case was settled, the apparently simple partnership between Knight and Carter had involved over a dozen litigants (counting plaintiffs, defendants, heirs, and their administrators and guardians), the testimony of ten witnesses, and an impressive stack of court orders, subpoenas, decrees, and affidavits.[12]

Lincoln was also called upon to deal with breach of contract disputes between entrepreneurs. This included the thousands of creditor/debtor disputes he litigated over the years, a promissory note being fundamentally a contractual agreement. But there were other possibilities under the law: Blackstone wrote of "formal" and "simple" contracts—that is, written or verbal agreements—for the exchange of things (horses, hogs, land) or performance of an action (building a house, hauling wood), in an expressed or implied manner, the latter "such as reason and justice dictate, and which the law presumes that every man undertakes a duty to perform."[13]

Lincoln litigated some relatively simple and straightforward contractual agreements. In 1858 he was hired by Thomas Gill, who was sued by Thomas Hildreth for breach of contract in failing to deliver $4,000 worth of hogs, a dispute that was settled out of court. In 1840 he and Stuart represented Archibald Hood, who signed a contract with John W. Gray to cut some stone but then was not paid for his work; Lincoln and Stuart won that case. In 1856 Lincoln was hired by Dick H. Phelps, who had contracted with Joseph McGee to deliver five thousand bushels of corn to Port Isabel, Illinois, but did not do so on a date that satisfied McGee, who won his case in the Cass County circuit court. Lincoln appealed the ruling to the state supreme court on a procedural issue; the court ordered a new trial and McGee won again, but the damages the second time around were several hundred dollars less than the original ruling—a victory of sorts for Lincoln's client.[14]

These were not difficult cases. But in the hands of overextended antebellum entrepreneurs, contracts could generate thorny legal disputes. Lorenzo Hamilton hired Lincoln to navigate one such dispute in 1855, concerning a 320–acre parcel of land in Peoria County. Hamilton bought the land from William Hassen of New York for $500. Before he actually gave Hassen the money, however, Hamilton transferred half his interest in the land to Aylett Buckner (who was in turn acting as a trustee for Ann Strother) and the other half to Joseph and Jabish Eddy. Buckner and the Eddys saw fit to guarantee their investment by having Hamilton sign an agreement—in legal terms, a "covenant"—that he would not do anything that might impair their interests. Hamilton then proceeded to do just that, canceling his original purchase of the land from Hassen and causing the entire deal to collapse. Buckner and the Eddys understandably saw this as a violation of their covenant with Hamilton and sued.

As Hamilton's lawyer, Lincoln probably thought at first that he had few options; his client had signed a legally binding contract not to do the very thing he did. But Lincoln noticed a technical defect in the proceedings. Buckner and the Eddys had filed their suit jointly, whereas the filings should have been separated, one for each of the half-interests they possessed in the deal—or at least Lincoln could make a plausible argument to that effect. He filed a motion with the circuit court, and won the case. The state supreme court later reversed the decision, but Lincoln was not involved in the appeal.[15]

Hamilton's motives in setting this affair in motion are impossible to divine. Perhaps he was just a careless businessman. But more likely he was another land speculator whose resources were stretched thin, who took a chance with those resources and lost. The case records suggest a plausible scenario: Hamilton thinks the 320–acre parcel is a solid investment, but lacks cash. At the same time, he owes money to Ann Strother—or rather, her deceased husband, R. T. Strother, which is why her trustee, Buckner, handles the transaction—and he owes a debt to the Eddys. So he covers the debts he owes Strother and the Eddys by shifting his "investment"—no investment at all, really, since no money has yet changed hands—in the 320–acre tract to them: not a bad deal, provided everything falls into place. But then some unknown circumstance forces him to cancel the original deal, and the whole house of cards comes crashing down.

The energy men seemed to habitually build these houses, out of credit, speculation, and risk. Lorenzo Hamilton did so. Lincoln represented him in several cases of a nature similar to *Hamilton v. Buckner*. In 1853 Hamilton hired Lincoln to sue the city of Pekin over land the city was supposed to purchase from him and a partner to build a ferry; the city reneged on the deal when it turned out that Hamilton did not have clear title to the land—eventually they settled the matter out of court. In 1858 Hamilton and Jefferson Dugger did not pay the balance due on a couple of notes they owed to the firm of Oliver B. Tweedy and Company. Hamilton hired Lincoln but failed to appear in court, and lost a judgment for over $1,100. In 1854 Hamilton found an error in the deed related to a foreclosed mortgage, hired Lincoln to bring the matter before the Tazewell County circuit court, and got the amount of foreclosure money substantially increased.[16]

There are enough of these men and their deals scattered throughout Lincoln's practice to suggest a business culture that encouraged risky, wheels-turning-inside-of-wheels dealings. In many ways, Lincoln's role in this culture was about negatives. Unpaid promissory notes and broken partnerships and contracts—Lincoln earned much of his living by picking up the pieces when things went wrong.

He likely cultivated a dispassionate image for Lorenzo Hamilton and others who came to him expecting legal solutions to their shattered business deals. In much the same way that he could not afford close inspection of the values and business judgment of those thousands of creditors and debtors he met during the course of his debt-collection practice, so too would he have been wise to avoid questioning too closely the values of clients who wanted him to fix the consequences of their business actions. Given his innate prudence and his abhorrence of personal debt—his avarice of the "keep"—Lincoln must have privately shaken his head in a what-were-you-thinking? sort of way as he went about performing legal heroics for overextended and often reckless men. But those head shakes would have remained private.

Besides, there were plenty of values Lincoln admired in the energy men. Representing them was about more than acting as their legal janitor; sometimes their cases concerned positives as well as negatives, embodying the principles of economic development and entrepreneurial spirit that he admired and wished to cultivate.

Lincoln saw himself as a walking, talking American success story, a self-described "friendless, uneducated, penniless boy" who used the skills of an entrepreneur—diligence, intelligence, perseverance, and a bit of luck—to climb into the ranks of middle-class society. He may not have been one of Tocqueville's restless class, exactly; he was not a wheeler-dealer. But Lincoln liked businessmen on the whole, and he believed he shared most of their basic values.[17]

As a politician, business and economic development was Lincoln's specialty—in fact his signature subject—during the 1840s and 1850s. Long before he cared or talked much about slavery, Lincoln talked about the economy. In particular, he wanted what Americans of the time called "internal improvements": government-funded roads, bridges, canals, navigation improvements to rivers, and subsidies for railroads and technological development. "That the poorest and most thinly populated countries would be greatly benefitted by the opening of good roads, and in the clearing of navigable streams within their limits, is what no person will deny," he declared in 1832.[18]

He supported an ambitious program created by the legislature during the late 1830s that would have funneled millions of state dollars into road and canal construction, railroad development, and river improvements. Lincoln led the way in garnering legislative approval of the plan, which was ambitious and in some ways irresponsible, for it committed Illinois to a long list of expenditures in the hopes that good economic times would follow. Normally a cautious and pragmatic man, Lincoln's embrace of the internal improvements scheme was an idealistic (and perhaps even a bit reckless) rendering of the American Dream; he enthused to one friend that he hoped he would someday be remembered as the "De Witt Clinton of Illinois."[19]

But the program was wrecked by a depression in 1839 that plunged Illinois deep into debt. Most of Lincoln's political allies saw the handwriting on the wall and chose to abandon the half-finished canals and roadbeds while they could still salvage something of the state's battered economic structure (not to mention their own political fortunes). Even so, Lincoln stuck to his guns, at considerable political risk, for the improvements program had become unpopular among voters who feared higher taxes. When the legislature finally scuttled what was left of it in 1840, Lincoln thought a golden opportunity to enrich the state and attract investment had been lost. "The Internal Improvement System will be put down in a lump, without benefit of clergy," he wrote sadly to Stuart.[20]

Nationwide, Americans debated these questions as matters of party political ideology. Whigs lined up on the side of internal improvements against Democrats who wanted curbs on government spending. The Supreme Court also wrestled with these issues, creating legal changes that generally favored economic development over attempts to impede the economy in the name of individual interests.[21]

All of that was high politics and constitutional law. In the courtrooms of Illinois' Eighth Circuit, lawyer Lincoln saw the grubby little details of internal improvements and economic development, and what he saw was more complicated than politics, party ideology, or his own personal preferences. Just as he could not chide entrepreneurs for their mistakes, so too he could not afford to pick and choose cases based on which forms of litigation best advanced his economic agenda.

If there was one overriding, fundamental concern for businessmen and investors in Lincoln's day, it was the need to move about the countryside. The energy men needed roads, clear rivers, canals, and railroads to act as sluiceways through which their ambitions could pour into the far corners of Illinois. Lincoln was all for this; road construction was a natural extension of the internal improvements plans he advocated. His name appeared on a number of county petitions for road construction throughout the 1830s and 1840s, and he helped sponsor legislation funding new roads in various locations throughout Illinois, as in January 1835 when he wrote a bill to create a road from Logansport, Indiana, across the state line and across Illinois, "thence to the Lower Yellow Banks on the Mississippi river."[22]

His practice sometimes brought him opportunities to help local officials do the things he advocated on the legislative level. In 1853 Woodford County was sued by William T. Adams, whom the county had paid $30 as compensation for building a road through his property. Adams thought this was not enough, and he sued the county for more money. Lincoln represented the county, but he lost, as the jury awarded Adams over $200 more than the amount he had already received.[23]

At other times, however, he represented clients whose actions limited municipalities in their attempts to build more efficient transportation systems. In 1850 he represented Gideon Hawley, who built a fence across a road in Tazewell County, near the town of Pekin. Hawley was one of Pekin's founding citizens. He obtained the town's first liquor license in 1829 and operated a hotel and tavern along with various other business and real estate ventures. Why he blocked the road is unclear, but he irritated county supervisors enough that they brought lawsuits to stop him. Lincoln represented Hawley, and got the supervisors' lawsuit thrown out, arguing that the commissioners had no legal standing to bring such a suit.[24]

On other occasions, he acted as mediator between the opposing sides. John Buckles hired him in 1857 to do what he had successfully accomplished for Hawley: stop a county road from being constructed through his property. In this case, Buckles not only objected to the road, but he also built a fence across its path, thus earning a lawsuit from the Logan County road commissioner. The two sides eventually negotiated a settlement, and the case was dismissed.[25]

In one interesting twist, Lincoln represented several men who were sued for their failure to keep clear the roads they were charged to oversee. In 1846, Menard County officials brought lawsuits against road commissioners Bennet Abell, Bluford Atterberry, and William P. Young for failing to do their jobs. Young, for example, was accused of not "keep[ing] well cleaned, smooth and in good repair so as to afford a safe and free passage to waggons [*sic*] and other carriages" the road from New Market to Athens. Abell and Atterberry faced similar charges. Given his fondness for transportation development and improvement, Lincoln might have been expected to sympathize with the county, and maybe he did; but he defended the three accused commissioners. He represented them well: Lincoln got Young acquitted in a jury trial, and a month later, the other two cases were dismissed.[26]

There is no identifiable pattern here, no underlying code of conduct in the way Lincoln approached this litigation. Sometimes he represented government officials who wanted to create better roads and other transportation improvements, and sometimes he represented people who, with or without good cause, had gotten in their way. And sometimes Lincoln was involved in cases that had no clearly marked lines between development and obstruction. In 1846, for example, he represented several citizens of Menard County who were battling county commissioners concerning the proper location of a road running between Petersburg and Sugar Grove. The commissioners, along with numerous other county residents, wanted a new road constructed that would bypass a hill that became muddy and nearly unusable in wet weather; Lincoln's clients wanted the old route preserved, and they eventually prevailed. Which side represented progress and which represented obstructionism? It is difficult to say.[27]

Perhaps Lincoln had some of these cases in mind when he gave a speech on internal improvements during his brief stay in Congress in 1848. The speech in general, while favoring internal improvements, focused not so much on the dreams of economic expansion that drove him in the 1830s, but rather on the need to surmount obstacles and overcome difficulties in prosperity's name. "That the subject is a difficult one, can not be denied," he declared, "All can recur to instances of this difficulty in the case of county-roads, bridges, and the like. One man is offended because a road passes over his land, and another is offended because it does *not* pass over his; one is dissatisfied because the bridge, for which he is taxed, crosses the river on a different road from that which leads from his house to town; another can not bear that the county should be got in debt for these same roads and bridges; while not a few struggle hard to have roads located over their lands, and then stoutly refuse to let them be opened until they are first paid the damages. Even between the different wards, and streets, of towns and cities, we find this same wrangling, and difficulty."[28]

His law practice tempered and educated his politics. Lincoln the diehard internal improvements Whig got a strong taste, as Lincoln the lawyer, of the ways in which government officials, private property owners, and businessmen could run afoul of one another in their zeal to either get ahead or protect personal interests. Road construction and location was not so simple a matter as it may have seemed in a stump speech or a legislative program.

Technological innovations likewise presented more ambivalence for Lincoln than we might expect. He loved gadgets, and even dabbled at being an inventor himself. In 1849 he applied for a patent on his design for "a new and improved manner of combining adjustable buoyant chambers with steam boats." His idea involved fitting river vessels with air bags made of metal, wood, and India rubber cloth that could be inflated to lift the vessel over sandbars or shallow water. Lincoln pursued the project with vigor, hiring an attorney to represent his patent rights and drawing up detailed sketches and descriptions for the patent officers. In the end, nothing came of the venture, but his interest in inventions persisted into the war, where he arranged demonstrations of new weapons on the White House lawn.[29]

Lincoln viewed patent law as a way of spurring innovation. Before the formation of the modern patent system, he pointed out that "any man might instantly use what another had invented; so that the inventor had no special advantage from his own invention." But "the patent system changed this; secured to the inventor, for a limited time, the exclusive use of his invention; and thereby added the fuel of *interest* to the *fire* of genius, in the discovery and production of new and useful things."[30]

Occasionally, patent cases crossed his path, almost all during the latter years of his law career.[31] Patent litigation was an obscure little corner of antebellum law. Blackstone devoted all of one sentence to the subject, observing in a parenthetical aside on the illegitimacy of monopolies that this was so "except as to patents, not exceeding the grant of fourteen years, to the authors of new inventions." Where Lincoln saw patents in the context of modern economic development, Blackstone's *Commentaries* functioned in the very different eighteenth-century world of ancient monarchial rights to grant monopolies, thus limiting the usefulness of that seminal book. There wasn't much reliable commentary on patents in the existing legal literature of the day, the available case law was relatively rare and scattershot—addressing, for example, the question of whether foreigners could be granted American patents—and because the Constitution and a 1790 act of Congress specifically empowered the federal government to address patent issues, patent cases often involved the federal judicial system. Take all this together, and patent litigation was a foreboding thicket into which an attorney might wander. There may well have been an unspoken professional convention that only more experienced lawyers should try to do so.[32]

This seemed to have been the case in 1855, when Lincoln became involved in a dispute related to the famous McCormick reaper. Cyrus McCormick, incensed that his design was being copied by numerous other manufacturers, brought a lawsuit against John H. Manny, another maker of farm machinery, for having stolen McCormick's designs for the reaper's divider, reel supporter, and rake supporter. When the case was moved to the U.S. district court in Cincinnati, Manny's attorney Peter Watson decided to enlist the services of a (relatively) local lawyer, and one with reputedly excellent jury skills, so he hired Lincoln. Lincoln was enthusiastic. He "prepared himself with the greatest care," wrote Herndon, because his "ambition was up to speak in the case and measure swords with the renowned lawyer from Baltimore," McCormick's attorney Reverdy Johnson. But when Lincoln arrived in Cincinnati, Manny's other attorneys, Edwin Stanton and George Harding, refused to allow Lincoln's participation. Harding was a specialist in patent law from Philadelphia, while Stanton (Lincoln's future secretary of war) was a highly regarded trial lawyer who privately described Lincoln as a "long, lank creature from Illinois" who had no business getting involving in such complex and high-profile litigation. Lincoln wandered around Cincinnati for a week and then returned home, "greatly depressed" and feeling "pushed aside, humiliated, and mortified."[33]

The reaper case aside, Lincoln—as a would-be inventor himself, and more generally as a progress-minded Whig—surely enjoyed the occasional patent case, not only as a breath of fresh air (what would be more interesting, a dispute concerning the rights to a self-rocking baby cradle, or yet another promissory note?), but also as a way to make a constructive contribution to Illinois' economic life. At the bottom of each patent case was an attempt by an inventive mind to fashion something positive, to inch humankind along toward a better and more efficient future. Lincoln's talk of patent law as having unleashed the "fire of genius" suggests what patents and inventions meant to him: human progress. Unlike contract disputes and partnership dissolutions, a patent case would have allowed Lincoln to feel a bit less like the businessmen's version of a divorce lawyer cleaning up after a nasty spat, and more like the man he wanted to be as a political leader: forward-looking, energetic, and practical, someone who took the lead in developing the state's economy—shades of the "De Witt Clinton of Illinois."

Or so it might seem. In reality, Lincoln's patent cases were rarely so straightforward. In 1849 he was hired by John Moffett, part of a three-man partnership to market and sell an "atmospheric churn," a device that created butter more quickly than conventional churns by injecting air directly into the cream. Moffett was not the churn's designer; that honor belonged to his partner Willis Johnson, a creative and busy Springfield inventor who also came up with new ways of processing flax and hemp, pumping water, and mixing cement. Moffett and a third partner, Thomas Lewis, did the sales work, selling the churns in Illinois, Missouri, Kentucky, and Tennessee. Lewis racked up over $50,000 worth of sales. St. Louis had been particularly fertile ground, where he displayed the churn in front of a saloon and on the sidewalk by his hotel.

Moffett's understanding was that the partners' arrangement called for selling the machine without him or Lewis earning any commission. He was therefore dismayed to learn that Lewis paid himself a $4,000 commission from the proceeds of his efforts. Moffett had Lincoln ask the court for an accounting of Lewis's earnings. For his part, Lewis argued that he acted not as a partner but rather as an agent for the partnership—a fine hair to split—and then demanded another $12,000 in compensation for his work. The court was not persuaded by the amount, but it did allow Lewis to keep $1,000, while paying Moffett $1,300. Lewis appealed the matter to the state supreme court, which ruled that he did not need to pay Moffett anything at all.

It would have been difficult for Lincoln to find a clear distinction between progressive economic development and its retardation in this case. Nor did the patent laws seem to do much for the "fire of genius" behind the atmospheric churn. Willis Johnson did not get anything out of the lawsuit (he tried to bring his own case against Lewis, but failed). The churn itself was worthless. During the appeal, the chief justice of the Illinois Supreme Court marveled at Lewis's ingenuity in earning so much money from peddling what was a dismal failure of a machine.[34]

And then there was the self-rocking baby cradle. In 1853, Alexander

Edmunds, a chair manufacturer from Mount Pulaski, obtained a patent for the design of what he called a "horological cradle," a baby cradle fitted with a clocklike device that, "being wound up, would rock itself until it run [sic] down, and so save the continual labor to mothers and nurses of rocking [a] cradle." Or, to be precise, Edmunds obtained only a partial patent to the cradle's ornamental design, and not the clock mechanism itself. Undaunted by this crucial distinction, he then peddled the cradle—design, clock, and all—in a dizzying series of transactions to investors who thought they were buying the rights to the entire device, and harbored visions of tired mommies with cash. "Mothers have the right to all the blessings of the day," enthused one of their advertisements, calling Edmunds one of the "scientific men" of the day and exhorting that "No mother should be without one of these beautiful and essentially useful articles of furniture."

When they discovered that the scientific man had not sold them a patent to the entire useful article, however, the investors sued him. The Logan County court tried to put the banana back in its peel, rescinding the investors' contracts and restoring the partial patent rights to Edmunds. He appealed the ruling to the state supreme court, and during the course of this appeal, one of the investors retained Lincoln. Lincoln was a latecomer to the whole affair, and in the end he lost the case—the supreme court decided that his client and the other investors should have known that Edmunds had only obtained a partial patent—but this did not impair Lincoln's sense of fun. He brought a model of the cradle to his office to play with, telling a visitor that the thing was "like some of the glib talkers you and I know . . . when it gets going it don't know when to stop."[35]

A patent case, like road construction and Lincoln's other economic-development litigation, complicated the notion that there were merely two sides to business growth and entrepreneurship. Politics encouraged such simplistic ideas, and while Lincoln was not a simplistic man, as a politician he functioned in a political culture that tended to divide the economic world into those who favored and nurtured improvement and progress (Whigs and Republicans) and those who impeded it (Democrats). But in their zeal to press outward in several directions, the energy men rarely created just two sides of anything.

This was all the more true when they rose above being merely men-on-the-make hawking flaxseed or atmospheric churns and became founders of industries and serious competitors in the business world. When they reached this level, Lincoln saw them less often. Banks, for example, were relatively infrequent clients for Lincoln; he represented their interests in only thirteen extant cases during his career. Insurance companies were also something of a rarity in Lincoln's practice; he represented them only five times. His industrial clients were usually of the smallish variety, like Robert McCart and Sons, who did bricklaying for a gasworks in Bloomington, Illinois, and hired Lincoln to represent them when the gasworks failed to pay them the full amount owed on the contract.[36]

Lincoln was not a "corporate lawyer," at least not on a regular basis. But there was one significant exception: railroads.

Railroads were American entrepreneurs' Mecca, the energy men's best hope for a rich future. No other endeavor represented quite the same mixture of cutting-edge technology, investment potential, and sheer economic power. "The city has been greatly benefited by the Sangamon and Morgan Rail Road," enthused a Springfield editorial. "Every citizen has acknowledged and felt it."[37]

They did have their downside; railroads were complicated, dirty, terribly expensive, and accident-prone. In later years, many Americans would wonder if they were worth the cost and the risk, and they would come to fear the railroad industry's mighty economic and political clout. But in the 1840s and 1850s most people, particularly those living on the frontier, fairly salivated at the opportunities they created. Property near a track or at a terminus skyrocketed in value, passenger cars brought people with dollars to spend in cash-starved local economies, and freight cars took products to faraway markets, tying local businesses into a thriving national market economy.[38]

Few people were more enthusiastic about railroads than Lincoln. They held a natural appeal for him as a way to bring into the state all the advantages of commerce he valued. "No other improvement that reason will justify us in hoping for, can equal in utility the rail road," he declared, "It is a never failing source of communication, between places of business remotely situated from each other." He boosted railroads as a legislator, thinking it in the state's best interests to invest tax dollars in their construction. Following the crash of the internal improvements program, Lincoln turned his energies to the private sector, helping develop railroads as private stockholding ventures.[39]

In the early years of his practice, Lincoln did not see much litigation related to railroads. Prior to 1850, in fact, there is no extant record of his having been hired by a railroad company, partly because railroads did not yet have a commanding presence in Illinois' economy, especially after the internal improvements project collapsed. But also there was the matter of Lincoln's stature. Railroads thought big, usually in terms of thousands of dollars, and they paid large retainers. They were unlikely to put such money into the pockets of an untried lawyer.[40]

His first steady railroad client was the Alton and Sangamon line, of which he possessed close firsthand knowledge. Residents of Springfield had been trying for years to get a line from their town westward to the state border at Alton, and Lincoln joined in their attempts to fund the project. He was part of a committee that in 1847 called the railroad "a link in a great chain of rail road communication which shall unite Boston and New York with the Mississippi" and urged citizens to invest in "this grand scheme of improvement." Lincoln himself was a stock subscriber in the Alton and Sangamon.[41]

As the line was nearing completion in 1851, his old partner John Stuart, now serving another term in the legislature, introduced an amendment to the railroad's charter that slightly altered the route, shortening it by twelve miles; a small change, but enough to bypass land purchased by James A. Barret. Barret was a land speculator who owned over four thousand acres in southern Sangamon county, acres upon which he had hoped to reap a handsome profit when the railroad went through that area. Barret was also a railroad stockholder, and he had purchased the stock on credit, paying for it in installments. When the altered route destroyed his land speculation scheme, Barret stopped making payments on his shares. The railroad retained Lincoln and sued him.

The case involved issues weightier than one speculator's pique. Two other railroad stockholders were following Barret's lead and threatening nonpayment as well; if this became a general trend, the railroad that Lincoln and other Springfield leaders had worked so hard to build might find itself in serious financial straits. There were also some troubling broader implications. Barret argued that he need not pay the rest of his stock subscription because the line's alteration voided his obligation to do so. If he prevailed, did that mean stockholders in any railroad project could abandon their obligations whenever the railroad altered its original construction plans? Future companies might hesitate to build new lines in Illinois, where a small change could hamstring the financial side of their operations. Or a company might become too brittle and inflexible, fearing to make necessary changes for fear of sparking new lawsuits.

Lincoln understood the stakes, and he put extraordinary time and effort into winning this case. He waited until the state legislative term was concluded before beginning his research, so as not to be distracted by politics. "I have examined the books, and reflected a good deal," he wrote William Martin, one of the railroad's commissioners. The books eventually included Chitty's *Pleadings* for insight into the proper form, precedent cases from Kentucky and Alabama courts, some relevant materials from the federal courts, and a search of the Illinois legislative files to find an act that had some bearing on the case. He also tried to construct a careful, airtight argument that left no wiggle room for Barret and the other recalcitrant stockholders. "To be entirely safe," he wrote Martin, "we must prove 1. the creation of the Corporation, 2. That the defendant is a Stockholder, 3. That the Corporation has been organized, 4. That the calls [for payment on the stock] have been made, [and] 5. That due notice of the calls has been given."[42]

The suit caused him a fair amount of aggravation. In order to prove his points, Lincoln wanted the minutes of the stockholders' meeting, the railroad's secretary to appear as a witness in court, copies of the newspaper notices concerning the stockholder's meeting, and a printer's certificate testifying to their authenticity. Isaac Gibson, the railroad secretary, thought this was overkill, particularly the matter of hauling both him and his books all the way to Springfield from New York to testify. Lincoln grew irritated at this. "I suppose it is a matter of interest to the Company that we should not fail in these suits," he wrote with a touch of sarcasm to Gibson. "The cases will be fiercely contested at all points. . . . Knowing the inconvenience of producing these Books I have struggled hard to convince myself that we could in some way dispense with them, but in vain. The Books *must* be here." In the end, Lincoln had to settle for a deposition of Gibson's testimony and copies of the stockholders' newspaper notices. His preparations and headaches paid off, however; he won the case.[43]

The Barret case was about a railroad businessman clashing with other railroad businessmen; he was a stockholder and an active participant in railroad expansion. But railroads also generated disputes with people who were on the margins of their business. With an eager ambition that was similar to Lorenzo Hamilton's land deals and James Reed's promissory notes, railroads sometimes wreaked a lot of unintended havoc as they rolled through the Illinois countryside. Hamilton, Reed, and other individual businessmen normally could not have too great an effect on their neighbors or their neighborhood, but a railroad could; and as usual, Lincoln was available to clean up the mess.

He was called in to help the Illinois Central Railroad deal with one such situation in 1855, when a DeWitt County farmer named Wilson Allen opened a one-man litigation war against the railroad. The Illinois Central built a rail line near Allen's property, and he accused their workers of using "shovels, pickaxes, ploughs . . . and other iron instruments" to excavate fifty thousand square feet of Allen's soil, leaving "mines, fills, shafts and holes of great depth and breadth." Allen wanted $50,000, and the railroad retained Lincoln. A jury found the railroad guilty, but assessed damages at only $762.50.[44]

This was only the beginning. Four years later, Allen sued the Illinois Central again, this time for filling a local waterway called Salt Creek with "filth and noxious water," then blocking it entirely and creating a fetid pool of water that, according to Allen, caused "sickness and ill health of his family" as well as a steep depreciation in his land values. Allen wanted $2,000, the railroad again retained Lincoln, and Allen again won—and, as before, the jury gave him considerably less compensation than he requested: $286. A third time, Allen took the railroad to court, arguing that its workers had destroyed grazing grass and herbage; this time the jury gave him $15. In still another suit, Allen wanted the railroad to construct fences and cattle guards near his land. Lincoln argued that the railroad had already done so; the case was eventually thrown out by the judge because Allen had since sold the land in question.[45]

Allen owned a substantial amount of land—about a thousand acres—and one wonders if he had so many complaints because he had speculated in the land being damaged, buying up parcels along the railway route in the hope of turning a profit. At the very least, his large landholdings and wealth gave him considerable clout in DeWitt County, so much so that Lincoln successfully petitioned for two of the lawsuits to be removed to Macon County because of Allen's "undue influence over the minds" of De Witt's citizens.[46] Allen was yet another one of Tocqueville's restless Americans; he had lived in four places prior to settling in DeWitt County, and in 1867 he would try his hand at carpetbagging, buying a farm in Georgia. His ongoing fight with the

Illinois Central illustrates the point that one American's economic development could be another American's threat.[47]

Riverboat operators felt the same way. Railroads were slowly but surely supplanting them as the most efficient way of moving people and goods around the country. Rivers had once ruled Americans' lives and livelihoods, and river towns like Cincinnati and St. Louis dominated entire regions because of their close proximity to waterways. But railroads could be built just about anywhere, barreling through a countryside belching smoke, noise, and money in a hell-bent-for-leather fashion that disturbed many people.

In May 1856, a vessel named the *Effie Afton* burned and sank after colliding with the Rock Island Railroad Bridge on the Mississippi River. The loss was considerable; not just the *Effie Afton,* an expensive new ship, "beautifully furnished," but also a cargo of "groceries, machinery, emigrants, and livestock," the whole valued at $50,000. Its owner sued the Rock Island Bridge Company to recover his loss, and the company in turn hired Lincoln.

The wreck and lawsuit received extensive newspaper coverage in St. Louis and Chicago, partly because it had been a spectacular wreck, making for good copy—"The outer end [of the bridge] burned off and fell upon the burning steamer; the other end of that span was cut away, and bridge and steamer floated down together, a sheet of flame"—and partly because the case involved more than just a railroad's liability for damages. It was to many observers a showdown between ships and railroads, between old-fashioned St. Louis, with its dependence on the Mississippi River, and the brash new town of Chicago, thriving commercial hub and booster of the iron horse. Railroad supporters mustered statistics to show that, dollar for dollar, the railroad crossing the Rock Island Bridge was worth more to the region's economy than the ships passing under it. The rivermen retorted that the railroad company should have built a better bridge, and that by creating a river obstruction, the railroad company was putting working men out of business. People in St. Louis "spoke of losses occurring to lumbermen and others by means of the bridge; of six planing mills at St. Louis being idle for want of lumber detained above the bridge—one person had lost four rafts at one time, and that it was with difficulty that vessels could pass the bridge at high water." Eyewitnesses claimed that the *Effie Afton*'s crew cheered when the burning bridge fell away: "It was a jubilee, a greater celebration than follows an excited election."[48]

As with so much else in his legal career, it is difficult to tell what Lincoln thought about all this. He was a riverman himself. He had unloaded cargo, push-poled flatboats, and piloted steamships in his early days, and he had pressed for river improvements as a state legislator. But he had also seen the town of New Salem die because of the Sangamon River's capricious navigation, and he knew railroads were the wave of the future. They carried more than just freight or people; they carried investment capital, dollars, and development, conducting energy to places otherwise stunted in their growth because, like New Salem, they happened to lack a decent river connection.

Because the case involved interstate traffic, it would be heard in a federal district court, a relative rarity in Lincoln's practice, and it would be closely watched in the press—again, a somewhat unusual circumstance for him. Lincoln therefore put in a great deal of preparatory work, understanding that the *Effie Afton* affair carried high stakes. Holding a railroad liable in such circumstances could set a precedent that might cause other railroads to hesitate before pushing their lines deeper into the countryside, for fear of leaving themselves open to lawsuits for the damage, inadvertent or not, that their equipment might cause. On the other hand, there were a lot of angry people in St. Louis. However the case went, there would be hard feelings.

Lincoln tried to smooth over the Chicago–St. Louis hostility created by the case, stating that "he had no prejudice against steamboats or steamboatmen, nor any against St. Louis, for he supposed they went about as other people would do in their situation." But even as he sympathized with the rivermen, he enthused about the benefits wrought by railroads. "There is a travel from East to West, whose demands are not less important than that of the river," he pointed out. "It is growing larger and larger, building up new countries with a rapidity never before seen in the history of the world. . . . There is, too, a considerable portion of time, when floating or thin ice makes the river useless, while the bridge is as useful as ever. This shows that this bridge must be treated with respect in this court and is not to be kicked about with contempt."

When Lincoln got down to the heart of the matter, his case rested on a central, key point: the *Effie Afton*'s crew was to blame for the accident, not the Rock Island Bridge Company—and surely not railroads in general. He mustered statistics showing that rivermen were learning to live with the bridge, and were slowly reducing the number of collisions with its piers: "The dangers of this place are tapering off, and, as the boatmen get cool, the accidents get less. We may soon expect, if this ratio is kept up, that there will be no accidents at all." He dwelt at length on the speed of the current under the bridge, whether or not there were eddies or crosscurrents created by the bridge, the precise angle of its piers, and eyewitness accounts concerning the *Effie Afton*'s speed and position. "The plaintiffs have to establish that the bridge is a material obstruction, and that they managed their boat with reasonable care and skill," and on this last point the plaintiff's case failed, Lincoln stressed.[49]

His arguments were successful enough to convince nine of the jurors, but three held out for the *Effie Afton,* producing a hung jury. The trial dragged on for weeks—Lincoln's jury speech alone took two days—and as it reached its unsatisfying anticlimax, there was a sense of frustration among the observers. "If the Rock Island Bridge is not declared a nuisance by the Courts those interested in the navigation of the Upper Mississippi will feel very much like removing the obstruction by force," warned one. Others railed against the "prejudiced, sore head pilots on the river," and pointed out that delays and new trials were in effect "a triumph for the bridge," which had been rebuilt and was steadily conducting traffic over the river once more. Rumor had it that the ship's owner wanted to retain Stephen Douglas for the new trial, but nothing came of this. For unknown reasons, the case was never again brought to trial.[50]

The *Effie Afton* and Barret cases were probably satisfying experiences in Lincoln's career. They were more important than most, establishing precedents for how courts would handle railroad liability issues in the future. And those precedents came down rather firmly on the railroad's side, where Lincoln probably preferred to stand, personally and politically as well as professionally. It was a relatively rare case of the different political and legal orbits of his life coming into close synchronization. He was helping railroads, and Lincoln wanted to help railroads and the economic development they represented.

But there were limits to the connections between Lincoln the political railroad booster and Lincoln the lawyer. The Illinois Central Railroad was Lincoln's biggest and most frequent client during his entire career: he litigated over fifty cases on their behalf. But in general, he was just as likely to oppose railroads in the courtroom as represent them.[51]

Railroads could be almost as vexing to him as they were to Mississippi River boatmen. In 1855 he and Herndon litigated a case for the Illinois Central Railroad that successfully prevented McLean County from levying a tax against the railroad's land holdings in their jurisdiction. The case was important ("the most important lawsuit Lincoln and I conducted," according to Herndon) because it headed off attempts by local municipalities to tax railroads and thus impede their growth. It was also lengthy and complicated litigation, involving multiple trials and appeals to the Illinois Supreme Court. By the time the dust settled and Lincoln had emerged victorious, he felt the railroad owed him substantial compensation. He presented a bill for $2,000. The railroad balked and, "stung by the rebuff," he successfully sued the railroad for a $5,000 fee. "Lincoln gave me my half," Herndon remembered, and "we both thanked the Lord for letting the Illinois Central Railroad fall into our hands."[52]

Lincoln also occasionally represented the interests of clients seeking damages from the railroads. For example, in 1857 he and Herndon were hired by Lewis Friedlander, who broke his leg when the railcar in which he rode struck another car. Friedlander won a $500 judgment from the Great Western Railroad Company. In a few other cases, Lincoln helped landowners get compensated for damage to the property caused by railroads.[53]

There is a school of thought that sees lawyers like Lincoln dancing with the devil of corporate greed and rapaciousness, helping transfer the costs of economic development to taxpayers, hapless stockholders, and victims of industrial accidents.[54] Whether this was so is debatable. But more to the point, a lawyer like Lincoln did not quite understand the world in this way. To him, economic growth was not really about rights talk, or weighing carefully the social costs involved in developing industries like railroads.[55]

What he saw instead was the energy: its hyper-embodiment in the growing railroad industry, and also, on a smaller, everyday scale, its manifestations in the business lives of everyday entrepreneurs like Robert Allen, Lorenzo Hamilton, or James Reed. It was on their level of personal investment, risk, and reward that Lincoln spent much of his time as an attorney. He was there to minimize their risks and to fix what got broken when they pressed matters too far.

Chapter Five

The Show

O
f course, some risk taking Lincoln could not fix. Some clients pressed their luck far beyond his capacity to be of any help. A few months after James Reed lost his debt case to William Butler, he decided that Springfield was no longer a promising business environment; the entire region had undergone an economic downturn. The far West looked better, as new ground for moneymaking and also a place where he hoped the climate might somehow fix his wife's headaches. In April 1846 he packed up and headed to Independence, Missouri, the staging area for the Oregon Trail. True to style, Reed outfitted his family in a gargantuan two-story wagon that sported its own cooking stove and a team of eight oxen. Reed's daughter called it the "pioneer palace car."

Maybe Lincoln watched the pioneer palace car trundle slowly away from the town square near his office. He surely heard about what happened next. The Reeds joined another Springfield family, the Donners, and together they traveled first to Independence and then westward to the Rocky Mountain passes. There the expedition went horribly awry, as the emigrants (urged on by Reed) took a disastrous shortcut, trapping them for the winter on Truckee Lake in the Sierra Nevada mountains. Their subsequent ordeal became the stuff of American legend—sickness, starvation, and eventually cannibalism.

If James Reed's imperious manner had not alienated many of his companions, history would remember this as the story of the Reed Party, for he was nearly elected its captain. As it happened, he was not present when events turned really nasty. Somewhere on the trail near the Humboldt River in Utah, he let his temper get the better of him when his cattle became entangled with another team driven by an emigrant named John Snyder. Snyder beat first the cattle and then Reed with a whip; enraged, the fiery Irishman drew his hunting knife and buried it in Snyder's chest. He died a few minutes later, with Reed standing, "dazed and sorrowful" beside his body.

The other members of the Donner Party were appalled. There was a general consensus that, however reprehensible Snyder's behavior had been, Reed had vastly overreacted. Murmurs ran through the camp about exacting retribution. One man turned his wagon tongue on end to use as a makeshift gallows.

Almost immediately, however, cooler heads prevailed. Reed and his family were taken to their tent and placed under guard. Then, according to one account, "an assembly was convened to decide what should be done. The majority declared the deed murder, and demanded retribution." Reed claimed he had acted in self-defense, and that he "was not prompted by malice," while another member of the party pleaded his case as well, citing extenuating circumstances and proposed that Reed be banished from the camp rather than hung. This sentence proved satisfactory to most. After extracting a promise that the party members would look after his wife and children, Reed "took leave of his friends and sorrowing family and left the camp." Spared the horrors of Truckee Lake, he made his way to California alone, returning later with an expedition to successfully rescue his family.[1]

A sentence passed by a makeshift jury, arguments of self-defense, intent, and malice aforethought, even a pseudo-lawyer to argue Reed's case—all occurred out in the middle of nowhere, where the only institutions were those rules of behavior carried by the travelers themselves. Nor was the Donner Party unique in its recreation of elaborate courtroom procedures; wagon parties often used courtroom-style trials as a way to resolve disputes. Frontier towns likewise quickly turned to trials and courtrooms, even when conditions rendered such efforts difficult and incongruous. One observer marveled at how Americans could put up the trappings of a courthouse as quickly as a lean-to or shanty. Faced with the lack of a formal building, a typical judge "therefore selects the largest room of a tavern or a spacious loft. . . . Upon a couple of planks are ranged twenty-four freemen, heads of families, housekeepers, forming the grand jury. . . . The judge makes his charge with as much dignity as if he sat in Westminster."[2]

It is a remarkable phenomenon, this reflexive American love of trials; they permeate American culture. Novels, films, and television shows create trials that are arenas of moral combat, with lawyers and judges acting the part of spokesmen for the national conscience: Harper Lee's Atticus Finch, fighting the good fight against southern racism in *To Kill a Mockingbird;* Jerome Tracy and Robert Lee's courtroom showdown between faith and science in their play *Inherit the Wind;* or Spencer Tracy's retired judge from Maine, Dan Haywood, struggling with the moral dilemmas posed by Nazism in *Judgment at Nuremberg.*

The interplay between theatrical drama and trials cuts both ways: if shows often turn to courtrooms, then courtrooms often turn into shows. Despite the best efforts of the law to pare away pretext and leave only the cold, unadorned issues of reason, fact, and evidence, trials have an unavoidable dramatic element. Lawyers to varying degrees stage scenes: for judges, jury members, witnesses, spectators, and even one another.[3]

Modern trial lawyers usually understand that they are part actors. Those with a flamboyant streak cultivate the actors within themselves to advance their careers and their causes. Antebellum attorneys were no different; the more astute among them grasped the theatrical aspects of their profession. They laughed, jeered, ridiculed, or scorned, as circumstances required. If they needed to sound folksy, they cracked down-home jokes. If they needed to sound aristocratic, they were urbane. If they needed to obscure a point, they might quote Latin. Some appealed to ethnic or regional prejudices. "Gentleman of the jury, do you think that my client, who lives in the pleasant valley of Old Kentuck . . . would be guilty of stealing?" asked one. Another lawyer from Missouri, defending a client against a charge of horse theft, bellowed at the jury, "Will you take from poor Coatjohn his only horse, and his only means of making bread for his poor starving children? . . . No gentlemen, you cannot do it, God forbid!" He then sat down next to his client, tears streaming from his eyes and, reportedly, from most of the jurors' as well.[4]

Lincoln earned the respect of his fellow lawyers at trial when he made solid logical arguments, but he also understood courtroom drama. Herndon claimed that other lawyers greatly feared Lincoln's abilities before a jury. "He brushed aside all rules, and very often resorted to some strange and strategic performance which invariably broke his opponent down or exercised some peculiar influence over the jury."[5] Billy's partner knew how to achieve a courtroom effect.

It started with his appearance. Homely Abraham Lincoln may have been, but his homeliness was itself a good way to get the attention of jurors and witnesses. He was not just tall and ugly, after all; he was prepossessing, in a way at once striking and difficult to describe. Herndon tried to do so at length, writing that Lincoln's "structure was loose and leathery . . . and looked woe-struck, the whole man, body and mind, worked slowly, as if it needed oiling." As he rose to address a jury, Lincoln was especially curious. "His body inclined forward to a slight degree," Herndon wrote, and "at first he was very awkward. . . . When he began speaking, his voice was shrill, piping, and unpleasant. His manner, his attitude, his dark, yellow face, wrinkled and dry, his oddity of pose, his diffident movements—everything seemed to be against him." But then Lincoln sort of unfolded himself in front of his audience's eyes. "As he proceeded he became somewhat animated. . . . By this time he had gained sufficient composure, and his real speech began."[6]

Added to this was Lincoln's clothing during a trial: usually a dusty black frock coat, dirt-splattered boots, tie a bit askew, mop of unruly black hair. "He was careless of his dress" in court, and "his clothes . . . hung loosely on his giant frame."[7] Given that he was by nature a slob (he drove Mary to distraction on this point), historians assume that Lincoln's slovenly courtroom attire was a function of his personality, a seamless meshing of his private and public personas. This is no doubt partly true; but it is equally likely that his sloppiness was also a court-room affectation. He always emphasized appealing to the "common people" who inhabited the juries and the witness chair. "Billy, don't shoot too high," he advised his partner, "aim lower, and the common people will understand you. They are the ones you want to reach. The educated and refined people will understand you, anyway. If you aim too high, your idea will go over the heads of the masses, and hit only those who need no hitting." As his words went, so did his clothes. "He had the appearance of a rough, intelligent farmer," noted another lawyer. That may be just the impression Lincoln sought.[8]

Lincoln knew that people judged cases as much by their hearts as by their heads. Politically and personally, he believed in the power of reason over emotion. He never liked overt displays of feeling, and he felt that emotions tended to get in the way when men of good will tried to make public policy. "Passion has helped us," Lincoln declared in his 1838 address to the Young Men's Lyceum of Springfield, "but can do so no more. It will in the future be our enemy. Reason, cold, calculating, unimpassioned reason, must furnish all the materials for our future support and defence."[9]

But in the courtroom he understood how to manipulate emotions in the name of (legal) reason. In 1846 he was presented with an unusual case involving a deceased Revolutionary War veteran named James Thomas. Thomas's widow Rebecca approached Erastus Wright, the local pension agent—and one of Springfield's leading citizens—to help her recover her husband's pension. Wright did so, but charged her a large sum for the service. Mrs. Thomas, "an old woman crippled and bent with age, came hobbling into the office and told her story," Herndon recalled, and "it stirred Lincoln up." According to Herndon, Lincoln became quite incensed. He immediately confronted Wright and demanded that the agent return the fee; when Wright refused, Lincoln brought suit. He asked his junior partner to find a good history of the Revolutionary War, "of which he read a good portion." "He told me to remain during the trial," Herndon wrote, "'For,' said he, 'I am going to skin Wright, and get that money back.'" During his address to the jury, Herndon wrote, "there was no rule of court to restrain him in his argument, and I never, either on the stump or on any other occasion in court, saw him so wrought up." Lincoln used the imagery he had gleaned from his perusal of the war's history to draw "a vivid picture of the hardships of Valley Forge, describing with minuteness the men, barefooted and with bleeding feet, creeping over the ice. . . . The speech made the desired impression on the jury. Half of them were in tears, while the defendant sat in the court room, drawn up and writhing under the fire of Lincoln's fiery invective. The jury returned a verdict in our favor for every cent we demanded."[10]

Billy's account should be treated with skepticism. Writing years later, he was fuzzy on the details. He claimed the suit was for $200, but court records reveal the amount was considerably less—probably half that amount—and the widow Thomas actually received only $35 in the judgment. It is also difficult to imagine Lincoln, a man who constantly extolled the virtues of compromise outside the courtroom and much preferred negotiation to litigation, storming into Wright's office and demanding the return of the entire fee without delay.

Herndon used this case to illustrate how emotionally overwrought

Lincoln sometimes became when presented with an obvious miscarriage of justice. Perhaps this was so. But *Thomas v. Wright* is more useful in illustrating not Lincoln's feelings but rather his skill in arousing the feelings of jurors. His notes for the closing argument read, "Describe Valley Forge privations—Ice—Soldier's bleeding feet—Pl[ainti]ff's husband—Soldier leaving home for army—*Skin Def[endan]t*—Close." Wright may or may not have aroused his ire; but blood, frostbite, and Valley Forge were dramatic enough metaphors for him to employ in arousing others' ire, and to put that arousal to good use in the courtroom.[11]

Sometimes Lincoln grew more creative in his attempts to put a vivid image in front of a jury. He once used a collection of chicken bones to make a point about the relative strength of young and old bones while representing a group of doctors in what was the first medical malpractice case ever brought before the Logan County circuit court.[12] Being Lincoln, he also knew the value of a good story. "His illustrations were often quaint and homely," remembered a colleague, "but always clear and apt, and generally conclusive. . . . His wit and humor and inexhaustible store of anecdotes, always to the point, added immensely to his powers as a jury advocate."[13]

He was also adept at using ridicule to win points with the jury. In an 1854 assault case he represented a man named James Dunlap, who was sued by Paul Selby, the editor of the *Jacksonville Journal*. Dunlap had beaten Selby with a cane after the editor published some disparaging remarks about Dunlap's character. Selby wanted $10,000 in damages. There wasn't much Lincoln could do about getting his client entirely off the hook; Dunlap had in fact assaulted Selby. When the time came for his turn to address the jury, Lincoln slowly stood, picked up a copy of Selby's motion, and then suddenly burst into a "long loud laugh accompanied by his most wonderfully grotesque facial expression." The very sight of this caused several members of jury to snicker, at which point Lincoln apologized. He said he had looked at the motion and noticed that the original amount of the suit had been only $1,000, but that this had been crossed out and replaced with the $10,000 figure. Lincoln snickered that, somehow, Selby had had second thoughts and "concluded that the wounds to his honor were worth an additional nine thousand dollars." His little joke was calculated to rob the assault case (and the plaintiff) of dignity. Apparently it worked; the jury returned a decision for damages of only $300.[14]

Lincoln also knew how to appear as if he was *not* angling for a dramatic display—when lack of theatricality was itself good theater. That same year he appeared in the Vermilion County circuit court on behalf of William Fithian in another case involving newspapers and slander. Fithian was a Danville physician who sued an editor named George Casseday after Casseday wrote an editorial disparaging Fithian's character and claiming that the doctor had abandoned the body of Casseday's deceased wife in the nearby town of Paris to be buried at the whim of the local authorities. Fithian responded with a $25,000 libel suit.

The trial had a tense quality because of the rather unusual nature of the accusation, the large amount of money involved, and the fact that Casseday retained a high-profile legal team: Orlando Ficklin, a noted lawyer from Charleston, Illinois, and Edward Hannegan, another noted lawyer and former U.S. congressman. The judge in the case, David Davis, predicted it would "excite a great deal of interest." He was right. During the two-day trial, the courtroom was packed. "The Ladies of town in great numbers were present all the time," Davis wrote to his wife (and then joked, "I gave your respects to them all").[15]

Lincoln felt low-key was the best strategy here; no "skinning the defendant" or bloody footprints at Valley Forge. He needed his client to seem calm and reasonable, the innocent and aggrieved victim of a wild-eyed newspaper editor. So he toned down his eccentric speaking style and traded in his trademark threadbare suit for something more dignified. "He was attired in a fine broadcloth suit, silk hat, and polished boots. His neck was encircled by an old-fashioned silk choker. . . . His clothes fitted him, and he was as genteel-looking as any man in the audience," according to one observer, who also thought that Lincoln "did nothing for effect." In reality Lincoln had produced the very effect he desired.[16]

So he knew how to pitch his stories, demeanor, facial expressions, and clothes. But when would he have had the opportunities to flex his dramatic muscles? Pension and libel cases were relative rarities in Lincoln's professional life. His practice was dull most of the time: it was not dramatic. He knew this, and resigned himself to the fact. "There is not a more fatal error to young lawyers than relying too much on speech-making," he believed, "if any one, upon his rare powers of speaking, shall claim an exemption from the drudgery of the law, his case is a failure in advance."[17]

Other lawyers likewise knew that the "drudgery of the law" was part and parcel of their existence, but the more dramatic-minded among them lived for the occasional opportunity to put on a show. And the best opportunities, the best shows in town, were criminal trials, the ones involving the sort of behavior that got James Reed kicked out of the Donner Party.

It is no coincidence that the truly high-profile lawyers of today, those who engage the media's attention and attain celebrity status, are more often than not criminal lawyers. Since colonial days, criminal trials have been "social drama" with "theatrical elements," according to historian Lawrence Friedman. Defendants are expected to play the role of penitent offender, lawyers act as passionate spokesmen for either the people's righteous anger or the principle of guilty until proven innocent, depending on which side of aisle they stand. Judges act the part of solemn dispensers of impartial and objective truth.[18]

This was so in any court case, of course; but criminal proceedings have a primordial quality, involving as they often do the base elements of human behavior: greed, lust, envy, avarice, and violence. Criminal trials lay bare those things we fear in ourselves, and the verdict, whatever it might be, offers a form of closure. People believe justice has been done and feel either that the genie of human depravity has been put back in its bottle or that the long arm of the law has not been allowed to harm an innocent person.

Blackstone did not dramatize criminal law (he did not dramatize much of anything), but most antebellum lawyers could figure it out for themselves. A few specialized in criminal cases. Edward S. Courtney developed a good criminal-law practice in Charleston during the 1820s and 1830s, as did Mississippians Roger Barton and Felix Grundy. Indiana attorney Daniel Voorhees—the "Tall Sycamore of the Wabash"—was "sought from every quarter to defend criminals in the most dangerous class of cases."[19] But for most lawyers, a criminal-law specialty was not feasible, in the same general sense that specialization in general was a bad idea.

Lincoln's career bears this out. Criminal law was only one piece of the multicolored mosaic that was his practice—a small piece. During his twenty-five years at the Illinois bar, he litigated only 194 extant criminal cases. Was this typical for an antebellum lawyer? It is impossible to tell. There is too little information available on other antebellum attorneys, and variations by region make the issue even more problematic. Was a southern lawyer, for example, more likely than most to see criminal cases because of his region's reputation for violence? Did frontier areas provide more opportunities to litigate criminal cases because of their (real or imagined) environment of lawlessness? Wrote humorist Joseph G. Baldwin in 1854 of a quasi-fictional attorney: "To the South West he started because magnificent accounts came from that sunny land of most cheering and exhilarating prospects of fussing, quarrelling, murdering, violation of contracts, and the whole catalogue of *crimen falsi*—in fine, a flush tide of litigation." Jokes aside, perhaps Southerners and Westerners generated a higher degree than usual of criminal litigation—or perhaps not.[20]

It may be that for a lawyer in Lincoln's particular situation—a general practice attorney in a western, largely rural region making the transition from frontier to a more settled environment—litigating relatively few criminal cases was typical.[21] Still, less than 200 cases—out of the over 3,800 extant cases in which he appeared as an attorney of record—seems remarkably few. Maybe Lincoln avoided criminal cases, though there is no direct evidence of this. Given his political sagacity and sensitivity to public opinion, he surely grasped the publicity value of a high-profile criminal case. On the other hand, Lincoln also knew the damage his defense of an unpopular defendant might wreak on his standing in the community.

Today's criminal-law attorneys are shielded by a professional structure that holds that all people, even the guilty ones, deserve a competent defense, and that good lawyers must sometimes defend bad people. Lincoln operated under no such protection. His neighbors had a remarkable ability to accept unpopular trial verdicts; foreign visitors marveled at Americans' faith in their own legal system, even when it went wrong and allowed the guilty to escape. Vigilante justice and mob behavior sometimes occurred, but usually at the fringes of polite society.[22]

This did not, however, necessarily lead to an unthinking acceptance of defense attorneys who helped acquit clients perceived as guilty or at least badly behaved. "Lawyers and jurists gained respect if they held themselves strictly accountable to the public will," according to one legal historian; people "considered the lawyer a public official and a conservator of the public will."[23] This attitude manifested itself in a variety of formal ways—election of judges, for example—but it also had an informal social dimension as well. There would have been countless small ways in which a lawyer's neighbors might have made his life miserable in the wake of a high-profile court case. People wondered if they could really trust their lawyer neighbors to make valid moral judgments, and that wonder would have an added edge when the issue in question was a criminal act like murder, assault, or theft. A poem called "The Lawyers' Ways" captured this ambiguity. As the poet wrote:

> "I've been list'nin' to them lawyers
> In the court house of the street. . . .
> First one fellow riz to argy
> An' he boldly waded in
> As he dressed the tremblin' prisoner
> In a coat o' deep-dyed sin. . . .
> Then the other lawyer started,
> An' with brimming, tearful eyes,
> Said his client was a martyr
> And brought to sacrifice. . . .
> And this aggrevatin' question
> Seems to keep a puzzling me
> So will someone please inform me,
> An' this mystery unroll,
> How an angel an' a devil
> Can possess the self-same soul?"[24]

So maybe Lincoln thought a little longer and harder before taking on a criminal case, especially one that might push a community's hot buttons.

Go back again to the initial client interview: not in Lincoln's office, but rather a jailhouse.[25] Lincoln's office possessed an almost gleeful carelessness; but a typical prison in his day was simply grim. Antebellum America was situated somewhere between the quasi-dungeons of old and the more humane rehabilitation centers envisioned by prison reformers.[26] Out West, prisons had a hasty, slapdash quality. In Rushville, Illinois, for example (where Lincoln litigated a few cases), the local jail was a two-story structure built of sandstone blocks. The lower floor was reserved for male prisoners; those deemed dangerous were chained to rings set in the center of the cell floor. A circular ladder made of iron led to the second floor, where female prisoners were kept, as well as quarters for the sheriff and his family. The kitchen at the Rushville jail was an afterthought, a wooden shack tacked onto the building's backside after the designers belatedly discovered they had made no provisions for feeding the inmates.[27]

Imagine Lincoln approaching the building, sometime in the 1840s. The place has a dark, sweaty dankness that seeps into the sandstone itself. As Lincoln enters he notices the smells more than anything else: human waste, sweat, tobacco, cooked meals, stale and new. Animal smells would have been stronger than usual; Schuyler County officials penned stray dogs, pigs, cows, chickens, and other loose fowl behind the jail. Some prisons burned tar in the cells to cover the stench. Lincoln is no prude, but maybe he tightens his jaw, clenches his fists just a little tighter, and thinks privately that he does not want to stay any longer than is necessary.

In one of the cells, standing or sitting or lying about, is his potential client. The dynamic partially resembles one of his many debt-collection cases. Lincoln needs to size up what is likely a total stranger, deciding whether the stranger will become a client. But the setting and the circumstances are far different. Normally Lincoln confronts someone who is at worst a lousy businessman. But now, in the fetid atmosphere of a small-town lockup, he faces someone whose alleged offense against society is more serious. Maybe the prisoner is a merely a drunkard or a horse thief; bad, but not as bad as some.

Or maybe Lincoln is staring through the bars at something much worse: an accused murderer, perhaps. Walter Bosley was a Vermilion County resident, indicted in October 1854 for shooting Egbart Barnett in the back with a rifle, "by the instigation of the Devil," in the archaic legal language of the grand jury indictment. Bosley apparently was a man of some means: he hired Lincoln and three other attorneys, who together got the charge reduced to manslaughter and their client eight years in prison at hard labor. Was Bosley a more (or perhaps less) genial client than Moses Loe, who bushwhacked James Gray along a lonely road near Lick Creek in De Witt County, beating him first with a club and then fatally stabbing him with a bowie knife? Or Bill Weaver, who in 1845 shot a man named David Hiltibran in a drunken rage?[28]

Whatever the case may be, the atmosphere is likely tinged with an emotional tension not normally present in Lincoln's professional life. Looming financial ruin is a dire strait for his many business clients, but a Bill Weaver or a Moses Loe faces an array of consequences more immediately frightening. He is already in jail, tasting the squalid lifestyle of a future in prison. His nerves are frayed.

It is in Lincoln's nature to play the role of peacemaker. Moreover, he likely has discovered what present-day criminal defense lawyers learn early in their careers: that generally speaking, the best approach, the best "show" for a client, is one that emphasizes gentle persuasion and recommendation over a pressing or take-charge attitude.[29]

Lincoln's primary goal is to gather information, so his questions are probably calm, simple, and pointed. What are you accused of? When did the incident take place? Were there any witnesses? He probably doesn't ask whether or not the man—his criminal clients were nearly always men—is guilty. Modern criminal law attorneys rarely do so. He probably does want to establish at the outset some measure of what is today called "client control"; that is, persuading the man in the cell that it is in his best interests to allow his lawyer the final say over what is done in his behalf: a jury trial, a plea-bargain arrangement, a change of venue, or some other courtroom stratagem. To get control, lawyers are often compelled to put on something of a show for their clients. If they sense that a person will react better to a nonconfrontational attitude, they will make it a point to speak in a calm, deliberate manner. If, on the other hand, a lawyer senses that his client may need a firmer approach, he may speak sternly and maybe even with a little passion, the better to communicate with and manage his client's behavior.[30]

As Lincoln looks at his potential client, perhaps Blackstone comes to mind. Crimes are committed, according to the *Commentaries,* because of "the infirmities of the best among us, the vices and ungovernable passions of others, the instability of all human affairs, and the numberless unforeseen events, which the compass of a day may bring forth." The law teaches its practitioners that human beings are capable of nearly any variety of behavior, and that there are no truly innocent people. "Very few billable hours are racked up in pursuit of vindication for such totally faultless clients," notes a present-day defense attorney. Given this lesson, defense lawyers do not want to know what lurks in the hearts of their clients.[31]

Modern criminal-law attorneys establish a degree of distance from their clients. Real empathy is not necessarily a valuable trait, though its affectation in a trial may be so. Criminal lawyers do want a degree of trust from their clients in order to win their cooperation and avoid any complaints or difficulties after the case is over; but in their more honest moments, most understand that a gulf separates them from their clients—a gulf of circumstances ("The defendants maybe are repulsive people," according to one criminal attorney) and often class differences ("I don't really identify with my clients. I'm not from that level of society," another admitted). It is not surprising that most modern criminal-defense lawyers don't want to get too close to the people they are defending. They must to a degree manipulate them to get control of them and their case, and they want in turn to avoid being manipulated by their clients for their own (possibly dubious) ends.[32]

Lincoln probably wanted something similar. Emotional distance was handy in a debt-collection case, where it did not make much sense to inquire whether the client was a prudent businessman. In a criminal case, it would have been at least handy and, in some respects, essential.

Most of his criminal cases did not push community hot buttons. Lincoln defended people accused of selling liquor without a license, keeping a "tippling house" open on a Sunday, perjury, receiving stolen goods, gambling, cutting wood on someone else's land, various minor acts of vandalism, a forgery case, and the like. A Christian County farmer named Sam Brown hired Lincoln to defend him against assault charges after he chased several people from his watermelon field and shot at them. In 1854, Lincoln represented Thomas Brewer, accused of running "a common ill-governed and disorderly house to the encouragement of fornication"; Brewer lost, and the court fined him $20. In 1842, he defended Andrew Charles against a charge of adultery (still an illegal offense in many parts of the nation); Lincoln apparently convinced Charles to plead guilty in the hope of receiving a lenient sentence. The strategy worked, to a point; Charles was fined $50 and jailed until he could pay, but he escaped from the Sangamon County jail and disappeared.[33]

Lincoln saw many sharp little altercations between neighbors who found various ways to get on each others' nerves. Isaac Moore hired Lincoln and Herndon to represent him in a case of malicious mischief after he broke into Chester Morris's home two different times and smashed its windows. In 1843 an entire family hired Lincoln to represent them after they were collectively indicted for assaulting a dinner guest. In DeWitt County, six women were represented by Lincoln and Stuart after being charged with riot. The ladies were disturbed by the establishment of a "doggery" (a saloon) in the town of Marion, and took matters into their own hands by breaking into the place and emptying its store of liquor onto the ground. On trial day, the courtroom was packed with women, most of whom sympathized with Lincoln's clients. From a purely legal point of view, there was not much he could do: his clients freely admitted their guilt. Judge Davis assessed a token $2 fine (which, rumor had it, he paid from his own pocket). "Huzzah for the ladies," wrote one local newspaperman.[34]

Some assault cases were not criminal prosecutions per se, but rather attempts by the victim to get civil damages by use of a writ called *vi et armis* (meaning literally "with force at arms"), a form of trespass. Whereas criminal prosecutions addressed the actual assault, civil damages dealt with the problems it subsequently created: lost income because injuries prevented the victim from farming or doing business, for example. As Blackstone put it, a criminal "indictment may be brought as well as [a civil] action; and frequently both are accordingly prosecuted: the one . . . for the crime against the public; the other at the suit of the party injured, to make him a reparation in damages."[35]

Whether criminal or civil, assault cases gave Lincoln a broad perspective on the many different ways his neighbors could find to hurt one another. He litigated charges involving axes, fists, feet, clubs, sticks, shotguns, pistols, pocket knives, hunting knives, a cane, a steel rasp, an iron rod, a two-pound scale weight (thrown in a fit of anger over a grocery bill), and a scythe. The stories Lincoln heard were brutal: one man attacking another with knife thrusts in his side and repeatedly kicking him in the head and back, another stabbing a man in the eye, a third going at his victim in a spasm of rage with his fists, sticks, firewood, a hoe handle, a mall, and a wedge—apparently anything readily at hand.[36] It took two weeks for Patrick Morgan to die from the shotgun blast to his neck, delivered by Lincoln's client, David Thompson—Thompson was sentenced to eight years in prison.[37] In 1841 Lincoln represented Alexander Edmunds, who accused Benjamin, John, and Lewis Simpson of beating him with their fists and a hickory stick, throwing him on the ground and kicking him, pulling his nose, and taking "divers [*sic*] large quantities of hair from and off [his] head." Benjamin claimed he sustained injuries to his "face, breast, back, shoulders, arms, legs, and divers [*sic*] other parts of his body," was unable to transact any business for weeks, and that his clothing—"to wit, one coat, one waistcoat, one pair of breeches, one cravat, one shirt, one pair of stockings, one pair of boots, one hat, and one fur cap"—had been spoiled. The jurors thought either Edmunds was exaggerating or he got what he deserved—they exonerated the Simpsons.[38]

Quite a few of Lincoln's assault cases ended without going to trial, suggesting that he put serious effort into finding acceptable out-of-court arrangements.[39] He tended to lose criminal-assault trials when they went to a jury, giving him added incentive to keep his assault clients out of the courtroom.[40] In October 1856 he persuaded Edward Barrett to accept a five-year imprisonment at hard labor for stabbing a man to death during a brawl.[41] Occasionally, he was able to pursue more creative strategies, as in the 1842 case *People v. Patterson,* in which he argued that his client, Allen Patterson, was subject to "mental alienation" when he attacked another man with an axe. The state attorney was convinced and dropped the case.[42]

Lincoln also saw a fair number of small-scale larceny cases (about seventy)—sometimes very small. In one case, he acted as a court-appointed attorney in Macon County to successfully defend David Adkin from charges that he had stolen a hog. Livestock theft was typical: pigs, horses, cows, and an occasional chicken rustler. Normally these were pro forma proceedings for Lincoln, but sometimes a case stood out for the odd nature of the theft. He once defended three family members who were indicted by the state attorney for stealing fruit trees; they lost and were sentenced to three months in prison and a $30 fine each.[43] Other cases stood out for the draconian quality of their sentences. Lincoln defended a teenager named Larry Bohen who was accused of stealing a sack of clothing, valued at about $15. Bohen was goaded into the deed during a drunken spree on Christmas Eve; and while the men who put him up to it escaped punishment, Bohen received a year in prison. The sentence was so harsh that over one hundred and forty people signed a petition to the governor asking that he be pardoned. There is no indication that the governor did so.[44]

Many of Lincoln's larceny cases simultaneously involved slander, with accusations of thievery leveled by one neighbor against another. Here again, Lincoln tried to play the role of peacemaker and keep things out of the courtroom if possible. As historian Mark Steiner points out, Lincoln (and, by extension, other antebellum lawyers) "helped to restore peace to the 'neighborhood' through his efforts to mediate and settle slander lawsuits."[45]

In 1845, he convinced his client, Wesley Gillenwaters, to retract an accusation of theft leveled against a neighbor named William Frost. Gillenwaters believed that Frost had stolen some money from him; Frost indignantly denied this, brought a slander suit against Gillenwaters, and lined up ten witnesses to prove his honesty. Gillenwaters apparently regretted having spoken out so rashly; or maybe Lincoln persuaded him that, whatever the truth of the matter, it was hardly worth a full-blown trial. He wrote out a retraction for his client to sign, stating that he never really believed that Frost had "ever stole, embezzled, or in any way appropriated to his own use" Gillenwaters's money—and there the matter ended.[46]

Lincoln saw many such legal tempests in teapots. Henry Overton accused Francis Boggs of stealing a clevis pin (a U-shaped device used in harnesses), and Boggs retaliated with a slander suit. Overton hired Lincoln, who pled justification for his client: Boggs had actually stolen the clevis pin. In the ensuing trial, no less than seventeen witnesses testified to this effect, ultimately convincing the jury that Boggs was a thief and finding in Overton's favor. By the time the dust had settled on *Boggs v. Overton,* the dispute over the whereabouts of a clevis pin involved forty-three different people: witnesses, jurors, judges, clerks, sheriffs, and four attorneys, two to each side (Lincoln teamed with Asahel Gridley, while Boggs retained David Davis and a lawyer named Wells Colton).[47]

Sometimes a criminal case touched close to home for Lincoln personally. In 1856, Thomas Johnson was indicted for stealing an expensive gold watch worth $125. Johnson was the son of Lincoln's stepbrother, a family branch of which Lincoln was not overly fond. "You are not *lazy,* and still you *are* an *idler,*" he once wrote his stepbrother, "I doubt whether since I saw you, you have done a good whole day's work in any one day. . . . This habit of uselessly wasting time, is the whole difficulty; and it is vastly important to you, and still more so to your children that you should break this habit." Still, Lincoln agreed to defend one of those children when he found himself in trouble.

As always, Lincoln tried to find a solution out of court. He approached Henry Whitney, his friend and sometime companion on the circuit, in an attempt to get the charges dropped. Whitney was apparently related to Alfred M. Whitney, the justice of the peace hearing Thomas Johnson's case. "I got it *rolled* for Lincoln," Whitney later boasted. Someone, perhaps Lincoln himself, talked the watch's owner into dropping the charges, and when he did so, the state did likewise. Lincoln rationalized the matter by telling Whitney, "'it all amounts to this: the watch was where he could have stolen it; and it was found where he might have left it.'" Whitney wasn't impressed. "That was a very superficial view to take of it," Whitney wryly observed, "because [Johnson] surely stole it and admitted it."[48]

When a case came close to Lincoln personally—a criminal case, too, in which the person in question would not just be out a few dollars, but possibly have to endure jail time—he had a tendency to fall back on this sort of hear-no-evil, see-no-evil reasoning, or what Whitney called going off "half-cocked." The criminal case that touched Lincoln on the most intimate personal level, a case in which some have thought him guilty of "half-cocked" behavior, was also arguably the most famous case he ever tried: the so-called Almanac murder trial, which landed on his doorstep in the fall of 1857.

Murder trials for Lincoln were rare; he was involved in twenty-seven, usually as a defense attorney.[49] The low number is an accurate reflection of Illinois society as a whole because, contrary to popular belief, the American frontier was rarely as violent as we think. Illinois was a comparatively tranquil place as far as murder went. "Our people are too moral to be caught in any serious transgressions of the laws," claimed a newspaper editorial from 1831, "the equilibrium of our social affairs is scarcely ever broken in upon." Statistics bear this out. Between June 1849 and June 1850, there was only one recorded murder in the state's thirty-two northernmost counties.[50]

Murder trials were the best show around precisely because they were unusual. They filled courtrooms, gossipy imaginations, and newspaper columns. If elements of race or sex could be tossed in, so much the better. The *Sangamon Journal,* for example, titillated its readers with lurid details of the murders committed by a "black fellow" who had allegedly assaulted several white women in the area. Springfield newspapers carried accounts of murders from as far away as Michigan and New Jersey, in some cases reprinting whole sections of the *National Police Gazette.* In 1850 the *Illinois State Journal* gave extensive coverage to Boston's infamous Parkman murder trial, including a complete transcript of the confession by Harvard professor John Webster.[51]

Lincoln received an education early in his career concerning the publicity that murder could generate when he helped try a case involving two locally prominent Democratic politicians, Henry Truett and Jacob Early. The men were bitter political and personal rivals, and Truett was an abrasive sort whom one neighbor called "a windy fool."[52] On the evening of March 7, 1838, he confronted Early at a hotel near Springfield, demanding to know if Early had authored a recent

Democratic Party resolution that criticized Truett's performance running the land-registration office in Galena. When Early failed to answer, Truett pulled a pistol from his pocket. Early jumped up, holding a chair in front of him. Truett positioned himself for an opening and then shot Early in the side, the bullet passing through his liver and stomach. He died three days later.

The case had all the ingredients of a riveting courtroom drama: political infighting, well-known participants, and a highly public shooting. Springfield buzzed with rumors and innuendos for days. "The gloom which this occurrence has thrown over our community can with difficulty be realized by those who have not witnessed it," intoned one newspaper editor. "There are many reports in circulation in relation to this affair," wrote another. "Mr. Truett is in the custody of the law, and we hope will receive a fair trial." It took two full days to empanel a jury. One report claimed that "twenty persons were challenged peremptorily, and three or four hundred for cause." As a newly minted junior attorney, Lincoln's role was limited. He did deliver the closing speech, however, telling the jury that Truett acted in self-defense because Early had threatened him with the chair. It was apparently an effective argument, because the jury acquitted Truett.[53]

But by the fall of 1857, it had been quite a while since Lincoln had been a participant in such a trial. The Truett affair was the most high-profile murder case he tried to that point, nearly two decades previously. Lincoln had since defended clients in only seventeen murder cases—and lost ten of them. So when he received a visit that fall from an old friend who asked him to defend her son in a murder case, he was understandably hesitant.

The visitor was Hannah Armstrong, a woman who had known Lincoln since his New Salem days, when she and her husband Jack had given him meals and a place to stay. Jack and Hannah had a son, William—nicknamed "Duff"—who was a bit of a difficult project because, like his father, who had once been a leader of a local roughneck gang called the "Clary's Grove Boys," Duff had a rowdy streak. On a Saturday night in August 1857, his carousing put him in the wrong place at the wrong time. Touring some makeshift bars that had been erected on the perimeter of a religious camp meeting, Armstrong and two friends, James Norris and James Metzker, got involved in an alcohol-enhanced tussle, during which Metzker sustained two serious blows to his head, one from the front and the other from the rear. The injuries did not

immediately kill him. He clambered up on his horse and rode slowly home, falling off several times along the way. He died three days
later.[54]

Eyewitnesses claimed that Norris and Armstrong had savagely beat-
en Metzker. Norris was said to have assaulted him from the rear with
"Some large Stick, resembling a neck yoke of a waggon [sic]," while
Armstrong delivered his blow using a makeshift bludgeon called a
"slungshot"—a chunk of lead wrapped in leather and attached to a
thong. Duff had made the thing himself, and it was a nasty weapon,
brought down with enough force on Metzker's face to smash the "inner
Corner of one Eye." Exactly which blow killed Metzker wasn't clear,
and at first it did not seem to matter very much. Norris was swiftly
convicted of manslaughter and sentenced to eight years. Duff seemed
sure to get the same or worse. It was at this desperate stage that Hannah Armstrong—now a widow—appealed to Lincoln for help.[55]

Lincoln was kindly disposed toward the Armstrongs. According to
Hannah, when he lived in New Salem he would bring the Armstrong
children candy, rock Duff in his cradle, "nurse babies—do anything to
accommodate anybody." Later, Lincoln offered to help Hannah keep
her land from "some men [who] were trying to get [it] from me," promising that, if the matter made it to the Illinois Supreme Court, "I and
Herndon will attend to it for nothing." Still, there seems to have been
limits to Lincoln's largesse. Hannah at first wrote to him, asking him
to defend her son. According to her, "he then wrote to me" but she
"lost the letter." It was after this that she traveled from her home in
Beardstown to Springfield to see Lincoln personally about the matter;
an odd and unnecessary trip, if Lincoln had already agreed to take the
case. Possibly Lincoln tried to beg off, citing his relative inexperience
in murder trials. Whatever she said to him in person changed his
mind, however, for he agreed to represent Duff at his upcoming trial
on May 7, 1858.[56]

Lincoln approached the case with diligence and a thorough attention to detail. Armstrong already had an attorney, William Walker, who
remembered showing Lincoln the evidence he had accrued: "This Mr.
Lincoln Scrutinized Closely and verry [sic] soon was fully posted in
regard to the case." Lincoln was also careful in the selection of the
jury. He wanted younger men, Duff's own age or thereabouts, who
would be inclined to sympathize with a fellow young rowdy whose
revelry had temporarily gotten out of hand. And there was, as always,

Lincoln's appearance. For this trial he dressed in an immaculate white suit, with a neatly arranged black tie and his hair carefully combed, the better to lend dignity and decorum to his client's cause.[57]

His courtroom persona was a crafty mix of drama and reason. The trial's high dramatic moment came when Lincoln confronted the prosecution's main witness, Charles Allen. Allen claimed to have clearly seen Armstrong deliver the fatal blow with his slungshot, despite the fact that the fight occurred late at night. Allen declared that the evening's full moon provided perfect illumination. Several other witnesses offered testimony about the fight, but Allen was the only one to mention the slungshot. Lincoln needed to wreck his credibility.

An experienced courtroom dramatist, he masterfully set Allen up for the fall. Prior to the trial's beginning, he handed an almanac to one of the court officers, "stating that he might call for one during the trial, and if he did, to send him that one." When Allen made his assertion about the full moon (Lincoln got him to repeat this several times) he called for the almanac—carried with appropriate gravity and suspense by the officer across the room, rather than, say, picked up from a table by Lincoln himself—and, triumphantly brandishing the book, declared that, according to the record, the moon had already set when the assault occurred. The courtroom erupted in laughter.[58]

When the time came for him to address the jury, Lincoln took by turns a low-key and emotional approach. Where the witness testimony was concerned, he wanted the jurors to use their heads more than their hearts; he needed them to get beyond the gut-level reaction to the eyewitnesses—they were there, so they must have seen what happened—to dissect the inconsistencies and improbabilities within each one's account. "He spoke Slow," Walker recalled, "and Carefully reviewed the whole testimony, picked it all to pieces, and Showed, that the man though kil[l]ed had not received his wounds at the place or time named by the witness, but afterwards and from the hands of Some one Els[e]." But when it came time to wrap up, Lincoln switched back to the heart, tugging the jurors' heartstrings by referencing issues that, judged by reason alone, had no bearing at all on the case. "He told of his kind feelings toward the Mother of the Prisoner, a widow," according to Walker, and "that she had been kind to him when he was young, alone and without friends. . . . I have never Seen, Such mastery Exhibited over the feelings and Emotions of Men." Lincoln got what he wanted; Duff was acquitted.[59]

The trial had unusual personal dimensions for Lincoln. Hannah approached him afterward and thanked him tearfully for saving her son. When the subject of a fee came up, Lincoln replied, "Why—Hannah I shan't charge you a cent—ever." Five years later, he again intervened on Duff's behalf, granting him a discharge from the Union army after Hannah implored the president to send her son home.[60]

Some have argued that the Armstrong case was so personal to Lincoln that it temporarily unhinged his sense of propriety. It is an argument based on thin evidence and a poor understanding of what was professionally proper for an antebellum attorney.[61] And in many ways, Lincoln's approach to the Armstrong case, once he agreed to represent Duff, was the opposite of personal. It was an expert manipulation of every aspect of the show that is an American criminal trial—from the white suit he wore to his mawkish closing argument—manipulation that came from a man who could coolly appraise the effect he needed to achieve in order to secure victory. "He handled and moved men *remotely* as we do pieces on a chessboard," Leonard Swett observed. Swett did not seem to mean this as an indictment of Lincoln—and in a courtroom, Lincoln would not have taken it that way.[62]

Chapter Six

Death and the Maidens

L eonard Swett followed Lincoln to Washington, D.C., when he became president, one of several old friends from the Illinois bar whom Lincoln brought with him. Some were officeholders like Ninian Edwards, who became captain commissary of subsistence, or Ward Hill Lamon, who was Lincoln's self-appointed bodyguard on the trip from Springfield, and who later became the U.S. marshal for the District of Columbia. Swett played the role of informal advisor to the president. His belief on the circuit that he knew what made lawyer Lincoln tick carried over into politics as well. He offered the president advice on matters ranging from Supreme Court nominees to how Lincoln might best manipulate the Washington press to his advantage.[1]

Swett saw Lincoln often, accompanying him on trips to the theater and generally hanging about the White House. "I remember one day being in his room when he was sitting at his table with a large pile of papers before him," Swett wrote. "After a pleasant talk, he turned quite abruptly and said, 'Get out of my way, Swett; tomorrow is butcher-day, and I must go through these papers and see if I cannot find *some excuse* to let these poor fellows off.'"[2]

"Butcher day" was Lincoln's regular review of the execution orders for soldiers convicted of desertion, cowardice, rank insubordination, and various other serious derelictions of duty. He brought a lawyer's-eye view to the task, parsing each document carefully for mistakes. "I was amused at the eagerness with which the President caught at any fact which would justify him in saving the life of a condemned soldier," his private secretary wrote. "Cases of cowardice he was especially averse to punishing with death. He said it would frighten the poor devils too terribly, to shoot them. . . . One fellow who had deserted and escaped after conviction into Mexico, he sentenced, saying, 'We will condemn him as they used to sell hogs in Indiana, as they run.'"[3]

Swett thought that Lincoln would sometimes "do things he knew to be impolitic and wrong to save some poor fellow's neck." He may have been exaggerating; recent scholarship suggests that Lincoln usually followed the thinking of his department commanders and Judge Advocate General Joseph Holt in reprieving or condemning soldiers to death.[4] Still, some of the men who were in charge of keeping the Union's armed forces functional did not appreciate the president's largesse. Ward Lamon recalled one commanding officer's anger reaching such heights that he directly confronted Lincoln and requested the president rescind his stays of executions for twenty deserters. According to Lamon, Lincoln replied with uncharacteristic heat, "General, there are too many weeping widows in the United States now. For God's sake don't ask me to add to the number; for, I tell you plainly, *I won't do it!*"[5]

Lincoln knew those weeping widows well. Like Hannah Armstrong, they wrote him letters and appeared at the White House, pleading with him to grant their sons, husbands, fathers, and loved ones leaves of absence, discharges, or stays of execution. They played on his sympathies, appealed to his sense of fair play, berated him as heartless and cruel, and sometimes called down the wrath of the Lord to punish his leadership of a pitiless and devastating war. "You stand on the hearts of widows and orphans and childless mothers to be," wrote one, "and the voice of their wailing goes up to God this day." Lincoln heard that wailing, too. In a way, every day of the Civil War was butcher day for him, in one fashion or another. "I have seen him shed tears when speaking of the cheerful sacrifice of the light and strength of so many happy homes," a reporter wrote.[6]

But Lincoln could make widows, and lots of them. He could knowingly order men to their deaths in ungodly numbers, and throughout the war he displayed little patience with generals who were overly squeamish about causing too many Union or Confederate casualties. And if he did sometimes shed tears for the war's terrible toll, he more often proved able to suppress those tears and send in fresh waves of soldiers to kill and be killed. During the war's most brutal time, that horrendous summer of 1864, when Ulysses S. Grant's Wilderness campaign resulted in thousands upon thousands of military graves, Lincoln betrayed no visible sense of uncertainty or anguish. "The President seemed in a pleasant and confident humor today," his private secretary wrote on July 12, the day he made a tour of Washington's fortifications, came under fire from Confederate forces, and saw a man shot at his side. A month later he famously told Grant to "hold on with a bull-dog gripe, and chew & choke, as much as possible." He knew that thousands of young men would die while they did the chewing and choking. "I sincerely wish war was an easier and pleasanter business than it is; but it does not admit of holy-days," he once wrote.[7]

Lincoln became a hard-hearted dealer of death when necessary, during an era when few subjects aroused quite so much raw emotion. Nineteenth-century Americans were morbidly obsessed with death, wrapping it in thick layers of ceremony and ritual. Town churches rang their bells a certain way to commemorate the dead, and there were elaborate local customs and rules for how family and friends should dress and behave during the grieving period. Cemeteries were laid out with extraordinary care, and their tombstones were decorated with appropriate signs and markers: crosses, cherubs, angels, Biblical sayings, and imagery. "Death was integrated, through a series of rituals and symbols, into the life of the community," noted one historian.[8]

Death tugged at Lincoln's elbow often enough. His mother died from food poisoning when he was nine, and his sister died during childbirth ten years later. Mary and he lost their first child, Edward, to tuberculosis in 1850, and their third child Willie to typhoid fever in 1862. Battle cost him close friend Edward Baker, a fellow lawyer for whom he had named his first son. "The death of his beloved Baker smote upon him like a whirlwind from a desert," wrote one observer. There was also Elmer Ellsworth, a handsome young law student who read for the bar exam in Lincoln and Herndon's office; he was shot by an irate southern sympathizer as he tried to haul down a Confederate flag in Alexandria, Virginia. The incident made national headlines, and it hit Lincoln hard. He had admired Ellsworth's dashing and bravery. "In the untimely loss of your noble son, our affliction here, is scarcely less than your own," he wrote to Ellsworth's mother, "so much of promised usefulness to one's country, and of bright hopes for one's self and friends, have rarely been so suddenly dashed, as in his fall."[9]

But Lincoln moved on. By the time he became president he knew how to bury whatever feelings death may have aroused in him, a task all the more difficult because he was blessed (or afflicted) with an extraordinary tenderheartedness, averse to harming even "animals and crawling insects." Stories circulated in New Salem and Springfield about his dislike for hunting and his habit of stopping along a roadside to replace birds that had fallen from their nests.[10]

He eventually learned to shove these private traits aside and elevate instead the task at hand—defending the Union, winning battles, winning the war—above the costs and the sacrifice in human lives. His religious fatalism proved useful here (people died because it was God's will that they do so), as did his fundamental patriotism and reverence for the heroic battlefield sacrifices of the Revolutionary generation. The battlefields of the War for Independence, he argued, meant that "a *living history was* to be found in every family—a history bearing the indubitable testimonies of its own authenticity, in the limbs mangled, in the scars of wounds received." Maybe some of Lincoln's less attractive qualities also helped him along: his intense ambition, for example, that "little engine which knew no rest" and that might have smoothed over the cost of the path he took toward becoming the Union's savior.[11]

But another source was his law practice. Until the Civil War, the law provided the most frequent means of contact between Lincoln and the dead. It brought Lincoln into close contact with death, and yet also it taught him to drain death of emotional content.

Death seeped into his practice in a variety of ways, some obvious, others less so. There were the cases arising directly and dramatically from a death, like Duff Armstrong's murder trial. Duff was spared (he would live until 1899), but another one of Lincoln's clients, William Fraim, was hung for a murder he committed while working as a riverboat laborer. Fraim was apparently the only client Lincoln ever lost to the hangman.[12]

Other cases posed death as a background issue. In June 1854, Lincoln and Herndon were hired by John Connelly and John Way, two Springfield citizens who discovered that a plot of land adjoining their property was owned by Chicago's Bishop Van de Velde; he planned to use it as a Catholic cemetery. Connelly and Way objected that the cemetery would be a nuisance and health hazard, its drainage posing a threat to their drinking wells. After a long and convoluted series of filings, the parties involved reached a settlement whereby Van de Velde agreed to sell the plot and locate the cemetery someplace else.[13]

Death also hovered over the cases involving wills and inheritance settlements. There were many of these. During the course of his career, Lincoln litigated over five hundred cases involving division of a dead person's property.[14]

The sheer variety of Lincoln's litigation in this area was astonishing. His clients sued estate administrators to collect unpaid promissory notes, compel the sale of land to pay estate debts, divide land among various heirs, and collect unpaid court judgments and fees. In one typical case, he was hired by the administrator of Henry Loutzenhiser's estate to sue Loutzenhiser's brother and heir Charles and force him to sell land to satisfy Henry's debts. In 1847 he represented the administrators of an estate seeking to collect an unpaid debt owed by a man killed during the Mexican War. Ten years later, he was hired by the administrator of Singleton Keeling, who had died in California in 1852 (possibly as part of the gold rush) and whose estate was embroiled in a controversy involving the differences between California and Illinois laws of descent.[15]

Death caused a variety of entanglements in his business litigation. Debt collection was more complicated when a creditor or a debtor passed away. After Zachariah Peter sold eighty acres of land to Mathew Martin in 1841, for example, he had to hire Lincoln and sue Martin's family (all eleven members, including several children) to collect his money.[16] Partnership dissolutions and land transfers also became more troublesome, particularly if a party to the transfer died before the paperwork was completed. Lincoln might then be called in when the court tried to sort out competing claims among partners, family members, and heirs. Sometimes multiple deaths among investors in a business venture wrought havoc, as in a case involving the establishment of a flouring mill in Tazewell County. One of the mill's investors, John Caldwell, sued the others (including Lincoln's client, William Finn) for expenses he accumulated when he paid for the transportation of a steam engine to the mill. The partner who had agreed to compensate Caldwell for his trouble died, however, and to make matters still more difficult, Caldwell himself passed away while the litigation was still pending in the Tazewell County circuit court. Eight years later, Caldwell's administrator dropped the suit entirely.[17]

Death also created a little niche area of business and property litigation on its own. Lincoln was involved in quite a few dower cases (more than seventy), as widows tried to get what they considered their fair slice of a dead husband's estate. Sometimes he represented the widow when she sued an administrator to either hasten the process of apportioning the estate's assets or to argue for a better settlement. But there were times when he approached dower from other points of view. In 1855 he was hired by John Danielle's heirs to force John's widow Margaret to assign her dower and then divide what was left among them. The court also occasionally appointed Lincoln as the guardian of young children's interests while it decided how best to apportion their father's estate among the widow and various heirs.[18]

In all of these cases, the exact conditions of death escaped his notice. Court documents normally did not indicate the precise cause of death, and Lincoln would have had no reason to make such inquiries. In its quest to get at the fundamental issues in a case, the law has a way of discarding superfluous information; in order to decide the amount of a dower, proper payment of a debt, or disposal of estate property, it was usually enough simply to know that, somewhere along the line, a person had died. The record did not show whether John Black died peacefully or in agony, whether Hugh Irwin was in the presence of family or loved ones when he died, or if William Wernwag was comfortable in the Indiana town where he passed on. Lincoln litigated their cases, and hundreds of others, probably without ever knowing the character and flavor of their last moments on earth. He did not know, and he probably did not want to know.[19]

For Lincoln's neighbors, this was not so. The various farmers, merchants, and laborers making up the bulk of his community had cause to know death in a direct and intimate manner: mothers and children lost at childbirth, parents killed by accidents or disease, or any of the other myriad ways a person could die. They lived in a romantic age, and the culture sentimentalized death in a variety of forms, bestowing deep emotional significance to the deceased's locks of hair, clothing, and portraits. People believed that these objects and the various rituals of death—the black crepe, the rules regarding proper mourning attire and public demeanor, the intricate ceremonies—were necessary rites of passage whereby family and friends could travel from their initial, painful encounter with mortality to some state of mind that was more comfortable and functional. They were necessary precisely because death was so raw on the Illinois frontier, where it was encountered often and under circumstances that wove it into the fabric of daily experience. People died not in faraway hospital beds and nursing homes but rather their own beds, cemeteries were ubiquitous and scattered throughout the countryside, and in a time before the advent of professional mortuaries, the same individual who tended dead bodies might also be the town carpenter or blacksmith. Rituals of mourning placed some distance between the dearly departed and their loved ones, a space in which they could grieve and also move on.[20]

This applied to Lincoln as well, at least when it came to the deaths of his own family members. He accepted the era's death rituals without question, and he grieved with as much feeling as anyone around him when he lost friends and family members, like his eldest son Edward, who passed away from what was likely tuberculosis in the winter of 1850. But even as Lincoln wept for his son, donned a black mourning band, and otherwise observed the death rituals of his time, his profession helped put death in a more prosaic perspective. During the year Eddie died, Lincoln's practice involved him in the deaths of Pascal Enos, James Louthan, Marvelous Eastham, Michael Glynn, William Kirk, John Pantier, Rufus Pope, Archibald Trailor, and George Trotter. Some of these people were familiar to Lincoln; Enos was one of Springfield's first citizens who ran the town's land office for years, and Trailor had once been Lincoln's client in a murder case. Others were likely not known by him at all. In the end, they were all reduced to names on a court docket.[21]

The law gave him at least a bit more distance from death than that afforded by the social rituals of his time. It routinized it, de-fanged it to a certain extent, and played a role in allowing Lincoln to shake off death's worst effects, or at least set them to one side so he could get on with his job, whatever that might be. Thus, a mere seven days after Eddie's death, Lincoln was able to engage in the routine correspondence of his work, betraying none of his inner anguish in the process. "Were our men actually in possession of the land at the time it was conveyed by Denny to Bradshaw?" he wrote to a Thomas J. Turner concerning a real estate matter. "Are we *obliged* to put Bradshaw on his oath? Can we not *prove* our case without?" Turner would never have known from the letter that Lincoln had just buried his son.[22]

Throwing himself into his work was a refuge, of sorts; even when death made its way directly into his law office, it was often denuded of its more disturbing aspects. Lincoln had no immediate knowledge, for example, of the grisly circumstances surrounding the death of George Anderson, found dead behind his house on Monroe Street in Springfield in May 1856. The image was surely burned into the memories of his family forever after; how his wife went looking for George when she discovered he had gotten out of bed (nobody ever knew exactly why); how she woke an eighteen-year-old apprentice living in their home named John Morgan and asked him to go look for her husband; and how John discovered George's body just beyond the back door and about five feet from the outhouse, face up, the back of his skull cracked and mashed in, "the result of a severe blow with a blunt instrument," probably a hammer found lying nearby. He had lain there a long time, for the body was cold when found.

By the time the case came to Lincoln—as defense attorney for Anderson's nephew Theodore, who was accused of conspiring with George's wife to murder him—the bloodstains were gone, the ground behind the back door cleaned up, and the body buried. The details of death were reduced to the clinical paraphernalia of what the circumstances proved or did not prove about the defendant's guilt or innocence. The exact position of the body ("his left hand was lying by his thigh and his right hand about six inches out"), the amount of blood ("there was a small clot of blood lying by his head"), his wife's attitude (she "commenced crying and taking on considerable")—all were shorn of their colors, their smells, and much of their feeling. The case aroused a good deal of local interest, particularly when it was discovered that George had possibly been poisoned with strychnine before he was beaten to death. To do his job, however, Lincoln had to press all of this aside. He had to anesthetize George's death so he could properly analyze it and use its details to his advantage in court. He did his job well: the jury acquitted George's wife and nephew.[23]

The law taught Lincoln that death could be made rational as well as emotional. It was a lesson he could never impart to Mary. Edward's death deeply affected her, to the point that she stopped eating and fell into a deep depression. Willie's death fell upon her even harder and was made all the more painful because it was so public; Willie was the only child of a president to ever die in the White House. Washington, D.C.'s rumor mill whispered that the First Lady was on the brink of a complete mental breakdown, and one story had Lincoln threatening to send her to the city's insane asylum if she did not gain control of her constant weeping and melancholy spirit. "Try and control your grief," he said to her, "or it will drive you mad and we may have to send you there."[24]

Not all women were as overwrought by the deaths of their loved ones, of course; but the culture of the time equated sentimentality and feminine emotion with death.[25] Lincoln was extremely patient with Mary, and he tried to at least be polite when the war brought other distraught ladies before him. But privately he chafed at the never-ending line of female suppliants, especially those who came to appeal for his mercy in releasing pro-Confederate men. "Oh yes, I understand," he snapped at a petitioner who sought mercy for a condemned rebel spy, "some one has been crying, and worked upon your feelings, and you have come here to work on mine."[26]

Lincoln was always uncomfortable around women. "He would Joke—tell stories—run rigs—etc. on the boys [but he] Didn't love the Company of Girls," remembered a cousin.[27] Women were socially defined by characteristics he distrusted. Nineteenth-century Americans believed that women were sentimental to a fault: "I am not a very sentimental man," Lincoln once wrote. According to an Indiana neighbor, he "didn't like girls much, [they were] too frivalous [sic]." Women were supposed to be domestic and settled; he loved the peripatetic life of the road. Courtships were defined by vague and shifting cultural customs, and Lincoln detested hazy rules.[28]

He spent much of his life as a bachelor tripping over one social foot after the other. "I don't know how to talk to ladies," he confessed to a group of women introduced to him by Henry Whitney at a train station, "Whitney can tell you that." It was no small admission, coming from a man for whom talking was the foundation of his social life. His marriage may have eased matters a bit, removing the factors of incipient romance (or lack thereof) from subsequent encounters with the opposite sex.[29] And once Lincoln got his law license, women usually had to come to him on his terms, in the masculine world of his law office and the circuit.

Although the overwhelming majority of Lincoln's clients were men, he did litigate a fair number of cases involving women—over six hundred.[30] In many cases, they appeared on the periphery of otherwise ordinary litigation. Lincoln represented women as creditors, debtors, landowners, and renters.[31] Widow Permelia Skinner joined Samuel Beam, a road supervisor in Logan County, to stop John Buckles from obstructing a road that paralleled her property with his fence. Sinai Ann Beerup appeared on the docket as a plaintiff alongside her husband Thomas in a lawsuit involving some town lots in Springfield. Anna Benedict hired Lincoln in 1855 to collect a $600 debt.[32]

Wives were sometimes pulled into the vortex of their entrepreneur husbands' business dealings, whether they deserved it or not. Nancy McDonald discovered this when she was successfully sued by Lincoln's client, James Barret, and compelled to pay off a large debt accrued by her dead husband William.[33] Mothers were also made party to the masculine world of business by their status as guardians of their children's rights and interests.[34]

The fact that debt-collection, probate, and other business clients were sometimes women had no discernible effect on Lincoln's approach to their cases. But when they moved closer from that periphery, female clients could pose special problems. Or, to be more precise, the mores of Lincoln's time made it seem so.

When women appeared as litigants in slander cases, there was almost always a sexual dimension. Men sued other men for accusations of thievery, dishonesty, and perjury; women brought slander suits when they were accused of adultery, prostitution, fornication, or promiscuity.[35] On occasion, women were also the accusers, as in an 1851 case in which Lincoln represented Elizabeth Kitchell and her husband Milden, who claimed Mary Ann Jacobus was a "whore" and had acquired "her fine clothes by whoring." Lincoln helped negotiate an out-of-court settlement.[36]

A woman accused of sexual misbehavior usually had more to lose than a man who had been called, for example, "a damned rogue" or a "damned little horse thief."[37] A reputation for being "loose" or "fallen" could stain a woman more permanently, regardless of the context or the consequences. Once such allegations were accepted as fact by the local community, there was little a woman could do—small indiscretion or large, the damage had already been done. Lincoln told a little joke about a wife accused of having three illegitimate children. "Now, that's a lie and I can prove it," replied the woman's outraged husband, "for she only has two."[38]

Jokes aside, there was a sharp edge to the female slander cases. Truth was a defense in a slander suit; it wasn't slander if she really was a "whore." Slander trials could therefore involve a wholesale public airing of neighborhood rumors, innuendos, and gossip concerning a woman's character. "Litigation in slander suits were involved in 'small politics' of everyday life: reputation, gossip, and insult," historian Mark Steiner points out.[39]

Schoolteacher Emily Fancher found this to be so when she sued

Daniel Gollogher, who claimed that she had been inflating the number of students on her roll to get more township money. He also told people that Fancher was a fornicator who "ran away with a married man . . . and lived with him as his wife." Warming to the subject, Gollogher then suggested that Fancher's father "had better take Emily back to the bad house where he found her and then the sores on her neck would vanish away." It is anyone's guess what he meant by this, but—along with the reference to a "bad house" (a brothel)—Miss Fancher did not take it as a compliment.

When she took Gollogher to court, he hired Lincoln, who subpoenaed various witnesses to confirm the truth of Gollogher's claims. Fancher called witnesses who attested to her status as "a good, true, chaste and honest citizen." The men in the jury box had to weigh a series of competing character references, whose accuracy was difficult to assess, in determining what was slanderous and what was not. In the end, the jurors decided that Gollogher was guilty of slander where the school rolls were concerned, but not guilty when it came to her status as a denizen of the "bad house," neck sores and all. It was an interesting conclusion, suggesting that the jurors believed Emily was a moral bookkeeper but an immoral woman, and that the latter was at least as verifiable as the former.[40]

The two sides in a slander case could marshal impressive forces in the name of proving or disproving a woman's character and worth. William Underwood responded to Nancy Martin's slander suit by calling no less than thirty-two witnesses to prove his claim that she was guilty of fornication and having sexual relations with him. As one of Martin's attorneys (she had three), Lincoln helped subpoena twenty-five people to bolster her claim that the assertions were false, and that Underwood had made them with malice. It became an agonizingly drawn-out procedure, culminating in a jury trial that must have roiled the entire community. Martin won her case, with the jury extracting a little over $200 in damages from Underwood.[41]

Throw race into the mix, and the results could be still more complicated. In 1844 a Mason County woman named Maria Patterson was hauled into the local circuit court by Ambrose and Tabitha Edwards for spreading the rumor that Tabitha was (in the stilted wording of the court plea) "guilty of indecent, open, criminal, and illicit intercourse with a negro, and raising a family of illegitimate children by said negro." The words suggested—though they did not actually assert—that Tabitha was guilty of committing fornication and adultery. Worse (from the perspective of her white neighbors), Tabitha was accused of crossing the racial divide. Her lawyer did an effective job of marshaling character witnesses; that, and the jury was apparently stocked with neighbors willing to give her the benefit of the doubt. Whatever the reason, she won her slander suit and the jury awarded her $220 in damages.[42]

Edwards hired Lincoln to represent her when Patterson appealed the ruling to the Illinois Supreme Court. Lincoln sensed that the case rested on thin ice. The jury had sympathized enough with Tabitha to produce a victory in the lower court, but where the actual letter of the law was concerned, the suggestion of adultery made by Patterson was only that—a suggestion, an innuendo that could only be inferred from the base allegation, "raising a family of illegitimate children." When it came time to argue the appeal, Lincoln admitted as much, telling the Supreme Court justices that, by itself, the innuendos in Maria Patterson's statements did not quite rise to the level of slander. Having conceded this, however, Lincoln nudged his case from the area of gender to that of race. "The inference is, that she had had children *by a negro*," he argued, and it was within this racially charged atmosphere that Patterson's statements should be understood. The court ignored the racial dimension, however; in reversing the lower court's decision, it chose to narrowly construe the law of slander by pointing out that Patterson's words "do not, in their plain and proper sense, or in common acceptation, necessarily amount to a charge of fornication and adultery."[43]

The white community's revulsion at sexual relations between blacks and whites, neighborhood gossip about a woman's sexual mores and character, vague words that might or not imply wrongdoing—this was all rooted in visceral, gut-level perceptions. Like nearly every man (and woman) of his time, Lincoln associated "feminine" with soft, sentimental, and emotional behavior. "Some one has been crying, and worked upon your feelings, and now you've come to work upon mine"—that was how Lincoln understood womanhood, as part of that squishy, intellectually indistinct world of feeling and emotion that this self-described unsentimental man normally wanted to avoid, or at least remove from his masculine circles of fellow lawyers, judges, and businessmen. When that world intruded on his legal life—a life defined much more often by the hard, cold legal instruments of promissory notes, contracts, and the like—one suspects he became at least a bit uncomfortable.

Lincoln had this contrast brought home to him with particular clarity during an 1845 seduction case, in which a Cole County man named Michael Ryan sued Elias Anderson for seduction and loss of services when he discovered that Anderson had impregnated his young daughter. At one time, "loss of services" was the foundation of a seduction case, as parents tried to recover damages when a seduced daughter became pregnant and could no longer do heavy farmwork or other chores. Ryan won his case and the circuit court jury awarded him over $600. Anderson appealed and hired Lincoln to represent him before the state supreme court.[44]

Going over the trial records, Lincoln noticed that the circuit court judge had told the jury they could infer Ryan's loss of service from the mere fact of his daughter's pregnancy; no actual damage needed to be proven. For Lincoln, that was the rub: the jury never considered whether there was in fact a "loss of service," or how much that loss might mean in concrete terms—dollars and cents, lack of production, or fewer work hours. He asked the judges to set aside the jury verdict on that count, arguing that "the court could not see whether the jury based their verdict as to loss of service on the evidence, or on the misdirection of the court, [and] a new trial should have been granted."

But the judges told Lincoln that times were changing. The old English common law made parents prove they had suffered some measurable economic loss arising from the seduction of their daughter; these days, however, the mere proof of a parent-child relationship was enough to establish that a loss of service had occurred. This was not a mere matter of money or labor lost; it was also a matter of what the justices called the "more enlightened and refined views of the domestic relations" between daughters and their parents. "As one of the fruits of more cultivated times, the value of the society and attentions of a virtuous and innocent daughter is properly appreciated," according to the court, "and the loss sustained by the parent from the corruption of her mind and the defilement of her person, is also considered." The courts were doing more than merely protecting a father and mother's right to their children's "menial labors." They were also protecting the flower of American womanhood. Seduction was really about "the loss of character and happiness of the unfortunate female, and the consequent injury inflicted on the heart of the parent."[45]

"Character," "happiness," and the "heart"—here was a realm quite different from the questions that normally concerned Lincoln, questions about whether a promissory note was valid or whether a businessman had properly accounted for a firm's assets. Those cases had their gray areas, but not in quite the same prominent manner. When women were added into the mix, the results could be unpredictable, the legal criterion vague.

If these cases made Lincoln squirm, they must have also posed some anxiety for the female clients themselves. Women entered a male arena when they ventured into the law. Its practitioners were all men, the jury box was filled with men, and the courthouses, courtrooms, and law offices were unrelievedly male in their sights, sounds, and manners. Women could often be found in and around the outlying edges of legal terrain. They sat in the galleries, were called upon to testify, and (more often than we might think) used the courts to protect their rights as wives, mothers, and daughters.[46] But the law's heartland was male. It was in an era in which Americans placed a heavy emphasis on creating distinct masculine and feminine spaces, and even if the separation of those separate spheres was not so absolute as many wanted to believe, still there was a palpable social and cultural difference between the parlors and drawing rooms of feminine domesticity and the houses of the law. Those women were crossing a line when they entered Lincoln's world, and they knew it.

What was going through the mind of Caroline Beerup, for example, when she climbed the steps to Lincoln and Herndon's office sometime in 1853 to relate her tale? She knew she wanted a divorce from her husband Stephen. In this era before the no-fault divorce, her lawyer (it is not clear which partner represented her) had to know why. Caroline replied that Stephen was a cruel man and an adulterer, who in February 1850 deserted her and their six children, leaving them with no means of support at all. She also claimed that Stephen had tortured her, inflicting that "which can never be seen by eyes here, but such as no man whose sense of love and humanity were not crusted and hardened by baseness and infamy would do, perpetrate, or commit."[47]

Caroline Beerup had to expose a humiliating fact of her intimate life not only for her lawyer, but also for the Sangamon County circuit court, which made it part of the public record in the court's divorce proceedings—proceedings including a newspaper notice in the *Illinois Daily Register* that advertised her divorce (its fact, if not the precise circumstances) for everyone to see. This was an age when such matters were not to be openly discussed, when there was as yet no larger

American culture of frankness about sexuality, venereal diseases, or violence within a marriage.[48]

What would have been Caroline's demeanor, and other women like her, as she spoke to her lawyer of desertion, cruelty, bigamy, and other tribulations? Many Americans of the time thought battered and abused wives were at least partly culpable for their plight—"blaming the victim," in modern terminology. A cloud of shame, potential or real, would have hung over a conversation between a female client and her male attorney, seated in a dingy law office with dust, ink stains, and other signs of indifference to "feminine" sensibilities. Clients would have reacted to this in different ways, as their personalities and circumstances dictated. Maybe a woman like Catherine Beerup affected an air of stoicism, erecting an emotionless façade. Or maybe there were tears, as she stumbled and choked through her story. Or perhaps she avoided having to speak of her plight altogether, sending a friend or relative to make arrangements with her attorney.

And what was going through Lincoln's mind? He heard many sad stories. Nancy Clarkson claimed her husband John had tried to rape their daughter, consorted with "lewd women," and eventually abandoned her. Desiree Duhamel claimed Edmund Duhamel had threatened to shoot her during a drunken rage. Sarah Hook hired Lincoln and Herndon in 1859 to divorce Richard Denton, whom she claimed had forced her to marry him after he drugged her with chloroform and spirited her away to Cincinnati, where he locked her in a room. Sarah was rescued by her mother, only to be again kidnapped by Denton and again rescued by her mother. Sarah got her divorce. In 1853 Lincoln helped Mary Beard attain a divorce from Martin Beard; Martin had "frequently severely beaten and bruised [Mary] with his fists and . . . with a switch," and he abused the couple's six-week-old son, William. Mary won her case and was given custody of William. Lucy Sinclair also won her case against John Sinclair, who was being cared for by a relative because of his deteriorating mental condition. Lucy accused John of cruelty, drunkenness, and adulterous "acts of beastliness [to]o polluting to state."[49]

Lincoln sifted through the remains of over one hundred wounded and dying marriages during the course of his career.[50] He did not always represent the wife's point of view. In 1852 he took the case of William Hill, sued by his wife for divorce because, she said, he had abused her and he was impotent, being "not a natural and perfect man." Solomon Goodman hired Lincoln and Logan to get a divorce from Nancy Goodman for adultery and desertion. David Enslow hired Lincoln in 1853 to sue his wife Hetty for abandonment; she in turn sued him for abandonment and cruelty, and won not only a divorce but also a $400 alimony settlement.[51]

Most of Lincoln's divorce clients prevailed, probably because he and other attorneys acted as gatekeepers for the system, weeding out weak cases before everyone involved was subjected to the scrutiny and embarrassment of a public trial. Illinois possessed more liberal divorce laws than most other states. Nevertheless, some clients with dubious cases made it as far as the courtroom and were turned away; George Caldwell, for example, claimed that a divorce from his wife Laura was "manifest destiny" because of her "fire and powder disposition," and because he suspected (though he admitted he could not prove) that she was cheating on him. He doesn't seem to have gotten very far with the judge, who later dismissed the case.[52]

Win or lose, with a husband or wife as client, Lincoln saw and heard things considered by people of his time to be intensely private. Modern Americans might find a prurient interest in the sexual adventures of a husband like James Graham, who declared of his wife Amanda's child that "he did not know whether he was the father . . . but that he had a chance to be," or of wives like Rebecca Waddell, accused by her husband Squire of committing adultery while he was away digging for gold in California. For that matter, quite a few of Lincoln's neighbors would have been titillated, had they cared to admit it. But the conventions of the time dictated otherwise.[53]

Those conventions were powerful enough to shape the very language used to describe various marital predicaments. Lincoln's clients and the court tried to camouflage them with circumspect language about behavior "too polluting to state," and the like. Harriet Jackson divorced her husband Andrew because his philandering had given her "that most loathsome and detestable disease [that was] improper for [her] to name." Susan Howey was thrown out of the house by her husband James because, in her words, "he wanted his house for other purposes"—an adulterous relationship with another woman. Joseph Kyle believed he had contracted the venereal disease he transmitted to his wife (who in turn sued him for divorce) in a Springfield "necessary." Dealing with these delicate matters of gender, sexuality, and intimacy, Lincoln found himself communicating in a quasi-code, designed to infer meaning with innuendo, to deflect as much as invite scrutiny, and to reveal only the barest possible facts and meanings.[54]

A divorce case cracked open the sentimental bond of marriage like an egg, exposing motives and passions that the era's romantic ideals did not encompass. Husbands and wives weren't supposed to be motivated by unhealthy greed, lust, envy, or jealousy. Whether he liked it or not, Lincoln saw these things, and more. When he peered inside Samuel and Laura Philbrick's broken marriage, for example, Lincoln saw not just extraordinary deception—Sam turned out to have another wife in New Hampshire—but violence and the myriad consequences of drug addiction. Sam refused to sleep with his wife, he said, because her opium habit made her "filthy, loathsome, and disgusting."[55]

Antebellum Americans made little room in their ideals for lies, revulsion, and the effects of substance abuse. Lincoln lacked the array of cultural and psychological tools we now take almost as second nature when confronted with these and other marital sins. He was a compassionate man, and this no doubt helped him ease somewhat the awkwardness of discussing matters "filthy, loathsome, and disgusting." But only somewhat.

Or so our modern sensibilities tell us. But perhaps reticence itself was a vocabulary of sorts, a valuing of silence and reserve that could be brought to bear on Lincoln's most sensitive cases. In his criminal practice, Lincoln had to cultivate a degree of emotional distance in order to serve people whose deeds and perhaps character he might have found revolting.

Something similar may have been at work when Lincoln dealt with divorces and the various other legal issues involving women. One New Salem neighbor described Lincoln's attitude toward women in general as "Kind and Condescending," and perhaps this captures the difference between his approach to accused criminals and female clients. The legal culture of his day in general took a benevolent master/paternalist approach to women, children, and others widely perceived as dependents when they ventured into the clutches of the legal system. It allowed judges, lawyers, and other legal officials to assume a stance that was compassionate and protective without compromising the law's elevated position of superiority over women and others who were further down the food chain of social and cultural deference.[56]

"Kind and Condescending" Lincoln would have found this approach appealing, as well, but perhaps for different reasons. Affecting a paternalist attitude toward his female clients would have allowed Lincoln to preserve both compassion and his sense of distance from female clients. The point here was not necessarily preservation of an unequal power relationship, but rather a desire to put events that were normally categorized by society as matters of the heart on the more coolly rational plane where Lincoln did his best work and where he was most comfortable.

Some people, after all, found Lincoln not kindly but remote—and those people were usually women, fellow attorneys, or in one case the wife of a fellow attorney. Ninian Edwards's wife Elizabeth described Lincoln as "a cold Man" who "had no affection." She saw him in a variety of social settings, and observed that he "Could not hold a lengthy Conversation with a lady [because] he was not sufficiently Educated and intelligent in the female line to do so." If it seemed thus in the drawing rooms and parlors of Springfield, how much more would Lincoln have felt his uneasiness with the "female line" in the private and delicate matters of marital relationships, sexual behavior, and the like that his practice periodically brought to his attention? "He has no heart," Mrs. Edwards claimed. Depending on the circumstances, Lincoln might not have found this to be such a bad thing.[57]

Chapter Seven

Storytelling

Elizabeth Edwards was a good talker; it was a trait that fit her lifestyle well. As one of the leading figures in Springfield society, she and her husband Ninian hosted frequent soirees at their large house on what was locally dubbed "quality hill," the high spot at the edge of town where Springfield's upper crust cloistered. Her wit and manners were valuable assets in such a setting. She assured her sisters in Kentucky that, if they came to Springfield, she could find them husbands, probably right in her own parlor. In 1837 her younger sister Mary Todd, age nineteen, took her up on the offer.[1]

When Herndon sought Elizabeth out after the war as part of his project to gather information for what would someday become his biography of Lincoln, she bubbled over with gossip, philosophy, and general chitchat, all strung together in a nonstop stream of observations and anecdotes. Her favorite subject, naturally enough, was the Lincoln marriage. "He was charmed with Mary's wit and fascinated with her quick sagacity—her will—her nature—her Culture—I have happened in the room where they were sitting and often Mary led the Conversation—Lincoln would listen and gaze on her as if drawn by some Superior power, irresistably [*sic*]. So—he listened—never Scarcely Said a word." On she went, Billy probably scribbling furiously to keep pace.

Like many of the people who had known Lincoln before the war, Elizabeth portrayed herself as a prime mover-and-shaker in his saga. "I did not in a little time think that Mr. L[incoln] and Mary were Suitable to Each other and said so to Mary," she claimed. Elizabeth then asserted that she and her husband could see trouble coming. "Mr. Edwards and myself after the first crush of things told Mary and Lincoln that they had better not Ever marry," she told Herndon. "That their natures, mind—Education—raising, etc. were So different they Could not live happy as husband and wife [and] had better never think of the Subject again." To hear Elizabeth tell it, the Lincoln courtship was a wild ride of conflicting impulses, with Abraham and Mary lurching between periods of self-doubt and passion, fueled by her volatile temperament—"Mary was quick, lively, gay—frivalous [sic] it may be, Social and loved glitter Show and pomp and power"—and Lincoln's unstable frame of mind—"he was a peculiar man."[2]

Ninian was more reserved than his wife. Years later, Herndon's collaborator Jesse Weik reinterviewed the couple, and Elizabeth told another tale about the Lincoln courtship and marriage, telling Weik that Mary and her family had prepared for the wedding in the Edwards home, only to find that Lincoln had gotten cold feet. "Even cakes had been baked," Elizabeth claimed, "but L[incoln] failed to appear." When Edwards heard this, he interrupted the conversation. He "cautioned his wife that she was talking to a newspaperman," Weik recorded (referring perhaps to Weik's brief career as a dispatch writer for the *Cincinnati Commercial*), "and she declined to say more."[3]

Despite the fact that he was Lincoln's brother-in-law, Ninian Edwards seems to have been less afflicted with the hubris of some others who had once known Lincoln. He was a rather stuffy sort, rich and politically influential. But unlike Leonard Swett, he did not pretend to have plumbed the depths of Lincoln's mind; unlike Herndon, he did not think he had peered inside Lincoln's soul; and unlike Henry Whitney, Edwards did not contemplate the nature of Lincoln's bile. But even he could not resist a little ride on Lincoln's now-famous coattails. "Edwards thinks that he always thought L[incoln] would be a great man," Herndon wrote in his notes. He "thinks that he thought"—that was an interesting qualifier. Whether the words were Herndon's or Edwards's, they offered an uncharacteristic reserve, for many of Lincoln's friends and neighbors assured anyone who would listen that they had always been certain Lincoln was destined for greatness.[4]

This included Lincoln's courtroom colleagues. There was Herndon, of course, who turned his dead partner's story into an obsession, beginning with the authorship of the Springfield bar's resolution of grief and mourning a few days after Lincoln's death. His *Herndon's Lincoln,* finally published in 1889 after a series of setbacks and frustrations, became a foundational account of Lincoln's legal career. Whitney and Lamon wrote books, too, offering anecdotes from their days trying cases with Lincoln on the Eighth judicial circuit. So did Isaac Arnold, a Chicago attorney who was opposing counsel in the Illinois Central Railroad case, and who claimed to have told Lincoln in early 1860, "Next time I see you I shall congratulate you on being President-elect." David Davis did not write a book, but he was good for an occasional Lincoln story. Like Edwards, he was the rare individual who avoided claims of foresight into Lincoln's bright future, or that he possessed an intimate knowledge of Lincoln's character. "I know it was the general opinion in Washington that I knew all about Lincoln's though[t]s," Davis mused, "but I knew nothing. Lincoln never confided to me anything."[5]

When the lawyers and judges who were Lincoln's contemporaries began to grow old and fade away, new generations of admirers took their place. He became a favorite subject at bar association meetings, like the gathering of the Illinois State Attorney's Association in Chicago in 1912, where Judge Joseph Benjamin Oakleaf told his audience that Mr. Lincoln would have made an outstanding criminal lawyer, had he chosen to pursue that specialty; or Judge John P. Hand's address commemorating the centennial of Lincoln's birth three years earlier, in which he painted a classic-style portrait of Abe the frontier barrister, taking small-time cases involving three-dollar pigs and the like, and all the while stocking his store of folksy pioneer wit and wisdom.[6]

It was all about storytelling: the saga of Abraham Lincoln, given whatever flavor the teller preferred. Elizabeth Edwards had her frenetic tale of romance and conflict. Hand had his prairie lawyer anecdotes, rooted in the lore of the Eighth Circuit spread by Lamon, Whitney, Davis, and their cohorts. For Isaac Arnold (and countless others), Lincoln's story was the great-man-in-the-making. For Herndon, Lincoln was a fellow iconoclast, a misfit who never really believed in God and whose greatness was more because of his odd, gloomy intellect than the sickly-sweet martyrdom thrust upon the world by misguided worshipers.

Herndon saw what he wanted to see, but he was hardly alone. Lincoln has always been in some respects a mirror Americans hold up to ourselves, trying to find in his familiar, careworn face what we want to know (or think we want to know) about the other politicians and presidents who have at various times been found in our midst.

And the lawyers? Following the lead of Herndon, Lamon, Whitney,

Arnold, and other lawyers and judges—who together formed the foundation on which most of Lincoln's biographers constructed their understanding of Lincoln's legal career—what did the keepers of the Lincoln saga think they thought when they looked at Abraham Lincoln, attorney-at-law?

They thought they saw a man of towering legal stature, "the recognized leader of the Illinois bar" who was acknowledged by his peers as their superior. "All the lawyers on the circuit feared Lincoln," according to one account, because deep down they knew they could never get the better of him in an argument, especially in front of a jury. Some declared that Lincoln was one of the best lawyers of all time, anywhere. A British jurist ranked him as one of the five greatest attorneys in human history. "He hardly had an equal," one biographer wrote, "unless we take into account the great legal instincts of [Supreme Court Chief Justice] John Marshall." Another wrote that Lincoln "was a lawyer in a class by himself—all alone."[7]

At the same time, Lincoln was a paragon of lawyerly virtue. He never took unfair advantage of his opponents; he never employed technicalities, what one writer called "quibbles and neat little tricks," to win a case; and he was courteous and respectful to colleagues, judges, juries, and witnesses. "He always met his opponents' case fairly and squarely," according to one observer, "and [he] never intentionally misstated law or evidence." He took ridiculously low fees (or none at all), and he never sued to get his retainer.[8]

He refused to defend guilty or mischievous clients. "I have often listened to him when I thought he would certainly state his case out of court," recalled fellow lawyer Joseph Gillespie, because "it was not in his nature to assume or attempt to bolster a false position." Lawyer-turned-historian Alfred Woldman followed Gillespie's lead, asserting that Lincoln had a difficult time defending guilty clients ("such was the compelling honesty of his nature") and that his arguments in defense of morally questionable clients were "spiritless" and "half-hearted."[9]

Lincoln could do this because the law schooled him in all the vicissitudes of the human heart, giving him "peculiarly close insight into the minds and hearts of men." In the courtroom Lincoln learned to penetrate all the façades and walls thrown up by the wicked and weak to hide their foibles. "No other pursuit could have given him a better background of life and conditions and manners of mankind," Woldman wrote. Another lawyer/historian, John Duff, agreed, writing that his practice gave Lincoln "a vast knowledge of the ways of the human race."[10] Because the law gave him a window into the souls of his neighbors, Lincoln could afford to be picky about who he represented. "His conscience would not permit him to support a cause which he believed to be unjust, or to defend a person whom he knew to be guilty," reads James Baldwin's 1904 *Abraham Lincoln: A True Life.*[11]

The traditional plotline for Lincoln the lawyer was his role as moral teacher. His most notable cases were little parables, each with a special point to make about honesty, ethics, justice, or the pursuit of higher truths. After a while, they acquired shorthand names familiar to Lincoln buffs everywhere: the Almanac case, the *Effie Afton* case, the Chicken Bone case, the Horological Cradle case, the Reaper trial, and the Sandbar case. As they told and retold the tales of these famous cases, Lincoln's chroniclers sat their audience in the galleries of courtrooms on the Eighth Circuit to learn what they could from the future author of the Gettysburg Address. "Hooking his fingers under his gallus straps, which held up his shapeless trousers, the cool, unruffled prairie lawyer took the chief prosecution over a cross-examination," intoned Duff's account of the Almanac case—and, he might have added, the unruffled prairie lawyer took later generations along for the ride, as well, learning something of life from the someday-to-be-recognized master of American frontier wisdom.[12]

All these claims originate from post-1865 reminiscences by lawyers who recalled Lincoln's accomplishments in light of his apotheosis as an American hero. Reading Lincoln's status as the author of the Emancipation Proclamation and savior of the Union backward into the courtrooms of antebellum Illinois, his friends and colleagues decided that there were surely glimmerings of the great-man-to-be in his law practice. So their memories conjured a Lincoln who was more colorful than, say, former clerk-turned-lawyer Asahel Gridley, sharper than Stephen Logan, or funnier than David Davis. The Lincoln in their mind's eye always had the last word in a court argument, knew how to sway a jury, and could be forever counted on for a good joke after a long day on the circuit.

The truth is different, however. Lincoln the great American was in reality a pretty ordinary attorney. Take any lawyer plying his trade in America before the Civil War, and chances are he will be indistinguishable from Abraham Lincoln. In fact, many of the familiar plotlines in Lincoln's story can be found in the stories lawyers told about other lawyers. One could rummage through the obituaries, bar association tributes, and other published reminiscences from the period and assemble something that looks very much like Lincoln from the spare parts of obscure, long-dead attorneys. His biographers have not fully appreciated the fact that many of his more famous attributes were the standard narrative devices employed by attorneys of his day to praise their brethren and liven up an after-dinner speech or a *Bench and Bar* compendium.

The town of Winchester, Connecticut, had Roland Hitchcock, for example—described by a contemporary as someone who "at times exhibited much wit and humor and enjoyed the funny side of things and contributed his share to the merriment of the bar," but who also had "a streak of melancholia in his nature which always made him sorrowful." So did Daniel Mayer, a Southern lawyer whose merry disposition was marred by "occasional fits of despondency." Tennessee's Hugh Lawson White argued cases not from precedent but his "strong natural sense of justice." John McRady was a circuit jokester, and Timothy Ford never used technicalities to win a case. John Smith Richardson of South Carolina was "firm and immutable in what he believed to be right," David Johnson foreswore ornate language in his purpose of "attaining the truth," and Theodore Gaillard "was capable of rousing and captivating the passions, when eternal justice cried aloud for vengeance on her insult." And any Lincoln admirer would have recognized Henry Foote's description of Mississippi lawyer Richard H. Webber, whose "figure was ungainly; his manners were marked with awkwardness to a degree very uncommon, almost ludicrous; in his dress he was not only untasteful but even slovenly."[13]

What keepers of the Lincoln myth took to be extraordinary affection for Lincoln at the bar were often merely examples of how American lawyers typically eulogized one of their own. But once we compare the anecdotes with the thousands of extant cases now available, it becomes clear that Lincoln was not by any reasonable measure a legal superstar.

Lawyers (then and now) possessed their own professional yardstick for success. An "office lawyer" did not command as much respect from his peers as a trial lawyer. Attorneys from large Eastern states tended to look down on their frontier counterparts; thus did Lincoln's secretary of state William Seward privately disparage him as a "little Illinois lawyer." And what sort of courtroom a lawyer used to ply his trade likewise mattered. An attorney who litigated only nickel-and-dime suits before a local justice of the peace might be disparaged as a "pettifogger," a word said to have originated at the English bar and denoting a barrister who used his skills in the name of pursuing very minor—"petty"—legal disputes. More respect was attached to the man who could function in the state's circuit courts, and more still if he could litigate cases at the state or federal appellate level.[14]

Lincoln did his share of "pettifogging" in local courts early in his career. During 1838, for example, he saw mostly debt litigation for small amounts and the occasional minor property dispute: a fight between two Sangamon County men over $31 worth of rock, for example, or a probate settlement for a man who died without enough cash to cover his debts.[15]

But once his practice matured, Lincoln settled rather comfortably into what might be described as a middle-class attorney's life. In any given year he spent most of his time in the state circuit courts, with an occasional foray to the Illinois Supreme Court. He also sometimes saw the inside of the federal circuit court rooms, and he was occasionally a part of litigation that made its way to the U.S. Supreme Court. This was a richer professional life than many have supposed, but it hardly floated in the rarified air of John Marshall.[16]

The truth is that Lincoln was a moderately positioned attorney with a steady income and a wide range of cases. His practice allowed him to live in a comfortable home, support a growing family, and pursue his interest in politics. While his cases occasionally impacted important areas of antebellum legal doctrine, the majority were commonplace and of little concern to anyone beyond the participants themselves and local members of the community. Even on those rare occasions when a case touched upon a sensitive or important area of American life—railroad liability in the Rock Island bridge case, for example—Lincoln's arguments rode the crest of larger currents in American law. He created no new waves himself.[17]

During his day, Lincoln did not profoundly impress his colleagues at the bar; only after 1865 would some claim otherwise. There are actually almost no surviving contemporary references to Lincoln in the letters and papers of other lawyers and judges; and when newspapers noted his presence in a courtroom, they nearly always did so in a matter-of-fact way, attaching no hyperbole to his name. In their more candid moments, Lincoln's colleagues admitted as much. "He did not make a very marked impression upon me, or any other member of the bar," Usher Linder recalled of his first encounter with Lincoln in 1835. "He had the appearance of a good-natured, easy, unambitious man, of plain good sense and unobtrusive in his manner."[18]

Lincoln was apparently unfazed by his mundane legal stature. His political career was a different story; he could sometimes grow despondent about lost elections or a lack of influence in some political circles.[19] But he expressed no recorded frustration about his legal career. Nobody intimated that his healthy political ambition spilled over into the law, or that he felt moved to push himself above the ranks of other workaday lawyers into a practice more oriented toward appellate work or an eventual judgeship.

He probably won more cases than he lost. It is difficult to tell, however, for "win" and "lose" are slippery and subjective concepts. If he kept a murder suspect from going to the gallows, a businessman from paying off his former partner, or a railroad from compensating a local landowner for damages, then he could fairly be called a victorious lawyer. When Jane Abrams got her divorce from William Abrams in 1856 because of his gambling and alcohol problems, for example, she surely felt she had prevailed, and her lawyer Abraham Lincoln marked down *Abrams v. Abrams* as a "win."[20]

But other cases were less straightforward. They resist the easy plot devices of justice served or denied, of the homespun frontier attorney/philosopher, thumbs in his gallus straps and all that. Lincoln's professional life was more complicated and messy. Did he count himself the victor in May 1842 when his client William Fithian, who had sued a man named Isaac Walker for an unpaid $200 promissory note, received only half that amount because of an eventual out-of-court settlement? Was Levi James satisfied enough with Lincoln's performance as his attorney to afford him a "win" when in 1853 Lincoln persuaded an Edgar County jury to award James a little over $100 in damages for an assault case he had brought against three men? James had asked for $500. Maybe he really believed the three men had inflicted $500 worth of pain and suffering when they assaulted him and felt cheated when Lincoln could coax less than half that amount from a jury of his peers. Or maybe he felt fortunate to receive any money at all.[21]

Lincoln was good enough at his job that many clients gave him repeat business. Fithian retained Lincoln in five other lawsuits, for example, and several Springfield merchants used him as their primary bill collector.[22] Later in his career, large railroad corporations like the Illinois Central had him on retainer. One client, Joseph Foster, saw Lincoln sitting across the Sangamon circuit courtroom as opposing attorney, saw him sitting on the bench as a judge, and was impressed enough to hire Lincoln for his own uses.[23]

His techniques in the courtroom were neither more or less devoid of technicalities or "neat tricks" than any other attorney trying to win his case. He did what he had to do, within the broadly accepted boundaries of professional propriety, to win a case. If he found a paperwork error that might help his client, he used it; if a client might benefit from a statute of limitations or a close reading of the law's language (rather than the actual right or wrong of the matter), Lincoln did not hesitate to exploit those circumstances in pursuit of a courtroom victory. He defended people trying to take advantage of improper signatures, faulty land-section numbers, misplaced deeds, poorly drafted wills, and courtroom declarations. No one suggested that he felt any reservations about using these "technicalities" when necessary. "He wanted to win as badly as any lawyer," Henry Whitney believed.[24]

But Lincoln's zealotry in defense of his client's interests was tempered by knowledge that there were boundaries, professional and moral, to his behavior. Whitney also thought that Lincoln was "unlike lawyers of a certain type" in that "he would not do anything mean, or which savored of sharp practice, or which required absolute sophistry or chicanery to succeed." If this sounds like yet another example of kicking over the traces by a friend and admirer, it should also be noted that, of all the many charges of inequity, duplicity, and fraud leveled by his political enemies over the years—people who accused him of everything from thievery to adultery—no one seems to have ever accused him of being an unethical attorney. A lawyerly workman he may have been, but he was a principled workman.

Nor did he cherry-pick his clients for their moral worth. Possibly he turned away unsavory clients and we have no record of the fact. There was no reason for him to record such instances for posterity, and they would not have generated legal paperwork historians could examine. But the thousands of clients he did choose to represent suggest, in their innumerable varieties of guilt and innocence, honesty and depravity, that Lincoln was open-minded on this score. Poet and Lincoln biographer Carl Sandburg had an eloquent way of expressing it: "Lincoln came to know in whispered consultation and public cross-examination the minds and hearts of a quarreling, chaffering, suspicious, murderous, loving, lavish, paradoxical humanity."[25]

There was a broad consensus of testimony among his fellow lawyers that Lincoln was constitutionally unable to represent a dishonest client or a bad cause. "He was not only morally honest but intellectually so," Samuel Parks claimed. Lincoln "could not reason falsely [and] if he attempted it he failed. . . . At the bar when he thought he was wrong he was the weakest lawyer I ever saw." Herndon went so far as to claim that Lincoln would actually throw a case "if he believed he was espousing an unjust cause." An oft-repeated tale had Lincoln deciding during a murder trial in Champaign County, *People v. Patterson,* that his client was guilty of the crime, suddenly turning to cocounsel Leonard Swett, and exclaiming "Swett, you defend him. I can't." He then supposedly either dropped the case entirely—which if true would have raised a lot of eyebrows at the bar, even in those fast and loose days—or gave a lackluster closing argument that cost his client three years in prison.[26]

But the criteria in such testimony is vague and the standards subjective and (as always) colored by Lincoln's postwar fame. Here again, the very same claim was put forth by other attorneys about their colleagues as a way of posthumously praising their character. It was said of South Carolina lawyer John Hooker, for example, that "when fully satisfied that a case on defence was founded in injustice, no fee could induce him to undertake it."[27]

Perhaps Lincoln did not perform at peak level before the *Patterson* jury, but was this because he had suddenly discovered, twenty-two years into his law practice, that he might be compelled to defend a guilty person? More plausible explanations suggest themselves. The case occurred during his campaign for the U.S. Senate against Stephen Douglas, a project that consumed nearly all of his time and energy. In fact, he had to request a continuance in *People v. Patterson* because of delays and scheduling problems caused by the campaign. "Swett, you defend him. I can't" might have simply reflected Lincoln's weariness and inability to focus during one of the most stressful periods of his life.[28]

Some have gone so far as to suggest that Lincoln's injection of personal morality into his law practice carried with it glimmerings of his future role as the liberator of slaves. Lincoln admirers focused their attention on an 1839 case in which he represented the interests of David Bailey, who purchased the services of an African American female indentured servant named Nance with a promissory note and then failed to pay because the seller never furnished written proof that the woman was actually held in servitude. The Illinois Supreme Court eventually ruled that Lincoln's client did not have to pay the note on fairly narrow technical grounds (the contract, the court ruled, lacked "consideration," and was therefore void). What captured the attention of Lincoln's admirers was not so much his skill in negotiating the complexities of contract law to win the case, but his use of the Northwest Ordinance's 1787 ban on slavery to argue that freedom was the presumed status of any individual who stood on Illinois soil unless proven otherwise.[29]

Some of Lincoln's critics, on the other hand, highlight the Matson case, in which Lincoln represented the interests of a slaveholder named Robert Matson, who in 1845 brought five slaves from the slave soil of Kentucky onto the free soil of Illinois. They subsequently sued for their freedom, arguing—shades of *Dred Scott v. Sanford* a decade later—that their time in a free state had automatically ended their slavery. On their owner's behalf, Lincoln argued that they should remain in bondage because they were only in transit; Matson intended to return with them to Kentucky. The court disagreed, and the slaves went free.[30]

Dedicated Lincoln-haters like Thomas DiLorenzo and Lerone Bennett pounce on this instance of Lincoln vainly defending the property rights of a slaveholder. "In twenty-three years of litigation he never defended a runaway slave, but he did defend a slaveholder," DiLorenzo wrote, while Bennett alluded to Lincoln being "blinded by his racism and the dissembling rhetoric he used to rationalize it" in agreeing to take up Matson's cause. Bennett and DiLorenzo have their own stories to tell, fueled by their single-minded conviction that he was a dictator (DiLorenzo) and a bigot (Bennett), convictions that warp their perspectives. DiLorenzo framed a statement that, while narrowly true, ignores the fact that in the Bailey matter Lincoln did indeed come awfully close to defending the rights of fugitive slaves (not to mention *People v. Kern, People v. Pond,* and *People v. Scott,* in which Lincoln came to the aid of men accused of harboring runaway slaves). Bennett practiced stealth character assassination on Lincoln by asking with sarcastic innocence whether, in taking the Matson case, Lincoln was "down on his luck? Did he need ready cash?"[31]

With equally dubious results, Lincoln's defenders either gloss over the Matson affair entirely or fancifully suggest that his performance in that case was substandard because his heart was not really in it. His arguments in the Matson matter were "pitiably weak . . . spiritless, half-hearted, and devoid of his usual wit, logic, and invective," Alfred Woldman wrote. Here we run into the same problem with similar assertions about his performance in the *Patterson* case; even if Lincoln was not in top form during the Matson affair, who could really identify the reason? Worse still, Woldman was attempting such a judgment from over a century's distance.[32]

In any event, the entire conversation about Lincoln, his practice, and race is almost beside the point. Race was a negligible presence in his practice. In twenty-five years, he litigated only twenty-four cases involving African Americans, a much too miniscule group from which to draw any reasonable conclusions about Lincoln's racial views.[33] They followed no particular pattern: a divorce case, debt collection (predictably enough), some probate and contract disputes, and several cases Lincoln undertook on behalf of William Florville, or "Billy the Barber," the African American man who regularly cut Lincoln's hair. Aside from his apparent personal regard for Billy, it is impossible to detect a pattern that reflects a private set of moral standards on Lincoln's part.[34]

Although some have questioned Lincoln's racial views, no one has plausibly challenged his consistent and urgent denunciations of human bondage. "I have always hated slavery, I think as much as any Abolitionist," he declared. So using the Northwest Ordinance to argue for freedom may well have given Lincoln a little twinge of inner satisfaction, but he would have buried that feeling under the strictly technical need to win his case. The Matson case, conversely, may have given Lincoln a moment of pause before he sighed and got on with his job; but got on with his job he did. Lincoln always drew a line between the moral and legal aspects of slavery, even in his capacity as a politician and president.[35] It is therefore futile to read moral choices about slavery into Lincoln's choice of litigation. There are too many variables to draw the conclusion that, because he represented clients with certain shared characteristics, he made a deliberate decision to represent those clients at the expense of others with different characteristics.

More generally, looking for *any* moral choices that drove Lincoln's behavior within his practice is problematic. The available records usually do not allow satisfactory answers; there is little if any evidence that Lincoln litigated cases based on some set of values that were separate from the conventions of his profession. The "parable" approach to Lincoln's law practice offers a fundamental misreading of his life as an attorney.

But what are the alternatives? History is fundamentally an act of storytelling, and all stories require a plot. Billy Herndon, Henry Whitney, Ward Hill Lamon, and the many other observers of Lincoln's law practice understood, if perhaps only on an instinctive level, that in order to tell the story of Lincoln the lawyer, they needed to find some sort of storytelling device, some form of narrative glue to connect the man's diffuse, sprawling practice into an understandable whole.

But Lincoln's life as a lawyer was a jumble of workaday images: Lincoln cramming paperwork into his hat as he heads out the front door in the morning, the smell of breakfast wafting down the hallway behind him as he ambles toward the other set of smells that defined much of his life—dust, maybe stale coffee and tobacco, and that peculiar musty aroma of old law books—collected in his office several blocks away; Lincoln standing in one corner of a crowded courtroom filled with the buzz of low-key, businesslike conversation, talking in an equally quiet monotone to Nathan Fletcher, Alvin Ackley, Augustus Pratt, Benjamin Turney, Major Packard, Milton Stapp, or some other now-faceless, anonymous soul about a long-forgotten promissory note, will, or deed; Lincoln in his shirtsleeves, seated at the baize-covered table in his office on a sweltering summer day, sweat beading his forehead as he writes down the particulars of Rachel Dennis's broken marriage or Nancy Burr's administration of her dead husband Saban's estate or Maria Bullock's mortgage foreclosure; Lincoln grabbing his faded green umbrella (the one with the broken handle) and working to get the contraption open while a cold October rain starts to pelt him on a backwater road in Tazewell County as he makes his way to the fall court term in Tremont. It is Judge Logan's pine shavings, David Campbell's fiddle playing, Ward Hill Lamon's off-color jokes, and Billy Herndon's rickety collection of eccentricities. It is writs, interrogatories, crossbills, and other esoteric legal paperwork, all written with monotonous exactitude and attention to every last detail of punctuation and syntax, lest a mistake cost a client his case.

The law is not important in Lincoln's life because of its drama, though he had his moments over the years. He probably felt a little extra rush when he donned that white suit and stood before a jury in the Almanac trial, doing his best to save the life of an old friend's son.

He knew what was at stake for the future of Illinois and his cherished cause of economic improvements when he defended the interests of the Rock Island Bridge Company. But those moments were few and far between, and they pale in comparison with his crucial "House Divided" speech, the address he gave before the Republican faithful at New York's Cooper's Union, and of course the thunderous tones of his words at Gettysburg and during his second inauguration.

Lincoln's admirers have done what they can to inject a little excitement into his legal life—perhaps too much so. Take, for example, an oft-repeated vignette from Herndon's account of Lincoln as he prepared to depart for Washington, D.C., in February 1861. "We ran over the books and arranged for the completion of all unsettled and unfinished matters," Herndon wrote, "He gathered a bundle of books and papers he wished to take with him and started to go; but before leaving he made the strange request that the sign-board which swung on its rusty hinges at the foot of the stairway should remain." Herndon remembered Lincoln saying in a low voice, "Let it hang there undisturbed. . . . Give our clients to understand that the election of a President makes no change in the firm of Lincoln and Herndon. If I live I'm coming back some time, and then we'll go right on practicing law as if nothing ever happened." Billy then ratchets up the melodrama. "He lingered for a moment as if to take a last look at the old quarters, and then passed through the door into the narrow hallway." After telling Herndon that he had a presentiment of his own death—a "feeling which had become irrepressible that he should never return alive"—Lincoln gave him a heartfelt handshake "and with a fervent 'Good-bye,' he disappeared down the street."[36]

How much of this is accurate would be impossible to say, but we all get the point of Herndon's story: Lincoln is not coming back, he senses death's icy breath whispering at his shoulder, and he feels foreboding for a future filled with tragedy on a Shakespearian scale. However appealing it may be, this is not Lincoln the lawyer. It is the presidential Lincoln, the Greatest American, read backward into his antebellum days and given life and a veneer of credibility with plot devices like presentiments, forebodings, and hunches.

Historians have tended to follow Herndon's lead—albeit with less pathos—looking at the law practice for signs of the master politician and statesman to come. This is not a vain search, for the law was in fact an important source of Lincoln's political skills. It made contributions in the form of networking and general people skills. It also shaped his use of language at various points throughout his political career, giving him a high degree of clarity and a judicious use of words.[37]

At times, Lincoln slipped into overtly legalistic formulas on the political circuit, writing in one speech (a reply to Stephen Douglas's charge of dishonesty) that "I demur to this plea. Waiving objection that it was not filed till after default, I demur to it on the merits. I say it does not meet the case." He occasionally set up his political arguments concerning slavery, emancipation, and freedom as if they were legal briefs in the moot court of American public opinion. "If A. can prove, however conclusively, that he may, of right, enslave B.—why may not B. snatch the same argument, and prove equally, that he may enslave A?" he wrote in an 1854 note.[38]

Looking closely at a lifetime of speeches and letters, astute observers have noted these and other instances in which Lincoln's law practice peeked through the surface of his political career.[39] Others suggest Lincoln possessed a lawyerlike concern for the rules and forms of policy making, even when those rules and forms prevented a more robust pursuit of grandiose ideals like racial equality, justice, or retribution toward the South's rebels. His legal training came to the forefront when he analyzed legislation like the Second Confiscation Act, which he signed but with an attorney's caveats concerning the precise legal status of slaves confiscated and then liberated under its provisions. Lawyerly dryness is also evident in the Emancipation Proclamation. Richard Hofstadter famously likened it to a "bill of lading" in its boring, uninspiring text, but he might just as appropriately have used "writ of garnishment" or some other legal tool to make his point.[40]

The law peeked through his presidential life on occasion, but we should be careful about how we portray cause and effect in these matters. Had Lincoln been, for example, a merchant his entire life, he would surely have used different words. He would have been less given to phrases that frequently appear in courtroom briefs—"demur . . . on the merits" and the like. But it is equally possible that the habits of thought expressed by the words, albeit in a different form, would have remained much the same, even if Lincoln had lived a lifetime of keeping ledgers and balancing books. There was more than one path to the qualities of mind identified by some scholars as lawyerly, and it is hard to tell whether his directness of thought was a product of his law practice or a preexisting condition that guided him into law—or whether something similar would have been evident had Lincoln chosen a different occupation.

Stepping back from the daily minutiae of his practice—the thousands of cases, clients, and causes Lincoln saw for a quarter-century of his life—the question we should pose is this: What qualities did the law give him that came primarily from the law, more so plausibly than from any other source? How do we answer that question without either trivializing a nontrivial thread in Lincoln's life or, conversely, awarding the law undue influence or dramatic license?

Chapter Eight

Grease

A s storytelling goes, it all comes down to a matter of metaphors. Various people have applied different metaphors to Lincoln the lawyer. He has been a giant (or, for some critics, pygmy) of the Illinois bar; a champion of freedom (or, for some critics, its nemesis) and future emancipator in the courtroom; a frontier philosopher; a moral redeemer of a suspect profession; and a keen-eyed student of human nature.

Each of these metaphors contains a kernel of truth. But there is a dimension of Lincoln's law practice—the most important dimension, because it was so prevalent—that none get quite right. Those who would describe Lincoln in terms of a towering professional or moral stature within the Illinois bar overlook the day-in, day-out grind, the grittiness of his legal career. This oversight is rooted in the post-1865 reminiscences, stories related by men and women who would not have recorded their recollections of Lincoln for posterity's sake in the first place had they not possessed the *a priori* assumption that Lincoln was special. Moreover, his admirers often seem to fear even a suggestion of ordinariness where Lincoln is concerned, wishing to avoid the impropriety of shrinking his appropriately lofty reputation in American history.

But taking into account not only the reminiscences but also the court records of Lincoln's more grubby cases—the debt-collection work, the minor lawsuits over smaller business and personal transactions, the small-scale criminal and civil matters—what sort of metaphor might describe the Lincoln law practice as a whole?

There are of course multiple possibilities. I would suggest that an appropriate metaphor is this: it taught him about the value of grease—that unglamorous, often overlooked but vital substance that lubricates and reduces friction to acceptable levels, that slips between the cogs and devices of machines and allows continuous movement without malfunction.

Lincoln's age sorely needed grease. A literal imagination can see it: the hard iron wheels of the Market Revolution, burred and rough in their newness, throwing sparks and heat from the clashes between old and new ways of farming, old and new ways of moving around, old and new ways of making and selling and exporting. Being so abrasive and new, the wheels threaten to come unbolted from their tracks and run amok, destroying traditional lives, values, and ways of doing things in their path, replaced by God knows what. Honor found itself in competition with commerce, businessmen strapped for cash cast worried glances over their shoulders at creditors, who wondered whether they would be paid so they might in turn meet obligations to *their* creditors, who were themselves debtors to yet other creditors. Teamsters were vexed about business taken from them on rivers and canals, where flat boatmen scowled at steamboat captains, who in turn scowled at railroad men, who in turn scowled at all those strangers catching rides westward to communities where people of different morals and codes of conduct mixed with other strangers to create all manner of violence, perfidy, and shame—a lot of worry and doubt here, a lot of heat and friction.

People with a religious bent turned to revival meetings and Bibles to calm their fears. People with a political bent formed parties designed to do much the same thing through the ballot box or legislation. Reformers created movements that agitated for (and sometimes achieved) changes in troubled social milieus like temperance, insane asylums, prisons, and prostitution, and so eased somewhat the difficult transitions from traditional to modern lifestyles. Americans had a lot of different ways to slap on some grease and quiet the screeching.

Abraham Lincoln the attorney applied his own form of grease, in a multitude of visible and not so visible ways.

Debt—its avoidance or, more often, collection—was Lincoln's primary function as a lawyer, and it is the arena in which his role as a lubricator is most clearly evident. Choose any case at random from the thousands of cases he litigated during his quarter-century at the

bar, and chances are that case will involve a litigant who owed someone money, goods, or services. Between June and December of 1850,
for example—roughly the midway point in Lincoln's law career—he
appeared as attorney of record in thirty-four cases: twenty involved
some form of debt relief, from cash to a mechanic's lien on a house.[1]

The dominating presence of debt in Lincoln's professional life is not
surprising. Debt made the Market Revolution's wheels turn. This was
particularly true out West, where so few people possessed ready cash.
The energy men who surrounded Lincoln in Springfield and Illinois
needed a free-flowing system of ready credit from which they could
launch their assaults on the American Dream.

Running for office or acting as an Illinois state representative, Lincoln encountered debt within the context of antebellum politics and
his own Whiggish economic ideology, a context that emphasized the
big, distant institutions of his age: currency policies, banking practices, and the state government's borrowing of money to fund large-
scale economic development. Lincoln followed the straight Whig line
on these matters, speaking out in favor of a national bank, aggressive
state promotion of internal improvements, and other manifestations of
his beloved Henry Clay's "American System." When Lincoln spoke of
debt as a politician, he did so in the context of public land purchases,
subtreasuries, and the condition of the state bank. He was not grease
here; rather, he was very much a part of the machinery of Jacksonian
economics and its consequences.[2]

But when he came down from the level of banks and subtreasuries
and entered the courtroom, Lincoln became something more prosaic.
His opinions about who should pay to develop the state and national economy, what sort of currency and banking policies lawmakers
should pursue, and what a Whig (and Republican) economic plan
should do for the state and the nation mattered very little. He was no
longer part of the political and policy-making process.

Instead, he became the grease lubricating the machinery created
by the economy and the statehouse. Lincoln was a fallback position
for those who had gotten swept away by the fast-moving currents of
that free-floating credit system, either as lenders who might lose their
hard-earned cash or borrowers who might face foreclosure on their
hard-earned possessions. He was like a branch poking out from the
bank that creditors and borrowers could grab as the credit system
rushed them by.

Granted, by modern standards, Lincoln was a weak stick. This was at least partly due to his own personality. Some lawyers may have been well-suited by temperament and character to dun people for money. Lincoln was not one of them. "I am the poorest hand living to get others to pay," he once wrote. It was a remarkable admission from a man who spent so much of his professional life performing that very service.[3]

But issues of personality aside, Lincoln's resources for tracking down errant debtors were limited. He was a creditor's last resort, more bluff than substance. Debtors could fairly easily avoid paying up when the bills fell due, by hiding assets or disappearing from the state entirely. Some may have employed even more creative means. Lincoln once told a joke, maybe or maybe not facetiously, about a debtor he knew in Illinois who was "terribly annoyed by a pressing creditor, until finally the debtor assumed to be crazy whenever the creditor broached the subject."[4]

Such dubious stratagems aside, Lincoln did not have private investigators at his disposal or the modern technology of the information age that can now find just about anyone who owes someone else money. There was no credit-rating system to speak of, nor were there very many ways of discovering the location of a debtor's property that might be sold to satisfy a debt. He could sometimes use information gleaned from his own personal knowledge or neighborhood gossip to help a creditor. "I have the impression that he is not able to pay any thing," Lincoln wrote to client William Crafts about a note owed to him by Asahel Thayer, "besides his brother Martin Thayer, of Philadelphia, he has a brother, Joseph Thayer, at Springfield, Illinois, who is pecuniarily, in good circumstances. Still, my impression of Asahel is as I have stated." More often, however, Lincoln possessed little real knowledge on a given debtor's circumstances, and could be of limited use to a creditor. "The deputy Marshall, who has the execution is out of town now, so that I can not give you particulars as to the prospect of collecting the debt," he wrote a client in a typical collection case in 1844, "I believe this is about all the information I can give you."[5]

Debtors found Lincoln to be an even more tenuous option. There normally wasn't much Lincoln could do, other than slow down the wheels of collection long enough for a debtor to gather his wits and what assets he possessed. Again, Lincoln's resources were limited. He usually could not stop foreclosures, sheriff's sales, and the other measures available for collection on a valid promissory note; nor does it seem to have been a regular occurrence for him to try to forestall collection by appealing to creditors for more time. The best he could do was encourage out-of-court negotiations or simply represent the debtor's losing cause in a courtroom.

But he was at least there, creating a bit of protection for wayward debtors from the implied threat of debt collection from creditors, long before the existence of skip tracers, credit counselors, or collection bureaus. Lincoln's role is hard to detect with the naked eye because it came only in relation to the minute decisions rendered by lone lenders as they sized up potential borrowers from across a table or a behind a handshake. William Ricketts loaned Josephus Goings $243; Thomas Maloney gave Mark Hamilton a bill of exchange worth $447, redeemable at the McLean County Bank. Fielding House gave a $59 promissory note to Robert Adams, who in turn gave it to John Andrews.[6] But maybe none of those deals would have taken place if Ricketts, Maloney, House, and Andrews did not each in the back of their minds know they had access to Lincoln, should their deals go awry. Perhaps they would have hesitated a bit longer, or put their pens back in their pockets.[7]

Or when things went wrong, maybe the social fallout would have been more acrimonious, harkening back to the days when loaning money was all about character, and gentlemen passed judgment on the souls of other gentlemen, rather than merely decrying their lack of good business sense. Unable to breathe even the slightest sigh of relief that Lincoln's efforts afforded him, maybe Wilson Owen squints harder or snarls with greater disdain at Samuel Ferrin when Ferrin can't pay back the $124 Owen loans him in the winter of 1842.[8] Or possibly a firm like Springfield's B. C. Webster and Company goes under when it cannot hire Lincoln to force its customers to make good on their bills, leaving behind the broken shards of a once-promising business that cut a little sharper, making other Springfield entrepreneurs think twice before extending credit to the people who come through their doors—or even think twice about launching a new business at all.[9] Then the wheels turn just an infinitesimal amount more slowly, and toss off an extra spark or two.

There are no dramatic trials here, no almanacs triumphantly waved or frightened clients saved from torment and ruin. The story is harder to tell because it does not have a narrative crescendo, an obvious high point that tells the audience when to clap; just all those transactions among local buyers and sellers, one largely indistinguishable from the other, endless little revolutions within the larger machinery of America's Market Revolution. Even within those movements, Lincoln is difficult to detect: a quiet presence in the background while others signed the promissory notes and took the risks.

And it wasn't just about the notes. Lincoln greased a variety of other business relationships: partnership dissolutions, contract disputes, arguments over payment for or possession of real estate, stocks, bonds, and just about every form of property imaginable, from cows to mulberry trees. In most cases, Lincoln was not present when the trees were planted, the farms plowed, or the stores opened their doors. He was called in only when the economic machinery began to sputter smoke and fly apart, to contain the damage and if possible salvage some of the parts for another day.

This was true even for big machines like the railroads. Some scholars emphasize Lincoln's role as a "railroad lawyer," the implication being that he was in on the building of one of the grand enterprises of his age: the conversion of America from a nation of wagons and flatboats to one of steel rails and steam engines.[10] As a politician who enthusiastically supported efforts to fund railroad construction in Illinois, this was true. But as a lawyer it would be more accurate to say that, on those occasions when he represented a railroad's interests in court, Lincoln's job involved destruction more than construction, in the sense that he acted to prevent problems and remove obstacles that got in the way of other men who did the funding and the building.

Lincoln wasn't always on the side of big business. He sometimes represented the interests of those who sought money from the railroads as compensation, and more generally clients who sued businesses, towns, and counties for damages and debtors who wanted to forestall payment on a loan. Although their points of view may have differed from the loaners and the builders, Lincoln's perspective remained much the same: to get his client some measure of satisfaction or just compensation without necessarily crippling the targets of the litigation. Suing Springfield on behalf of Andrew Browning in 1853, for example—Browning had broken his leg and hauled city officials into court for failing to keep its streets in good repair—Lincoln and Herndon surely had no intention of bankrupting the city. They may even have felt they were doing some measure of civic good by forcing Springfield to fix its streets.[11]

Or, more likely, Lincoln tried to make no value judgment at all when

prosecuting such cases. Some accuse him and other antebellum lawyers of abetting the growth of big-market capitalism by representing railroads, banks, and creditors, and generally acting, in historian
Charles Sellers's words, as "the shock troops of capitalism."[12] Others
might be inclined to portray him as a lawyer who fought the good fight
by standing up in court for the rights of those who were trodden upon
by those same big corporations.[13]

Both perspectives possess a bit of truth. Easing the Market Revolution's friction helped the machinery of the market grow and develop.
Lincoln would not have been troubled by this; in fact, he would have
rather liked being described as one of capitalism's "shock troops." He
believed in the system, believed in a robust free-market economy, and
was probably pleased when his law practice dovetailed with market
expansion.

On the other hand, it is not too great a stretch to suggest that at least
some of Lincoln's litigation helped the "little guys" take their tilt at the
windmills of capitalist America: Lewis Friedlander, for example, who
retained Lincoln in 1857 to sue the Great Western Railroad following a
depot accident that broke his leg. Lincoln asked for $10,000 in damages
for his client (no doubt trying to set a high bargaining position), and
ended up getting a $500 out-of-court settlement for his client.[14]

But the fact that Lincoln could represent both business interests and
a litigant like Lewis Friedlander indicates that efforts to portray him
as either pro- or anticapitalist, pro- or antimarket development, are
misguided. Grease does not favor one cog over another; it is a third set
of values, favoring smooth operation of the whole machine, both big
and little parts. The enemy is not capitalism, nor is it the gadfly who
gets in the way of economic growth and progress.

The enemy is friction. This, at bottom, is the lesson Lincoln took
away from his twenty-five years at the bar, a lesson he would not likely
have learned from tilling soil or piloting riverboats or pursuing any of
the other occupations available to him on the Illinois frontier. Nearly
any other way of earning a living would have placed him on one side
or the other in the eternal creditor/debtor combination. As a lawyer,
Lincoln was part of both and neither at the same time.

The lessons about friction extended to his valuation of settlements
that never made it into the courtroom. A trial is inevitably abrasive,
and Lincoln tried whenever possible to pursue negotiated settlements.
"Discourage litigation," he admonished. "Persuade your neighbors to

compromise whenever you can. Point out to them how the nominal winner is often a real loser—in fees, expenses, and waste of time. As a peacemaker the lawyer has a superior opportunity of being a good man. There will still be business enough."[15]

His admirers praise this as evidence of Lincoln's essentially peace-loving nature, as well they should. But we should also pay attention to that last sentence: "There will still be business enough." Lincoln did not expect the friction of American life to dissipate. He never thought that one particular segment of the economy could or should dominate the other. He detested farming, but did not look with relish to the day when few Americans would be farmers. He liked railroads, but as a means to the end of growing Illinois' economy, not as an end in themselves. He did not see his job as a lawyer to be hastening the domination of one occupation or one economic sector over another. If such domination came—if, say, railroads really did end up putting other carriers out of business—then in the courtroom the best Lincoln could do would be to smooth over the difficulties involved, if and when they generated lawsuits.

As business went, so did the other facets of Lincoln's practice. Observing people at loggerheads with one another over probate settlements, slanders real and imagined, divorces, fisticuffs, and a myriad of other problems, Lincoln normally betrayed no sympathy with one or the other neighbor. Although there were cases that aroused his ire or compassion, far more often no one could tell what he thought about the plaintiff's or defendant's character.[16] His professional correspondence evoked a dispassionate tone, with Lincoln calmly explaining the circumstances of this or that facet of litigation. "We are willing to attend to your cases as you propose," went a typical letter to Garland B. Shelledy in February 1842. "Thinking it may aid you a little, I send you one of our blank forms of Petitions. . . . The schedules, too, must be attended to. Be sure that they contain the creditors' *names,* their *residences,* the *amounts* due each, the *debtors'* names, their *residences,* and the *amounts* they owe, also all *property* and *where* located."[17]

It was crisp, orderly, and to the point, with no obvious record of Lincoln's feelings—if he had any feelings. Part of this was simple self-preservation. Lincoln had to live with these people, at a time when professional identities were not well-enough developed to protect him from the social consequences of defending an accused thief, ne'er-do-well, or bad businessman. He could face his friends and neighbors (not to say potential voters) in the streets of Springfield and elsewhere only by maintaining the front that he did not, for example, sympathize with Jane or William Abrams when he helped Jane sue Bill for divorce, or think that his client Jacob Williams was a fool for publicly challenging a man named Horneback to duel, thus earning himself an indictment in Menard County. Lincoln was required to help Jane Abrams win her case and Jacob Williams avoid a fine or jail, but these were largely matters of legal tactics, not Lincoln's assessment of their characters.[18]

Then again, maybe it wasn't a front. Lincoln the lawyer was in but not of the machinery of his times, more so even than other lawyers. Unlike many other members of the bar, he did not have many sideline investments. He did not put much of his money or time into the business opportunities that surrounded him. Aside from purchasing stock subscriptions in an Illinois railroad and a brief investment in a German-language newspaper, Lincoln was not an entrepreneur. He rarely bought real estate or speculated in land. He shipped nothing by steamboat or wagon or rail; he sold no crops, and he raised no horses or livestock. He planted nothing, built nothing from wood, hammered nothing from metal, or made anything that could be bought or sold. Aside from politics, Lincoln pursued no living other than the law.

This placed him at a distance from the largely agricultural, manual-labor community in which he lived. He did not have to sniff the pungent odor of the one thousand hogs his client John Madux was hired to deliver for the firm of VanBrunt and Watrons in 1859, or shake off the sawdust from Edmund John's carpentry business when John became entangled in a lawsuit over a $230 promissory note in 1838. However much he may have employed his rail-splitter image to good political effect, not much dirt clung to his fingernails after he became an attorney. Lincoln left all that behind in the days of his youth, choosing instead to pursue a profession that removed him from the visceral experiences many of his neighbors took for granted.[19]

He therefore could not convince himself that he saw any form of business from an insider's point of view. Harkening back to the days of his failed venture with Berry and his "national debt," he might have felt a twinge of sympathy for a client who had likewise begun a general store venture and seen it fail. But memories like these would have faded as time went by, and the values instilled by his profession discouraged overt displays of empathy. Lawyers in Lincoln's time may have lacked the elaborate professional and institutional structures available to modern members of the bar, but certain features remain largely unchanged then and now: the essential human interaction between a general-practice attorney and clients who have made poor business deals, require extrication from complex contractual obligations, feel wronged by neighbors or other associates, or who stand accused of some crime. The circumstances of these interactions suggest, in their multiple contexts, the need for the attorney to create some form of emotional separation from the people in question, to focus on the negotiations, the settlements, or other solutions that keep the machinery of the community intact and functioning smoothly.

The law did not afford Lincoln the luxury—the delusion perhaps—of intimate knowledge of his neighbors' circumstances. Other available professions might have done so. Medicine would have given him knowledge of his patients' bodies and would have allowed him to probe details of their private lives. The ministry would have given him the hope and perhaps the belief that he could penetrate the depths of his followers' souls. Even a military career could have afforded him the comfort that, as a soldier, he knew his brother soldiers' values and sense of esprit de corps.

Instead, the law gave Lincoln a turn of mind that was quite the opposite. Far from teaching him to plumb the inner depths of humanity, it taught Lincoln that there were many things he could not know about clients, witnesses, and other participants in the legal system. Nathan Jones, Napoleon Mayall, David Enslow, Nancy Plummer—all those clients line up in a seemingly endless line, leaving little for historians other than their names and perhaps a line in a census count someplace. We know so little about them; and everything Lincoln experienced as a professional attorney would have persuaded him to discover relatively little about his clients as well. There was no need for him to probe whether, for example, Nancy Plummer's husband Nathan really was "totally worthless," or the reasons Nancy thought so, except insofar as it was necessary to pursue victory in court as Nancy's attorney. He needed only to know enough about the Plummer marriage to honor his client Nancy's wishes and legally end that marriage—which happened in November 1856.[20]

Billy Herndon, David Davis, Leonard Swett, Stephen Logan, Ward Lamon—those were names from his lawyer's life that Lincoln knew more closely. They shared office space, courtrooms, hotel rooms, dining tables, buggy rides, and even beds with him on the "mud circuit."

But the law also taught him that it did not pay to look too closely into the heads and hearts of his colleagues at the bar, men with whom he would possibly make common cause one day and then oppose the next. Grease required at least some separation from the machinery, all of it, with which Lincoln had to contend. "There will still be business enough"—it was the point of view of the professional, perpetual lubricator.

Modern lawyers understand this. "In the American legal system, a lawyer's job is not to seek justice," argues one. "Indeed, the primary objective of our legal system is not to determine the truth, but to resolve disputes peacefully. Besides, in most cases where the facts are disputed, no one but the clients know for sure where the truth lies, and often they aren't really sure."[21] Another legal expert calls this the "attorney's exclusive focus on manifest behavior." When a lawyer acts in a client's behalf, he does so "on the basis of what he does and what he sees the client do," not "the potential impact on the client's thinking and private actions."[22]

These are lessons that present-day attorneys learn largely from experience. Lincoln did so, as well. But if he recalled his Blackstone, he might have remembered that Sir William warned him from the outset not to draw private and public behavior too closely together. "Let a man therefore be ever so abandoned in his principles, or vitious [*sic*] in his practice, provided he keeps his wickedness to himself, and does not offend against the rules of public decency, he is out of the reach of human laws," he had once read in Blackstone's *Commentaries.* "But if he makes his vices public . . . it is then the business of human laws to correct them."[23] As a lawyer Lincoln learned the utility, indeed the necessity, of separating the public from the private, the knowable from the unknowable, that which is necessary from that which is superfluous. He learned not to overreach. "In law it is good policy to never *plead* what you *need* not, lest you oblige yourself to *prove* what you *can* not," he cautioned Usher Linder.[24]

His profession, his personality, and his political avocation meshed well here. It may be that there were certain psychological traits Lincoln brought to the law that fed these tendencies; an intense need for privacy or a desire to wall off his public persona from his private feelings. But if this was so, where else but the law could these traits have been so fully realized? Any other way of earning a living would have required, sooner or later, that he abandon a comfortable persona for him, the persona of a lifelong lubricator who was always between and around but not quite of the people who surrounded him.

More than anything else, Lincoln seemed comfortable in the law. He was in his element on the circuit, acting the part of a "poke-easy" in his office, or putting on one of his well-calculated performances before a jury. In all of the secondhand accounts of Lincoln's legal career left behind by Herndon, Swett, Lamon, Whitney, Davis, and others, not one hints that Lincoln felt dissatisfaction with his job. He went elsewhere—the statehouse, Congress, and eventually the White House—to feed his ambition. But he used the courthouse to feed his family, and maybe to feed some part of himself, to find a degree of personal security unavailable elsewhere.

In the other major facets of his life, Lincoln often lacked such comfort. His marriage, and relations with women in general, required either an affected sentimentality that he did not wear very well, or a degree of partnership intimacy that likewise did not quite fit. He and Mary may or may not have had a happy marriage, but it is difficult to escape the conclusion that, however much he loved his wife, the day-to-day requirements of closeness in their relationship were not always congenial to him.[25]

As a lawyer he could embed himself in the masculine world he preferred. Much has been made of Lincoln's predilection for male company. Whatever his motives, he satisfied that preference in the predominantly masculine spaces of his office and all those courthouses on the Eighth Circuit. His ideas about manhood were formed within the context of the law as much as anywhere else.

Politics offered a heavily masculine environment as well, of course; but politics also brought discomfiting moments. An antebellum political career was such an emotional enterprise, with its rollicking penny-newspaper press, its feuds, catcalls, occasional brawls between opponents, and, above all, the emotional hot buttons of race and culture that the era's predominant political crises pushed. Politics required Lincoln to be both committed and compromising. Lincoln supported Zachary Taylor for the presidency in 1848, for example, despite his preference for Henry Clay. He acknowledged white Southerners' legal property rights in slaves while at the same time passionately denouncing the institution itself. He remained at once both passionately committed to the causes represented by the Republican Party, while flexible enough to function within an American polity that was peppered with men and women who disagreed with him, sometimes violently so.

He tacked pretty well between the need for passion and the need for distance in his politics: better than most, probably, in that unstable time of hotheads, zealots, and martyrs. The political machinery of antebellum and Civil War America was every bit as prone to dysfunctional meltdowns as the economic and social machinery, and likewise cried out for some sort of lubricant to ease the way: an overarching spirit of compromise, some political entity that played the lawyer's role of valuing none of the wheels so much as their relatively noiseless operation. But in the end, no such lubricant existed—and the war came.

When he entered the White House in 1860, Lincoln brought a myriad of different influences to bear on his new job. On paper he was shockingly unprepared for the presidency; he had never held an executive position of any kind. But Lincoln possessed an important set of skills that would stand him in good stead during the trying years to come. His political instincts had been honed by decades of laboring in the trenches of the Illinois statehouse and among the rank and file of the state's Whig and Republican parties. His people skills had likewise been developed by long years of storytelling, speechmaking, backslapping, and glad-handing in general stores, streets, and other public venues.

As an influence on his behavior, the law assumed a background role in his presidential life, but it peeped through occasionally. There were the sneers leveled at him by political enemies—and even some supporters—who saw in him an unappealing representative of an unappealing profession, a "second-rate Illinois lawyer," according to Ohio congressman (and future president) James Garfield. From time to time, similar sentiments would surface among those who imagined the president to be nothing more than a mere frontier pettifogger, unequal to the task of leading a great nation during a civil war.[26]

President Lincoln was sometimes overtly attorneylike in his approach to the job. His weekly review of soldiers' court-martials certainly made him look a great deal like a practicing attorney as he carefully examined court records searching for ways to ease their sentences. He possessed a legalistic point of view on some of the more controversial issues of the war, worrying about the long-term ramifications of measures like Congress' Confiscation Act, which he dissected with an attorney's eye for detail and returned to Congress for revision, noting in particular the act's possible violation of the Constitution. "It is the sum of those provisions which results in the divesting of title [in confiscated slaves] forever" to which Lincoln objected, he wrote. "For the causes of treason, and the ingredients of treason, not amounting to the full crime, it declares forfeiture, extending beyond the lives of the guilty parties; whereas the Constitution of the United States declares that 'no attainder of treason shall work corruption of blood, or forfeiture, except during the life of the person attainted.' True, there is to be no formal attainder in this case; still I think the greater punishment can not be constitutionally inflicted, in a different form, for the same offence. With great respect, I am constrained to say I think this feature of the act is unconstitutional." A less lawyerly president might have overlooked this matter altogether.[27]

He was also aware of the legal dimensions of the Emancipation Proclamation, which he understood would possess definite (and perhaps fatal) limitations inside a courtroom, should the measure ever be subjected to a lawsuit. Lincoln may well have had the possibility of a legal challenge before a hostile U.S. Supreme Court in the back of his mind when he limited the proclamation's scope to only those areas not directly in the Union's control (thus eliminating border state slaveholders as possible litigants). He also understood, better than many who did not possess his lawyer's perspective, that the Emancipation Proclamation absolutely had to be superseded by a constitutional amendment outlawing slavery forever, if freedom for African Americans was to have any sort of permanence. "All would bear him witness that he had never shrunk from doing all that he could to eradicate Slavery by issuing an emancipation proclamation," Lincoln told a group of well-wishers in 1865, who had gathered at the White House to congratulate him on passage of the Thirteenth Amendment, "that . . . falls far short of what the amendment will be when fully consummated. A question might be raised whether the proclamation was legally valid. . . . But this amendment is a King's cure for all the evils."[28]

Laws, amendments, constitutions, soldier's court-martials—they brought out the attorney in Lincoln, in ways easy to spot. Less obvious, however, was a more understated set of values he brought to life as America's chief executive, values rooted in his courtroom days. Those values were so subtle that many of the people around him—and historians ever since—mistook both their nature and their source.

If there was one quality of Lincoln's presidential leadership that engendered consistent commentary from colleagues, journalists, and

168 · Lincoln the Lawyer

other observers, it was the president's magnanimity. His secretary of war (and erstwhile antagonist in the McCormick reaper case) Edwin Stanton, to cite one of many examples, remarked on "the kindness and humanity of [Lincoln's] disposition, and the tender and forgiving spirit that so eminently distinguished him." Lincoln's fellow Americans were amazed at his profound generosity, his calm evenhandedness, and his unwillingness to either take or give offense. "It seems utterly impossible for the President to conceive of the possibility of any good resulting from a vigorous and exemplary course of punishing political dereliction," Lincoln's private secretary John Hay marveled. "His favorite expression is 'I am in favor of short statutes of limitations in politics.'"[29]

It was a trait all the more pronounced because Lincoln lived in a time when magnanimity was in short supply. Men who held political office routinely nursed grudges and slights, and often brought a hyperemotional sensitivity into the public arena. The Civil War, of course, tended to exacerbate such things. But in a turbulent sea of angry men and women, Lincoln always seemed able to maintain a high degree of emotional distance from his enemies, to readily overlook slights and insults, and to keep his mind focused on the task of victory without an excessive focus on his own pride and its possible wounding at the hands of others who were far less discreet and unemotional.

At the same time, however, astute observers saw what looked to be a contradiction between the president's kindheartedness and his steely-eyed determination—even an occasional streak of ruthlessness. The same man whom some saw moved to tears by the sight of a soldier's suffering could with grim enthusiasm countenance the harsh measures advocated by William Tecumseh Sherman and the dogged, bloody persistence of Ulysses S. Grant. As a politician, Lincoln went out of his way to avoid giving offense to his enemies or to indulge in the sort of rough-and-tumble name-calling and strife that marked the politics of his age; and yet he found himself repeatedly immersed in the most passionate political quarrels of his age. Lincoln himself marveled at the contradiction of his situation and his times. "It is a little singular that I who am not a vindictive man, should always have been before the people for election in canvasses marked for their bitterness," he mused during the election of 1864. "The contests in which I have been prominent have been marked by great rancor."[30]

It is jarring; perhaps it is the central contradiction of Lincoln and his presidency. How could a man who felt so deeply the suffering of others, who all knew to be fundamentally kind and singularly averse to violence, order thousands of young men to their deaths and embrace—if reluctantly—the tremendous destruction endemic to the Civil War?

The problem here lies, I think, in a misunderstanding of Lincoln's behavior when it is sentimentalized as a form of kindliness. Yes, he was by nearly all accounts a genial man; but there was more to it than that. His magnanimity was also a function of his lawyerly sense of distance from other people's motives, and his appreciation—honed by decades of witnessing nearly every imaginable form of strife in Illinois' courtrooms—of the value of reducing friction as much as possible.

If we look closely, we can see Lincoln the president trying hard to apply a lawyer's grease to the shrill machinery of war that surrounded him. We see it in his almost desperate appeals to white Southerners for a calm appraisal of their situation, appealing to their feelings the way he would a reluctant jury ("We are not enemies, but friends. We must not be enemies"). We see it in his steadfast refusal to fully identify with one of the most clanging wheels of all, radical abolitionism, a movement with which he privately sympathized ("I have always hated slavery, I think as much as any Abolitionist") but that he felt compelled publicly to keep at arm's length, lest its passions become his. We see it even in Lincoln's little decisions, like his approval of a name change for the Republican Party during the 1864 election (to the National Union party) as a means of easing the transition of moderate Democrats into his camp.[31]

Nothing produced more friction than the racial politics of emancipation, and here Lincoln applied grease with an alacrity that has left him the target of criticism ever since. His calls for a gradual, compensated emancipation system, and his support of colonization as a solution to the nation's vexed problems of race relations—a support long predating the Civil War—suggested to some critics that, deep down, Lincoln possessed a racist's heart.[32] It is far more accurate to say that Lincoln possessed an attorney's heart. There is a subtle lawyerly tone to his colonization schemes, and a not-so-subtle legal dimension to his calls for Congress in the fall of 1862 to compensate white slaveholders for their losses, including draft proposals for constitutional amendments to that effect. And, of course, there is the writ of garnishment quality in his Emancipation Proclamation.

Most of all, Lincoln refused to impugn the motives of his detractors or speculate on the state of their hearts and souls. Recalling a conversation between Lincoln and his postmaster general Montgomery Blair, in which the latter lambasted some of the president's congressional critics as having "interested motives and hostility to Lincoln," Hay heard his boss coolly admonish that "it is much better not to be led from the region of reason into that of hot blood, by imputing to public men motives which they do not avow."[33] This was not kindliness or magnanimity. It was, rather, the hard-won lessons learned by an attorney who came to understand that clients, witnesses, courtroom colleagues, and opponents were all essentially unfathomable in their innermost agendas and purposes. In a courtroom, it was best for the lawyer to concern himself with "manifest behavior"—procedures, overt agreements, and that which could be proven (or disproven) via tangible evidence. Reckless speculation about what lay underneath the legal surfaces led nowhere, and could only impede the smooth operation of the system.

But Lincoln's valuation of grease did not give him pause in his moral judgment; he was no relativist. It did give him, and properly so, a deep appreciation of the damage a pell-mell rush to reform might cause to the nation's already delicate and overtaxed political and social structure. Having spent much of his adult life trying to minimize the harm caused by collisions between debtors and creditors, family members, friends and business partners, he could not ignore the potential for friction between whites and blacks, North and South, Republicans and Democrats, and Unionists and Confederates.

But when matters finally came to a head during the war, and an embattled Union required leadership from its president, Lincoln to his everlasting credit chose to embrace the machinery of emancipation and its attendant frictions, come what may. His lawyerly valuing of grease did not qualify as a quiet dogma, exactly; but he came to know that a mere lack of friction and the smooth operation of the Union machinery, of themselves, were inadequate to his stormy present. "The occasion is piled high with difficulty, and we must rise with the occasion," he famously remarked to Congress, "As our case is new, so we must think anew, and act anew."[34]

In this sense, one could argue that Lincoln transcended "grease," outgrowing his careful tacking back and forth between and among the more emotive people and institutions in his life to embrace one of the most emotionally charged and sensitive issues of all: emancipation and racial equality. But even so, the various lessons he learned in the

courtroom about the dangers of friction and its attendant disloca-
tions served him well as president. The lawyer in him kept Lincoln
from pressing forward too fast and too recklessly, even as the moralist
in him kept moving forward toward his particular vision of a nation
without slavery and human bondage.

Of course, other presidents have been lawyers; over half, in fact. But
no other president spent quite so much time inside a courtroom; and
the law had never exercised quite so exclusive an influence over a chief
executive. Other presidents had college degrees of some sort, and even
those who did not (Washington, for example) possessed at least the
framework of a classical education in which the seminal works of philosophy, history, and society could be brought to bear on any given
subject.

Lincoln knew great works of literature—Shakespeare most promi-
nently—and he read with an eclecticism that made his a far from
narrow-minded or isolated intellect. But his quarter-century at the
bar was a weightier influence, quiet but forceful in the lessons it had
driven home about the ways in which people function and interact
within a community. The primary lesson the law practice imparted
to Lincoln—the most important message it conveyed to this future
president and savior of the Union—was the simple fact that the motives, desires, and appetites of his fellow Americans were ultimately
unknowable. This was true in the courthouse, and it was equally so in
the White House. Any attempt to penetrate the hearts and minds of
the men and women who surrounded him was futile and, in its hubris,
counterproductive.

It is a staple of the vast literature on Abraham Lincoln that he possessed a unique and peculiar insight into the minds and hearts of his
fellow human beings. Historian Doris Kearns Goodwin summarized the
accepted wisdom of historians when she wrote that Lincoln "learned
from early mistakes, transcended the jealousy of rivals, and his insight
into men and events had deepened with each passing year."[35] There
has always been a sense among Lincoln's many admirers that he possessed some ineffable quality of seeing deeper and understanding better what made people tick than anyone else of his time.

In fact, however, Lincoln's insight rested on the entirely opposite
belief that there were a great many things he could not know, and
did not really need to know, about the people around him, whether
they were debtors, energy men and divorcées, or (later on) cabinet

members, generals, and fellow politicians. His magnanimity—if that is what it was—his generosity, and his humility were not manifestations of saintliness or an inordinately pure character. Rather, they were the products of a quarter-century spent in a law practice that taught Lincoln some difficult but exceedingly valuable lessons about limitations, boundaries, and the tremendous societal value of grease.

Conclusion

Let's take Billy Herndon at his word, and imagine that Lincoln really did want nothing more than a return to his law practice at the end of his second term; a return to the rusty shingle, "hanging there, undisturbed . . . as if nothing had ever happened," including John Wilkes Booth's bullet.

This would probably have occurred sometime during the spring of 1869, after he had been replaced by the voters the previous November and remained until March to escort the new president to his swearing-in ceremony. Mary later recalled that she, Lincoln, and the boys planned to travel to Europe "when he was through with his Presidential terms," and perhaps they do so before returning home.[1] Then Lincoln, Mary, and Tad (and perhaps Robert) board a train and make their way back to Springfield. The town hosts the inevitable homecoming celebration; and after he shakes many hands and the well-wishers finally go away, former president Abraham Lincoln again stuffs papers into his hat, opens the door with the brass nameplate, and heads toward his downtown office.

He is now sixty years old, and maybe he calculates that, if the war hasn't aged him too much, he has five, maybe ten good years of law left in him. He needs those years, too. He was not a rich man when he left for Washington, D.C. (one wonders if he could really have afforded a trip abroad), and he would not have been rich when he returned. "We will go back to Illinois," he told Mary, "and I will open a law-office in Springfield or Chicago, and practice law, and at least do enough to help give us a livelihood."[2]

Perhaps he is able to parlay his fame into a higher income bracket within the law: a judgeship, maybe even at the appellate level. He had been a judge often enough in his circuit days, filling in for David Davis, so the idea was plausible. But then again, maybe he doesn't really want a seat on the bench. Normally not a nostalgic man, Lincoln nevertheless may pine a bit for the old days of the "mud circuit" and its camaraderie. Mary also later recalled that, on the day Lincoln was killed, he ruminated wistfully at length on his "law office, the courtroom, the green bag for his briefs and law papers," and most of all "his adventures when riding the circuit."[3]

But it is not "as if nothing had ever happened," not nearly so. David Davis is gone, off to the U.S. Supreme Court where Lincoln put him in 1862. Henry Whitney is practicing law in Kansas. Leonard Swett is in Chicago, and Ward Hill Lamon is back in Virginia. His office is different now, too. Billy Herndon will eventually quit the law in disgust, restlessness and the whiskey slowly getting the better of him, so that maybe Lincoln is forced to go looking for a new junior partner.

The Old Eighth has changed, as well. This would probably not have been quite so disconcerting—the circuit's borders underwent constant tinkering throughout Lincoln's antebellum years, as the legislature added and subtracted counties. But as litigation in a complex world becomes increasingly more complex itself, and as the state grows and develops and settles in, the days of the itinerant circuit lawyer handling cases with whatever books he could stuff into his saddlebags are numbered.

The cases are different, too. As time goes on, there would likely be fewer debt collections, and fewer promissory notes, as an increasingly sophisticated economy becomes more cash-rich and less prone to using IOUs as a crude form of currency. If Lincoln practices law long enough, he may start to see the rudiments of specialized debt services appear: collection firms and the primitive attempts at a credit-rating system. Eventually, new bankruptcy legislation will make that option again available to harassed debtors. In any event, he is likely to see fewer notes crossing his desk.

At the same time, maybe he sees more lucrative business in the form of ongoing railroad litigation. The practice had been pointed in that general direction anyway before he left for the White House. Possibly Lincoln finds himself searching for a niche, some area within the law that he can make his own in his twilight years. As litigation increases in scope and complexity, lawyers begin to specialize. Far away in Texas, for example, another old-time Whig attorney, Nathaniel Hart Davis, turns to divorce cases as a way of supplementing his income from other areas. It is hard to imagine Lincoln deliberately choosing to specialize in an area like divorce—one that would give him a surfeit of female clients—but it is quite easy to see him turning to railroads and their legal concerns as his primary source of income.

Just as he begins to reestablish his practice, halfway across the country Harvard University appoints Christopher Langdell as the dean of its law school, who in turn introduces the rigorous "case law method" that finally shifts legal education's focus away from old texts like Blackstone and toward a rigorous investigation of court opinions. A few years after that, seventy-five lawyers meet in Saratoga, New York, and found the American Bar Association, thus creating a national umbrella organization for lawyers that will eventually either control or heavily influence nearly every major facet of a lawyer's professional life, from bar examinations to disbarments.[4]

The country still needs grease, now more than ever. The machines have become much bigger, the wheels turning, screeching, and belching the black smoke of industrial progress. Only now, with its bar associations, structured law-school systems, case methods, and growing collection of paraphernalia, the law may seem to Lincoln like just another machine.

Maybe he's comfortable with that, even as his circle of circuit friends steadily dwindles, as he sees fewer and fewer young men emulating him by simply picking up the books and going at it seated on a woodpile somewhere, and as he sees law libraries in offices around the community replacing his eclectic collection of treatises, Byron, and Shakespeare with row upon row of state and federal case reports.

Maybe they are changes Lincoln does not find much to his liking. But he could see them coming already. Years before, while he was still in the White House and a civil war raged outside its doors, his son Robert came to him and told him that he intended to enter Harvard Law School. Thinking back to those days on the circuit, shrouded in a nostalgic haze perhaps made all the more wistful by the deadly carnage of the war, Lincoln replied, "If you do, you should learn more than I ever did, but you will never have so good a time."[5]

Notes

Preface

1. Mark E. Neely, Jr., *The Last Best Hope of Earth* (Cambridge: Harvard University Press, 1993), 34.

2. Carl Sandburg, *Abraham Lincoln: The Prairie Years*, 2 vols. (New York: Harcourt, Brace and Company, 1926), 2: 328.

Introduction

1. For examples of Lincoln attending such meetings, see the descriptions of Lincoln chairing bar association meeting for lawyers in Peoria, McLean, Sangamon, and Tazewell counties, April 11, 1845; chairing bar meeting in Petersburg, Illinois, October 28, 1848; and attending bar meeting for the entire Eighth Circuit on April 17, 1855, all in Lincoln Legal Papers DVD-ROM database (Urbana: University of Illinois Press, 2000; hereinafter referred to as LLP).

2. The editors of the Lincoln Legal Papers speculate that the notes may be related to an 1858 invitation to speak at Ohio State and Union Law College, but again, evidence is lacking on this score; see entry "Lincoln prepared lecture on law," LLP.

3. Lincoln to George W. Rives, May 7, 1849, Roy P. Basler, ed., *The Collected Works of Abraham Lincoln*, 9 vols. (Urbana: University of Illinois Press, 1955; hereinafter referred to as *CW*), 2: 46.

4. Lincoln to Jesse W. Fell, December 20, 1859, *CW* 3: 512.

5. This is based on a search query in LLP, with a beginning date of September 1, 1836, and an end date of June 31, 1850; the database lists 2,447 cases.

6. Lincoln, Notes for a Law Lecture, [July 1850], *CW* 2: 82.

7. For such use of the "honest lawyer" passage, see Frederick Trevor Hill, *Lincoln the Lawyer* (Littleton, Colo.: Fred B. Rothman, 1986; originally published in 1906), 33–34; Clark P. Bissett, *Abraham Lincoln: A Universal Man* (San Francisco: John Hall, 1928), 77; William E. Curtis, *The True Abraham Lincoln* (Philadelphia: J. B. Lippincott, 1903), 71; "Lincoln's Contacts with Law Students," *Lincoln Lore* 280 (August 20, 1934): 1; Henry Oliver Evans, *Abraham Lincoln as a Lawyer* (Pittsburgh: Smith Brothers, 1927), 9.

8. Curtis, *True Abraham Lincoln*, 71.

9. Emanuel Hertz, *Abraham Lincoln: A New Portrait*, 2 vols. (New York: Horace

Liveright, 1931), 1: 48; Linus P. Brocket, *The Life and Times of Abraham Lincoln, Sixteenth President of the United States, Including His Speeches, Messages, Inaugurals, Proclamations, etc. etc.* (Philadelphia: Bradley, 1865), 81; Richards, *Lincoln, the Lawyer-Statesman,* 25; Moores, "Abraham Lincoln: Lawyer," 528; Kranz, *Abraham Lincoln: A New Portrait,* 26; also Hay and Nicolay, *Abraham Lincoln: A History,* 157; Nathaniel W. Stephenson, *Lincoln: An Account of His Personal Life* (Indianapolis: Bobbs-Merrill, 1922), 45; and Frederick T. Hill, *Lincoln, Emancipator of the Nation* (New York: D. Appleton, 1923), 88; Tarbell, *Life of Abraham Lincoln,* 2: 42, and 44–45. Lincoln did have one critic among his early biographers; Edgar Lee Masters, *Lincoln the Man* (New York: Dodd, Meade, 1931), 121–23, was generally quite disparaging of Lincoln's legal skills.

10. Stephenson, *Lincoln: An Account of His Personal Life,* 67; J. G. Holland, *The Life of Abraham Lincoln* (Springfield, Ill.: Gurdon Bill, 1866), 78; Stoddard, *True Story of a Great Life,* 127; also Hill, *Emancipator of the Nation,* 87–88; and A. Bergen, "Lincoln as a Lawyer," *Journal of the American Bar Association* 5 (June 1926): 390–91.

11. Notes for a Law Lecture, [July 1850], *CW* 2: 81.

12. Ida M. Tarbell, *The Life of Abraham Lincoln* 4 vols. (New York: Lincoln History Society, 1903), 2: 155.

13. *Tuthill v. Tuthill,* April 1850, LLP.

14. Brief Autobiography, June 1848, *CW* 2: 459.

Chapter 1: "Great God Almighty"

1. Godbey biographical information in *Illustrated Atlas Map of Menard County, Illinois* (Chicago: W. R. Brink, 1874), 39.

2. Russell Godbey, interviews with William H. Herndon, [1865–66], *HI,* 449–50.

3. Chris Goodrich, *Anarchy and Elegance: Confessions of a Journalist at Yale Law School* (Boston: Little, Brown, 1991), 51; see also Mark Simenhoff, ed., *My First Year as a Lawyer* (New York: Walker, 1994), 2–3.

4. Goodrich, *Anarchy and Elegance,* 51; Clarence Darrow, *The Story of My Life* (New York: Da Capo Press, 1996; originally published in 1932), 29.

5. Webster's Law Diary, entry for September 17, 1804, in Konefsky, *Webster Legal Papers,* 1: 36; Archibald MacLeish to Francis Hyde Bangs, January 25, 1916, in R. H. Winnick, ed., *The Letters of Archibald MacLeish* (Boston: Houghton Mifflin, 1983), 23; also generally Richard W. Moll, *The Lure of the Law: Why People Become Lawyers and What the Profession Does to Them* (New York: Penguin Books, 1990), quotes at 24, 25.

6. See, for example, Robert W. Johannsen, *Stephen A. Douglas,* 2nd ed. (Urbana: University of Illinois Press, 1997), 88–97.

7. W. H. Ward, "The Legal Profession," *Southwestern Quarterly* 1 (March 1852): 158; see also E. Anthony Rotundo, *American Manhood: Transformations in Mas-*

culinity from the Revolution to the Modern Era (New York: Basic Books, 1993), 165–75.

8. Charles Richard Williams, ed., *Diary and Letters of Rutherford Birchard Hayes,* 5 vols. (Columbus: Ohio State Archaeological and Historical Society, 1922), 1: 107.

9. Lincoln, Notes for a Law Lecture, [July 1, 1850], *CW* 2: 81–82; first debate with Douglas, August 21, 1858, *CW* 2: 29.

10. See, for example, evidence in Samuel L. Treat, interview with Jesse W. Weik, c. 1883, *HI,* 725; James Gourley, interview with William H. Herndon, c. 1865–66, *HI,* 451–52.

11. Hardin Bale interview with William H. Herndon, May 29, 1865, *HI,* 13.

12. Autobiography, written for John L. Scripps, c. June 1860, *CW* 4: 65.

13. Lincoln to Jesse W. Fell, December 20, 1959, *CW* 3: 511.

14. "Blackberries" quote in Warren, *American Bar,* 301; saying quoted in Daniel Boorstin, *The Mysterious Science of the Law: An Essay on Blackstone's Commentaries,* 2nd ed. (Chicago: University of Chicago Press, 1996), xiii; see also Maxwell Bloomfield, "The Texas Bar in the Nineteenth Century," *Vanderbilt University Law Review* 32 (1979): 261–62; Webster to James Hervey Bingham, May 18, 1802, in Alfred S. Konefsky and Andrew J. King, eds., *The Papers of Daniel Webster, Legal Papers, Volume I: The New Hampshire Practice* (Hanover, N.H.: University Press of New England, 1982), 1: 18.

15. On Gridley, see Samuel L. Knapp, *Biographical Sketches of Eminent Lawyers, Statesmen, and Men of Letters* (Boston: Richardson and Lord, 1821), 199–200; Usher Linder, 390, describes Smith's career; on Hatch, see Alderson, *Courts and Lawyers of New York,* 3: 1264; Foote, *Bench and Bar of South Carolina,* 162–74, describes four lawyers who abandoned the law for planting; on Patterson, see Foote, *Bench and Bar of South Carolina,* 444; on Seward, see Doris Kearns Goodwin, *Team of Rivals: The Political Genius of Abraham Lincoln* (New York: Simon and Schuster, 2005), 78–79.

16. O'Neall, *Bench and Bar of South Carolina,* xv–xviii, 164–66; Warren, *American Bar,* 196–203; English, "Pioneer Lawyer and Jurist in Missouri," 9; Lincoln to John L. Scripps, [c. June 1860], *CW* 4: 65.

17. *Bench and Bar of Massachusetts,* 117,123; *Bench and Bar of South Carolina,* 522–23; Foote, *Bench and Bar,* 25–26; Kenneth C. Kaufman, *Dred Scott's Advocate: A Biography of Roswell M. Field* (Columbia: University of Missouri Press, 1996), 33; Alderson, *Courts and Lawyers of New York,* 3: 1250.

18. David Davis, September 20, 1866, *HI,* 351.

19. David Donald, *Lincoln* (New York: Simon and Schuster, 1995), 24, suggests that Thomas was too poor to fight these claims in court; but other sources speculate that Thomas and his son both saw the inside of Kentucky courtrooms on this score; see "Lincoln's Decision to Become a Lawyer," *Lincoln Lore* 226 (1948): 1. Earl S. Miers and William E. Baringer, *Lincoln Day by Day: A Chronol-*

ogy, 1809–1865 (Dayton, Ohio: Morningside, 1991), 3–7, offer a succinct overview of Thomas's various legal entanglements.

20. An oft-repeated tale has the young Lincoln being struck by the speaking talents of an Indiana attorney named John Brackenridge, who gave such a rousing defense of his client during a murder trial that Lincoln, eighteen years old at the time, is supposed to have sought him out afterward to congratulate him on his oratory. Another legend has Lincoln borrowing law books from a Hoosier lawyer named John Pitcher, to whom he expressed a desire to study the law, "but his family being verry [sic] poor he could not give his time off the farm." I have my doubts on both stories; the Brackenridge legend is based on a supposed encounter with Lincoln while president, but there is no firm record of such a visit; see Herndon, *Herndon's Lincoln,* 50–51; and S. T. Johnson, interview with William H. Herndon, September 14, 1865, *HI,* 115. The Pitcher story also appears in *Herndon's Lincoln,* 53, and is based on a letter from Oliver C. Terry to Herndon, July 14, 1888, *HI,* 658; but Pitcher was very old when he related this tale, and at any rate, Lincoln's subsequent behavior does not suggest a man who had already settled on his chosen occupation by age eighteen.

21. See Whitney, 63; O. H. Smith, *Early Indiana Trials and Sketches* (Cincinnati: Moore, Wilstach, Keys, 1858), 7. There is also a legend, equally dubious, that Lincoln read a copy of the *Revised Statutes of Indiana* from cover to cover, and was by this also convinced to pursue the law; but this seems farfetched; see Duff, *A. Lincoln,* 5–6, for the tale, and Duff's own well-placed doubts; for a different perspective, see Woldman, *Lawyer Lincoln,* 10.

22. See generally Jason Duncan to William H. Herndon, [1866–67], *HI,* 540–41; and Abney Y. Ellis to William H. Herndon, January 23, 1866, *HI;* Herndon, *Herndon's Lincoln,* 93. I qualify the statement about Lincoln arguing cases in Green's court because some of the testimony involved has a ring of hyperbole about it, with Green struck by Lincoln's supposedly brilliant, innate lawyerly abilities; see especially *HI,* 540.

23. Dennis Hanks, interview with William H. Herndon, September 8, 1865, *HI,* 105; while Hanks's testimony has been rightly treated with skepticism by many scholars (he had a tendency to exaggerate his importance in Lincoln's life), on this point his observation is borne out by others; see, for example, Nathaniel Grigsby, interview with William H. Herndon, September 12, 1865, *HI,* 114; Anna Caroline Gentry, interview with William H. Herndon, September 17, 1865, *HI,* 131; Sara Bush Lincoln, interview with William H. Herndon, September 8, 1865, *HI,* 107; "awful lazy" quote from Nathaniel Grigsby, Silas Richardson, Nancy Richardson, and John Romine, interview with William H. Herndon, *HI,* 118.

24. Ward, "Legal Profession," 161.

25. Alexis de Tocqueville, *Democracy in America,* 2 vols. (New York: Alfred A. Knopf, 1945; original English translation in 1835) 1: 272; Lincoln, Notes for a Law Lecture, c. 1850, *CW* 2: 82.

26. Lincoln, autobiography written for John Scripps, [c. June 1860], Notes for a Law Lecture, *CW* 4: 65.

27. *Bench and Bar of South Carolina,* 443–44; James Allen Brent, "The Arkansas Bar in the Age of Sectionalism, 1819–1861" (Ph.D. diss., Auburn University, 1996), 37; Charles Warren, *A History of the American Bar,* 3rd ed. (New York: Howard Fertig, 1966), 185–87; see also John M. Palmer, *Personal Recollections of John M. Palmer: The Story of an Earnest Life* (Cincinnati: R. Clark, 1901), 28; Dwight C. Kilbourn, *The Bench and Bar of Litchfield, Connecticut, 1709–1909* (Union, N.J.: Lawbook Exchange, 2002; originally published 1909), 24, 133; and Michael H. Harris, "The Frontier Lawyer's Library: Southern Indiana, 1800–1850, as a Test Case," *American Journal of Legal History* 16 (1972): 239–51. John Marshall also read Blackstone as a seminal text; see Charles T. Cullen, "New Light on John Marshall's Legal Education and Admission to the Bar," *American Journal of Legal History* 16 (1972): 347; Boorstin, *Mysterious Science of the Law,* 2.

28. Williams, *Diary and Letters of Rutherford Birchard Hayes,* 1: 109.

29. Blackstone, *Commentaries* 1: 4.

30. Joseph Chitty, *A Treatise on Pleading, and Parties to Actions, with Second and Third Volumes, Containing Precedents of Pleadings, and an Appendix of Forms,* 3rd American edition from the second English edition (Philadelphia: I. Riley, 1819), viii, 1, 55, 122; on Chitty's importance to lawyers of the period in general, see Friedman, *A History of American Law,* 145.

31. Joseph Story, *Commentaries on Equity Jurisprudence, as Administered in England and America,* 2 vols. (New York: Arno Press, 1972; originally published in 1835), 1: 1.

32. Story, *Commentaries on Equity,* quotes at 2, 121.

33. On these and other titles available to lawyers of Lincoln's day, see Friedman, *A History of American Law,* 327–30.

34. Deed for Cox et al., June 1834, LLP; deed for Colson et al., July 1834, LLP; deed for Baker et al., April 1834, LLP; Lincoln to Thomas J. Nance, December 10, 1835, *CW* 1: 38; bill of sale for Ferguson and Trent, January 25, 1832, LLP. Other lawyers-to-be did similar tasks; see Palmer, *Personal Recollections of John M. Palmer,* 28.

35. One New Salem eyewitness, Mentor Graham, claimed Lincoln never "charged a cent" or was given anything at all to write up deeds and so on, but Graham's testimony is shaky in general; see Graham, interview with William H. Herndon, *HI,* 8–11.

36. J. Rowan Herndon to William H. Herndon, July 3, 1865, *HI,* 69; *Close v. Ritter,* December 1832, LLP; see also *State Bank of Illinois v. Parkinson,* April 1833, LLP; *Green v. Purcaple,* March 1836, LLP; subpoena, *Harrell v. Woldridge,* March 1835, LLP; in these last two cases, Lincoln appeared as a witness in slander proceedings; and appearance bond, *People v. Edwards and Edwards,* June 1834, LLP; see also *People v. Edwards et al.,* June 1834, LLP, whereby the defendants

were to be indicted for riot and attempted rape; here again, the state attorney later dropped the matter.

37. John A. Moretta, *William Pitt Ballinger: Texas Lawyer, Southern Statesman, 1825–1888* (Austin: Texas State Historical Association, 2000), 22–30; on Chase's experiences, see Friedman, *American Law: An Introduction,* 2nd ed. (New York: W. W. Norton, 1998), 278. Daniel Webster also took four years, but his preparation—including lengthy readings in international law—seems to have been more thorough than most; see Konefsky, *Webster Legal Papers,* 1: 46.

38. "Slow" quote from David Davis; see *HI,* 351; James A. Herndon, interview with William H. Herndon, [1865–66], *HI,* 461; "steel" quote from Joshua F. Speed to William H. Herndon, December 6, 1866, *HI,* 499.

39. Lincoln, autobiography for John Scripps, c. June 1860, *CW* 4: 64–65.

40. *Bench and Bar of Massachusetts,* 117,123; *Bench and Bar of South Carolina,* 522–23; Foote, *Bench and Bar,* 25–26; James Allen Brent, "The Arkansas Bar in the Age of Sectionalism, 1819–1861" (Ph.D. diss., Auburn University, 1996), 16.

41. Description of the law office in Duff, *A. Lincoln,* 41; the description refers to the office after Stuart and Lincoln became partners, but presumably its appearance was much the same as it had been during the days of Stuart and Dummer; William H. Townsend, "Stuart and Lincoln," *American Bar Association Journal* 17 (February 1931): 82.

42. Lincoln to Jesse Fell, December 20, 1859, *CW* 3: 512; autobiography for John Scripps, c. June 1860, *CW,* 4: 65.

43. Lincoln would later fill this role himself; see the examination of McRoberts et al., for admission to the bar, July 1841, LLP; Paul M. Angle, *One Hundred Years of Law* (Springfield, Ill.; Brown, Hay and Stephens, 1928), 374; Weik, *The Real Lincoln,* 133–34.

44. Sangamon County Circuit Court, admission of Lincoln to the bar, March 24, 1836, in LLP; Wayne C. Temple, "Lincoln's First Step to Becoming a Lawyer," *Lincoln Herald* 70 (Winter 1968): 207; and Robert M. Jarvis, "An Anecdotal History of the Bar Exam," *Georgetown Journal of Legal Ethics* 9 (1996): 374. Eastern states seem to have been more stringent; see, for example, Kilbourn, *Bench and Bar of Litchfield, Connecticut,* 83.

45. James G. Baldwin, *The Flush Times of Alabama and Mississippi* (Baton Rouge: Louisiana State University Press, 1980), 28; *Illinois State Journal,* March 4, 1850; on the struggles to establish procedures for admittance to the bar in early America, see Alan M. Smith, "Virginia Lawyers, 1690–1776: The Birth of an American Profession" (Ph.D. diss., Johns Hopkins University, 1967).

46. Ward, "Legal Profession," 166.

47. See generally Richard W. Moll, *The Lure of the Law* (New York: Penguin Books, 1990); John C. Tucker, *Trial and Error: The Education of a Courtroom Lawyer* (New York: Carroll and Graf, 2003), especially ch. 2.

48. Foote, *Bench and Bar,* 194; Alderson, *Courts and Lawyers of New York,* 3: 1046.

49. On this point of the desirability of partnerships, see Maxwell Bloomfield, "The Texas Bar in the Nineteenth Century," *Vanderbilt Law Review* 32 (1979): 269–73.

50. My characterization of Stuart is based on the following: John Todd Stuart Papers, Illinois State Historical Library, Springfield, Illinois; Usher F. Linder, *Reminiscences of the Early Bench and Bar of Illinois* (Chicago: Chicago *News* Co., 1879), 347–48; John Palmer, *Bench and Bar of Illinois* (Chicago: Lewis, 1899), 1: 187–90.

51. H. E. Dummer, interview with William H. Herndon, c. 1865–66, *HI*, 442–43.

52. Duff, *A. Lincoln*, 35, reaches a similar conclusion to my own, while other scholars simply observe that Stuart and Dummer dissolved without speculating on the reasons.

53. Lincoln did this himself, with Ward Lamon; see *Iroquois Journal*, December 1, 1852, in LLP; and Lamon, *Recollections of Abraham Lincoln*, 15.

54. See generally Linder, *Early Bench and Bar of Illinois*, 347–48; Palmer, *Bench and Bar of Illinois*, 1: 187; Stuart, interview with William H. Herndon, [June 1865], *HI*, 63–64.

55. *Hawthorn v. Wooldridge*, March 1837, LLP.

56. This sketch of Logan was taken from *Memorials of the Life and Character of Stephen T. Logan* (Springfield, Ill.: H. W. Rokker, 1882); "Stephen Logan Talks about Abraham Lincoln," *Bulletin of the Abraham Lincoln Centennial Association* 12 (September 1928): 1–5; Linder, *Early Bench and Bar of Illinois*, 158; Albert Y. Ellis to William H. Herndon, January 30, 1866, *HI*, 179; and William W. Thomas to William H. Herndon, *HI*, 391–92. A useful if overly laudatory obituary may be found in the *Illinois State Journal*, July 19, 1880.

57. Linder, *Early Bench and Bar of Illinois*, 158–59; Herndon, *Herndon's Lincoln*, 147.

58. Herndon, *Herndon's Lincoln*, 147–48.

59. Lincoln to Levi Davis, March 15, 1838, *CW* 1: 116.

60. Several observers noted Lincoln's penchant for slipshod legal work during the Stuart years; see Townsend, "Stuart and Lincoln," 85; see also Spiegel, *A. Lincoln, Esquire*, 24; and Duff, *A. Lincoln*, 79. The Englishman incident is related in Whitney, *Life on the Circuit*, 56–57.

61. Herndon, *Herndon's Lincoln*, 149; the case involving the coat was *Ely v. Edmund R. Wiley and Co.*, October 1838, LLP.

62. Herndon implied that Lincoln had neglected the practice during this period; see Herndon, *Herndon's Lincoln*, 178.

63. Lincoln to John T. Stuart, January 20, 1841, *CW* 1: 228; see also his letter to Stuart on January 23, 1841, *CW* 1: 229. Spiegel, *A. Lincoln*, 24, suggests from this letter that Lincoln may have been having second thoughts about his law career, but there is little evidence of this; on the general subject of Lincoln's depressions, see Joshua W. Shenk's excellent treatment in *Lincoln's Melancholy: How Depression Challenged a President and Fueled His Greatness* (Boston: Houghton Mifflin, 2005).

64. Herndon, *Herndon's Lincoln,* 210; Stephen T. Logan, interview with William H. Herndon, [1865–66], *HI,* 468; Linder, *Early Bench and Bar of Illinois,* 158.

65. See, for example, *Allen v. Maxey,* July 1840, LLP; *Atwood et al. v. Links,* June 1840, LLP; *Bailey v. Cromwelland McNagton,* September 1839, LLP; *Ball et al. v. Lockridge et al.* July 1839, LLP; *Bell v. Mitchell,* September 1839, LLP.

66. *People v. Truett,* October 1838, LLP.

67. Logan quote in "Stephen Logan Talks about Abraham Lincoln," 2; this sort of arrangement between partners, whereby one focused on rhetoric, the other research, was apparently not at all unusual; see, for example, the partnership between Henry Smith and Nathaniel Mook, described in Alden Chester, *Courts and Lawyers of New York: A History, 1609–1925,* 3 vols. (New York: American Historical Society, 1925), 3: 1012.

68. Stephenson, *Lincoln,* 46, characterized the Logan years as his "true student period"; Luthin, *Real Abraham Lincoln,* 67, made a similar claim, as did Woldman, *Lawyer Lincoln,* 39–40; but Frank, *Lincoln as a Lawyer,* 12–13, disagrees, arguing that there is little direct evidence of Logan's having played such a role; I tend to find a middle ground here, as suggested in the text.

69. Linder, *Early Bench and Bar of Illinois,* 158, quotes Logan as observing that Lincoln was not familiar with "the common affairs of ordinary life," but the context of these remarks is too vague to draw conclusions; see "Stephen Logan Talks about Abraham Lincoln," 3.

70. Linder, *Early Bench and Bar of Illinois,* 155. Woldman, *Lawyer Lincoln,* 45, speculates that Logan and Lincoln had personality clashes, but there is little evidence to support this; Herndon, *Herndon's Lincoln,* 211, likewise implies an "acrimonious" relationship between Lincoln and Logan because of political jealousies; but again there is no corroborating evidence.

71. "Stephen Logan Talks about Abraham Lincoln," 5.

72. There are a variety of theories concerning why Lincoln chose Herndon as a partner; see Donald, *Lincoln's Herndon,* 20–21; Woldman, *Lawyer Lincoln,* 51; and Duff, *A. Lincoln,* 98.

73. Herndon, *Herndon's Lincoln,* 211.

74. *Ibid.*

75. For this sketch of Herndon's early life, I have relied on Herndon, *Herndon's Lincoln,* introduction and passim; Whitney, *Life on the Circuit with Lincoln,* 400–405; the best secondary source is still David Donald's seminal biography, *Lincoln's Herndon,* ch. 1.

76. See generally Herndon, *Herndon's Lincoln,* ch. 3–4; I have generally followed Donald's characterization of their relationship, as well; see Donald, *Lincoln's Herndon,* ch. 2–3; and his more recent analysis in *We Are Lincoln Men: Abraham Lincoln and His Men* (New York: Simon and Schuster, 2003), 65–73.

77. Jesse W. Weik, *The Real Lincoln: A Portrait* (Lincoln: University of Nebraska Press, 2002), 301.

78. Herndon, *Herndon's Lincoln,* 268.

79. *Ibid.,* 468, 470.

80. Russell Godbey, interview with William H. Herndon, [1865–66], *HI,* 450.

Chapter 2: The Brethren

1. Manuscript, U.S. Census, Sangamon County, 1850; on the large number of lawyers in general, see Friedman, *American Law,* 268.

2. *Sangamon Journal,* August 27, 1841; *Illinois Daily Journal,* January 9, 1850.

3. Lincoln, Lyceum Address, January 27, 1838, *CW* 1: 108.

4. Jesse Higgins, "Sampson against the Philistines (Philadelphia, 1805)," in Dennis R. Nolan, ed., *Readings in the History of the American Legal Profession* (Indianapolis: Michie, 1980), 95.

5. See generally Charles M. Cook, *The American Codification Movement: A Study of Antebellum Legal Reform* (Westport, Conn.: Greenwood Press, 1981); Jarvis, "Anecdotal History of the Bar Exam," 377; Gawalt, "Massachusetts Lawyers," 110–14 and passim; also Maxwell Bloomfield, "Lawyers and Public Criticism: Challenge and Response in Nineteenth-Century America," *American Journal of Legal History* 15 (1971): 269–70.

6. Massachusetts had a statewide bar association structure in place as far back as 1764, but it ran into problems with the state legislature and democracy-minded reformers; see Gerard W. Gawalt, "Massachusetts Lawyers: A Historical Analysis of the Process of Professionalization, 1760–1840" (Ph.D. diss., Clark University, 1977), 17, and passim. Brent, "Arkansas Bar in the Age of Sectionalism," 76–86, discusses an interesting early attempt to create a state bar association in that community, but it seems to have quickly collapsed.

7. Gawalt, "Massachusetts Lawyers," 110; Lincoln chairs bar association meeting, April 11, 1845, LLP; *Illinois State Register,* January 1, 1859, in LLP; for similar bar association tasks in other states, see Kilbourn, *Bench and Bar of Litchfield County, Connecticut,* 139.

8. On the problems local and state bar associations encountered on this score, see Gawalt, "Massachusetts Lawyers," esp. ch. 2, 3, and 5; Friedman, *American Law,* 282–83.

9. Reference entries for law office, LLP; also Paul M. Angle, "Where Lincoln Practiced Law," *Lincoln Centennial Association Papers* (1927): 22–28.

10. "Lincoln's Law Library," *Lincoln Lore,* February 17, 1941; William H. Townsend, "Lincoln's Law Books," *American Bar Association Journal* (March 1929): 125–26; Browne, *Everyday Life of Abraham Lincoln,* 223; *People v. Anderson and Anderson,* November 1856, LLP.

11. Angle, "Where Lincoln Practiced Law," 41; Weik, *Real Lincoln,* 104–6; Gibson W. Harris, "My Recollections of Abraham Lincoln," *Farm and Fireside,* December 1, 1904.

12. See generally Rotundo, *American Manhood*, ch. 9.

13. For a good general description of the home and its furnishings, see Jean H. Baker, *Mary Todd Lincoln: A Biography* (New York: W. W. Norton, 1987), ch. 5; New Yorker quote on 116.

14. Herndon, *Herndon's Lincoln*, 255.

15. *Ibid.*, 256; Browne, *Everyday Life of Abraham Lincoln*, 220–21.

16. "Poke easy" quote in Milton Hay to Mary Hay, April 6, 1862, Hay-Stuart Papers, Lincoln Library Manuscripts Collection; Herndon, *Herndon's Lincoln*, 52, 256, 282, 494–95.

17. Herndon, *Herndon's Lincoln*, 256.

18. *Ibid.*, 269.

19. See, for example, Foote's characterization of lawyer George Coalter in Foote, *Bench and Bar*, 74.

20. Comments here are based on illustrations of the various courthouses in LLP.

21. For a good general discussion of the courthouse and its development as a physical space, see Martha J. McNamara, "Disciplining Justice: Massachusetts Courthouses and the Legal Profession, 1750–1850" (Ph.D. diss., Boston University, 1995).

22. *Bench and Bar of South Carolina*, 414; "unadorned" quote in Kilbourn, *Bench and Bar of Litchfield, Connecticut*, 27; see also comments at 28; for similar sentiments, see also Palmer, *Recollections of John M. Palmer*, 28; Right Hon. Viscount Alverstone, *Recollections of Bar and Bench*, 4th ed. (London: Edward Arnold, 1915), 15.

23. Foote, *Bench and Bar*, 5.

24. *Bench and Bar of South Carolina*, 192; Ward, "Legal Profession," 165.

25. Daniel Webster to Thomas Abbott Merrill, November 11, 1803, *Legal Papers of Daniel Webster*, 1: 21–22.

26. Linder, 264; *Bench and Bar of South Carolina*, 419; Foote, *Bench and Bar*, 213; Kilbourn, *Bench and Bar of Litchfield, Connecticut*, 96; Alderson, *Courts and Lawyers of New York*, 3: 1272.

27. *Bench and Bar of South Carolina*, 197, 414; Linder, 26.

28. Henry C. Whitney to William H. Herndon (with Swett's description enclosed), August 29, 1887, *HI*, 636.

29. Henry C. Whitney to Jesse W. Weik, September 17, 1887, *HI*, 644; Herndon, *Herndon's Lincoln*, 273; Isaac N. Arnold, *Life of Abraham Lincoln*, 84.

30. On these points, see generally Michael Burlingame, *The Inner World of Abraham Lincoln* (Urbana: University of Illinois Press, 1994); Donald, *"We Are Lincoln Men"*, esp. preface and ch. 1.

31. See, for example, the description of Arkansas circuit riding in Brent, "Arkansas Bar in the Age of Sectionalism," 19–20; and Missouri circuit riding in English, "Pioneer Lawyer and Jurist in Missouri," 65.

32. For other circuits, see, for example, Alderson, *Courts and Lawyers of New York,* 3: 1249.

33. See generally Whitney, *Life on the Circuit with Lincoln,* 53, 55; Herndon, *Herndon's Lincoln,* 280; Weik, *Real Lincoln,* 189–90; and Isaac N. Arnold, *The Life of Abraham Lincoln* (Lincoln: University of Nebraska Press, 1994; originally published in 1886), 339.

34. Whitney, *Life on the Circuit with Lincoln,* 63; Duff, *A. Lincoln,* 179; see also Linder, *Early Bench and Bar,* 183.

35. Linder, *Early Bench and Bar,* 41,111; *Bench and Bar of South Carolina,* 156–57.

36. *Bench and Bar of South Carolina,* 291; Whitney, *Life on the Circuit with Lincoln,* 62–64, 69

37. Robert L. Wilson to William H. Herndon, February 10, 1866, *HI,* 205; statistics are from reference section on cases by county, LLP.

38. Linder, *Early Bench and Bar,* 182.

39. Herndon, *Herndon's Lincoln,* 280; also Whitney, *Life on the Circuit with Lincoln,* 63–64, 100.

40. Based on data in the reference section, LLP; I base these numbers on cases litigated in all the various counties that made up the circuit from 1839 to 1861; according to extant data, Lincoln (or his partners) litigated 2,302 cases in Sangamon county and 1,492 cases in the counties that, at one time or another, made up the Eighth Circuit; I have excluded cases from the First Judicial Circuit, in which Lincoln litigated some cases early in his career (before the Eighth was organized); also, I qualify this with the term "around 40 percent" because, as the editors of the LLP point out, courthouse fires and other accidents destroyed records in several of these counties.

41. Herndon, *Herndon's Lincoln,* 344.

42. Duff, *A. Lincoln,* 177; Woldman, *Lawyer Lincoln,* 96; similar observations could be found in Burlingame, *Inner Life of Abraham Lincoln,* 319–20.

43. Herndon, *Herndon's Lincoln,* 348–50; "sea" quote on 348; also Donald, *Lincoln's Herndon,* 354–56.

44. Alteration in Herndon, *Herndon's Lincoln,* 344; last quote on 249 (emphasis added).

45. Herndon, *Herndon's Lincoln,* 149; Lamon, *Recollections of Abraham Lincoln,* 14–15.

46. Swett to William H. Herndon, January 17, 1866, *HI,* 167.

47. Whitney, *Life on the Circuit with Lincoln,* 1–4 and passim; Henry C. Whitney to William H. Herndon, June 23, 1887, *HI,* 617.

48. Henry C. Whitney, statement to William H. Herndon, c. 1887, *HI,* 647–48; Henry C. Whitney to William H. Herndon, August 27, 1887, *HI,* 631; Voorhees information from biographical sketch by T. B. Long in *Forty Years of Oratory,* 2 vols. (Indianapolis, Bowen-Merrill, 1898).

49. See generally Willard L. King, *David Davis, Lincoln's Campaign Manager* (Chicago: University of Chicago Press, 1974); Herndon, *Herndon's Lincoln,* 280–84; Whitney, interview with William H. Herndon, c. 1887, *HI,* 648.

50. Herndon, *Herndon's Lincoln,* 283; Swett, interview with Jesse W. Weik, c. 1887–89, *HI,* 732.

51. Henry Clay Tilton, "Lincoln and Lamon: Partners and Friends," *Transactions of the Illinois State Historical Association* (1931): 180; Whitney, *Life on the Circuit with Lincoln,* 78.

52. Herndon, *Herndon's Lincoln,* 283.

53. Henry C. Whitney, interview with William H. Herndon, c. 1887, *HI,* 647; Whitney, *Life on the Circuit with Lincoln,* 152.

54. The Lincoln Legal Papers database lists 321 cases in which Lincoln served as a judge; in the LLP's statistical reference guide, however, it puts the number at 320.

55. Whitney, *Life on the Circuit with Lincoln,* 179.

56. Jonathan Birch, interview with William H. Herndon, c. 1887, *HI,* 727–28.

57. Whitney to Herndon, August 27, 1887, *HI,* 632; Swett to William H. Herndon, January 17, 1866, *HI,* 165–66, 168; Whitney to William H. Herndon, August 23, 1887, *HI,* 626.

58. Herndon, *Herndon's Lincoln,* 247. Lincoln also claimed to be consumptive and thus averse to big city life.

Chapter 3: Promissory Notes

1. See bond signed by Lincoln and Berry to keep tavern, March 1833, LLP; also *Watkins v. Lincoln and Berry,* December 1833, LLP; sources generally agreed that Berry was of a low character; see, for example, statement of Abner Y. Ellis, January 23, 1866, *HI,* 170 (though other parts of Ellis's story concerning the Berry store are clearly false).

2. William C. Greene, interview with William H. Herndon, May 30, 1865, *HI,* 20.

3. Lincoln autobiography written for John L. Scripps, c. June 1860, *CW* 4: 65–66; *Watkins v. Lincoln and Berry* December 1833, LLP; appeal to Sangamon County Circuit Court in April 1834, LLP.

4. *Sangamon Journal,* June 28, 1832.

5. *Ibid.,* December 15, June 21, and June 28, 1832.

6. *VanBergen v. Lincoln et al.,* April 1834, LLP; Hardin Bale to William H. Herndon, May 29, 1865, *HI,* 13; James Short to William H. Herndon, July 7, 1865, *HI,* 74; also brief biographical sketch of Van Bergen at *HI,* 774. William Greene claimed that he had paid the entire debt, and that Lincoln lost his surveying equipment because of "some of the other debts"; but this conflicts with the court evidence cited above, and to my mind casts the rest of Greene's story about the Berry store into doubt; William Greene to William H. Herndon, May 30, 1865, *HI,* 20.

7. J. Rowan Herndon to William H. Herndon, May 28, 1865, *HI,* 7.

8. *Ibid.*, 90.

9. See, for example, *VanBergen for Use of Speed et al.*, November 1842, LLP; *Gray for Use of VanBergen et al.*, August 1852, LLP; *VanBergen v. Ball and Long*, March 1841 and July 1841, LLP; *VanBergen v. H. M. Armstrong and Co.*, March 1839, LLP; see also Wilson, *Honor's Voice*, 99.

10. On the national economy's general dependence on credit, see Balleisen, *Failure*, 5; on lack of money on the frontier, see Warren, *Lincoln's Youth*, 123.

11. Herndon, *Herndon's Lincoln*, 88–89.

12. Clark, *Roots of Rural Capitalism*, 214–16; David A. Skeel, *Debt's Dominion: A History of Bankruptcy Law in America* (Princeton: Princeton University Press, 2001), 151; Bruce H. Mann, *Republic of Debtors: Bankruptcy in the Age of American Independence* (Cambridge: Harvard University Press, 2002), 137–46; quote in Bertram Wyatt-Brown, *Southern Honor*, 23.

13. Charles Sellers, *The Market Revolution: Jacksonian America, 1815–1846* (Cambridge: Oxford University Press, 1991), 87–88; Clark, *Roots of Rural Capitalism*, 218–19; see also Mann, *Republic of Debtors*, 59, 110, and Balleisen, *Navigating Failure*, 166; and Peter Coleman, *Debtors and Creditors in America: Insolvency, Imprisonment for Debt, and Bankruptcy, 1607–1900* (New York: Beard Books, 1999), 42–45, 60–62, 248.

14. *Illinois State Journal*, February 19, 1850.

15. Coleman, *Debtors and Creditors*, xi, 42–45, 117–18.

16. Christopher Clark, *The Roots of Rural Capitalism: Western Massachusetts, 1780–1860* (Ithaca: Cornell University Press, 1990), 200.

17. Clark, *Roots of Rural Capitalism*, ch. 6; Edward J. Balleisen, *Navigating Failure: Bankruptcy and Commercial Society in Antebellum America* (Chapel Hill: University of North Carolina Press, 2001), ch. 3; Mann, *Republic of Debtors*, 259–60.

18. Blackstone, *Commentaries*, 2: 466, 470, 474.

19. *Ibid.*, 2: 467.

20. Although conclusive data are lacking, debt collection seems to have been a fairly common foundation for American lawyers' careers; see, for example, Kaufman, *Dred Scott's Advocate*, 37; early correspondence of John Stuart, 1829–31, in John Todd Stuart Papers, Lincoln Library Manuscripts Collection; and English, "Pioneer Lawyer and Jurist in Missouri," 110; also, my own research into the career of Texas attorney Nathaniel Hart Davis bears this out; see Dirck, "'Right and Ready,'" 10–24.

21. Based on database search, debtor and creditor heading in which Lincoln was listed as an attorney in the extent files, LLP.

22. Data search from January through December 1837 and January through December 1842, LLP, omitting cases in which Lincoln's name was not mentioned or in which the nature of lawsuit was unclear.

23. The exceptions were *Burrass v. Hewitt*, October 1842, LLP; *Donaldson v. Bailey*, June 1842, LLP; *Doughty v. Campbell*, November 1842, LLP; *H. E. Bridge and Co. v. Clark*, November 1842, LLP; *Hill v. Yocum and Ferguson*, November

1842, LLP; *Hummer v. Mcgraw,* October 1842, LLP; *Jayne v. Smedley,* June 1842, LLP; *Pence v. Jewett and Hitchcock,* November 1842, LLP; *Saunders for the use of Ford v. Busher,* July 1842, LLP; *State Bank of Illinois v. Corwith,* November 1842, LLP; *State Bank of Illinois v. Silverburgh,* November 1842, LLP; *Taylor v. Wash,* November 1842, LLP.

24. The exceptions were *Fitch et al. v. Pinckard et al.,* April 1842, LLP; *Gains v. West,* November 1842, LLP; *Grable v. Margrave,* July 1842, LLP; *Payne and Alexander v. Frazier and Frazier,* December 1842, LLP; *People ex. rel. Harris et al. v. Browne,* October 1842, LLP; *People v. Babbitt,* June 1842, LLP; *People v. Charles,* June 1842, LLP; *People v. Charles and Busey,* June 1842, LLP.

25. *Logan v. Garth,* September 1842, and *Logan v. Wilbourn,* September 1842, LLP; there were also three other cases in 1841 when Logan used Lincoln in a similar fashion; *Logan v. Payne,* July 1841, *Logan v. Whitney,* July 1841, and *Logan v. Grubb,* November 1841, LLP.

26. See, for example, *Garrett et al. v. State Bank of Illinois,* July 1842, LLP; *Brown et al. v. Montgomery et al.,* December 1842, LLP; *State Bank of Illinois v. Corwith,* November 1842, LLP; *State Bank of Illinois v. Silverburgh,* November 1842, LLP.

27. *Hardin v. Ralston,* November 1842, LLP.

28. *Grant v. Combs,* April 1857, LLP.

29. *Woodworth v. Cox,* April 1854, LLP.

30. *James Bell and Co. v. Elkin,* July 1839, LLP; for similar cases, see, for example, *Burt Bros. and Co. v. H. Bell and Co.,* March 1858, LLP; *Butler v. Grubb,* November 1845, LLP; *Butler v. Reed,* March 1846, LLP.

31. These conclusions are based on a general data search for cases involving negotiable instruments and identifiable attorney's fees, with Lincoln as an attorney of record in the LLP; note that these are generalizations only; the extant records make it very difficult to be precise.

32. Numbers here based on search string in LLP, identifying Lincoln as the attorney of record, for defendant and plaintiff, subsumed under the "debtor and creditor" heading.

33. The classic work here of course is Morton J. Horwitz, *The Transformation of American Law, 1780–1860* (Cambridge: Harvard University Press, 1979); Sellers, *Market Revolution,* 47; see also Steiner, "Learning from Lincoln," esp. 432.

34. *Billington v. Cannon,* March 1854, LLP; *Billington v. Mattlen,* May 1853, LLP.

35. Balleisen, *Navigating Failure,* 28.

36. A. W. B. Simpson, *A History of the Common Law of Contract: The Rise of the Action of Assumpsit* (Oxford: Clarendon Press, 1973), 3–5.

37. *Goddin v. Richmond,* September 1842, LLP.

38. *Hart v. Dean,* October 1856, LLP.

39. *Bryan v. Smith,* October 1837, LLP.

40. On the legal and business definition of a promissory note, see Mann, *Republic of Debtors*, 11.

41. For similar cases, see, for example, *Brown v. Allin*, October 1839, LLP.

42. See, for example, *Bevan v. Davis*, May 1859, LLP.

43. See, for example, *Carlin for use of Sangamon County, Illinois v. Calhoun et al.*, November 1846, LLP.

44. *Alexander v. Parrish*, May 1851, LLP; *Bailey v. Robbins*, April 1838, LLP; unfortunately, the extant documents do not indicate how Lincoln made the jurisdiction argument.

45. See generally Mann, *Republic of Debtors*, 168–69, 255–56; Skeel, *Debtor's Dominion*, 23–27, 31; Coleman, *Debtors and Creditors in America*, 35.

46. The cases were *Atwood et al. v. Links*, June 1840, LLP; *Brown et al. v. Little*, December 1841, LLP; *Gould et al. v. Allen*, June 1840, LLP; *Hooper, Martin, and Smith v. Haines and Son*, December 1839, LLP; *Montelius and Fuller v. Blankenship*, December 1841, LLP; *Porter v. Porter*, June 1840, LLP; *W. and C. Fellows v. Kellar and Snyder*, December 1841, LLP.

47. Data search for bankruptcy cases, LLP; *in re Craw*, October 1842, LLP.

48. See generally Skeel, *Debt's Dominion*, 3, 26–31; Mann, *Republic of Debtors*, 255.

49. That case was *in re Legier*, June 1843, LLP.

50. Lincoln to Frederick A. Thomas, July 11, 1842, *CW* 1: 290; *in re Gambrel*, March 1842, LLP; during its brief existence, the Act of 1841 did become a lucrative moneymaker for some American lawyers, however; see Skeel, *Debt's Dominion*, 34.

51. Data searches for 1853, 1856, 1858, LLP; note these numbers do not include a case in which the precise outcome cannot be ascertained from the extant records; see *Tinsley v. Masterson*, March 1853, LLP; Lincoln to James W. Somers, June 19, 1858, *CW* 2: 469–70.

52. *McCollom v. Allen*, May 1856, LLP; see also Mann, *Debtor*, 20–22, on debtors' use of litigation as a delaying tactic.

53. *Ayers v. Griffin et al.*, September 1847, LLP.

54. *Fairbairn v. Potts*, December 1820, LLP.

55. *Barrett v. Spear*, November 1840, LLP; *Atwood, Cole, and Crane v. Cosby*, March 1846, LLP.

56. Data search, 1,842 cases involving creditor and debtor with Lincoln as an attorney of record, LLP.

57. Dozens of cases could be cited for each of these types of debt litigation; typical examples are *Clemons v. Allen*, March 1853, LLP; *Chambers and Garvin v. Maxey*, October 1837, LLP; *Elder v. Nigh and Perce*, November 1854, LLP; *Wright for use of Davidson v. Bennett and Bennett*, June 1845, LLP.

58. See, for example, *Center v. Whitney*, January 1838, LLP; *Bacon v. Ohio and Mississippi R.R.*, March 1856, LLP; *Campbell v. McCoy and Blatchford*, March

1859, LLP; *Columbus Machine Manufacturing Co. et al. v. E. R. Ulrich and Co.,* April 1859, LLP; *Hayward v. Perley et al.,* March 1845, LLP; *Hoffman v. Wernwag,* November 1839, LLP; *Lockwood v. Wernwag,* November 1839, LLP; *Radcliff et al. v. Crosby and Waggoner,* October 1858, LLP; *Scott v. Winkel and Scott,* November 1854, LLP; *Bennett v. Radford,* March 1838, LLP.

59. *Sangamon Journal,* November 10, 1831, July 5, 1832, December 29, 1832, June 14, 1832; on the general practice of creditors and debtors avoiding litigation, see Mann, *Debtor,* 18.

60. Lincoln to R. S. Thomas, August 24, 1854, *CW* 2: 226; Notes for a Law Lecture, [July 1, 1850], *CW* 2: 81; the 380 figure is based on a search query in LLP involving the heading "settlement" with debtor and creditor cases in which Lincoln appeared as an attorney of record, yielding 383 cases.

61. Lincoln to Peter Ambos, June 21, 1859, *CW* 3: 386–87; Lincoln to Samuel Galloway, July 27, 1859, *CW* 3: 393.

62. Foote, *Bench and Bar,* 74.

63. Henry S. Foote, *The Bench and Bar of the South and Southwest* (New York: William S. Hein, 1994; originally published in 1876), 207.

64. Higgins, "Sampson against the Philistines," 96.

65. Foote, *Bench and Bar,* 54–55. Interestingly, some lawyers acquired a reputation as friendly to debtors, in an altruistic fashion; see, for example, the description of New York lawyer Benjamin Smith in Alderson, *Courts and Lawyers of New York,* 3: 1062–63.

66. Foote, *Bench and Bar,* 56.

67. See generally Austin Sarat and William L. F. Felstiner, "Law and Social Relations: Vocabularies of Motive in the Lawyer-Client Interaction," *Law and Society Review* 22 (1988): 737–54, and "Lawyers and Legal Consciousness: Law Talk in the Divorce Lawyers Office," *Yale Law Review* 98 (1989): 1663–87; and Roy B. Fleming, "Client Games: Defense Attorney Perspectives on Their Relations with Criminal Clients," *American Bar Association Research Journal* (1986): 253–70.

68. Harrison v. Greer, January 1859, LLP; *Purvance for Use of Warren and Carothers,* May 1864, LLP; *Blane v. Strawbridge,* June 1842, LLP.

69. *Thompson v. Crane,* March 1859, LLP.

70. Lincoln to Joseph Galloway, July 27, 1859, *CW* 3: 393–94.

71. *Shields v. Matthews et al.,* October 1854, LLP; *Allin v. Douglas,* May 1840, LLP; *Atwood and Jones v. Douglas and Wright,* November 1839, LLP. On the Speed-related litigation see the variety of cases involving James Bell and Co., LLP; also *Speed v. Boice,* March 1843, LLP; *Speed v. Branson and Branson,* November 1843, LLP; and *VanBergen for use of Speed and Others et al.,* November 1842, LLP.

72. Lincoln to Joshua F. Speed, February 3, 1842, *CW* 1: 267; and February 13, 1842, *CW* 1: 269; a good accounting of their friendship may be found in David Donald, *"We Are Lincoln Men": Abraham Lincoln and His Friends* (New York: Simon and Schuster, 2003), 29–64.

73. Lincoln to Joshua Speed, May 18, 1843, *CW* 1: 323; and October 22, 1846, *CW* 1: 390–91.

74. Data search for 1857, LLP; these numbers do not include cases in which Lincoln's name does not appear as an attorney of record, or cases in which the nature of the litigation is unclear; also, this does not include several cases in which Lincoln served as a judge during the proceedings; Frank, *Lincoln as a Lawyer,* 41, made similar observations about Lincoln's later practice.

75. *Backhouse v. Grider,* May 1857, LLP; *Colean v. Davis,* October 1857, LLP; *Constant v. McDaniel,* August 1857, LLP; *Elliott v. Cassidy,* October 1857, LLP; *Miller v. Melton,* May 1857, LLP; *Miller v. Pinkley,* October 1857, LLP; *Newlin v. Roberts and Fleming,* August 1857, LLP; *Rager for use of Wilcox v. Rhea and Rhea,* April 1857, LLP; *Stephenson v. Moore et ux.,* October 1857, LLP; *Tappert v. Ives and McIntire,* October 1857, LLP; *Quinn v. Thompson,* May 1857, LLP; *Tonica and Petersburg Railroad v. Myers,* November 1857, LLP; *Williams v. Booth et al.,* May 1857, LLP; *Wilson and Parks v. Fisher,* May 1857, LLP; these cases do not include several cases in 1857 whereby Herndon was a litigant in a debt-related matter; 1860 data based on search entry, debtor and creditor cases, in which Lincoln was an attorney of record, LLP.

76. Lincoln may also have been aware that his beloved stepmother's first husband had serious debt problems, too; see Warren, *Lincoln's Youth,* 61.

77. Whitney, *Circuit,* 83; Herndon, *Herndon's Lincoln,* 279; a rare exception was an incident in 1833, when Lincoln cosigned a promissory note with Nelson Ally, and was sued with Ally for failure to pay; the precise circumstances of this matter are unclear: see *Henry for Use of McCandless and Emmerson v. Ally and Lincoln,* September 1833, LLP.

Chapter 4: The Energy Men

1. See generally Winkle, *The Young Eagle,* 270–73; and Paul M. Angle, *"Here I Have Lived": A History of Lincoln's Springfield, 1821–1865* (New Brunswick, N.J.: Rutgers University Press, 1950); and Donald, *Lincoln,* 67.

2. The foregoing sketch of Reed's life and personality was derived from *History of Sangamon County, Illinois, 1881* (Chicago: Inter-State, 1881), 853; C. F. McGlashan, *History of the Donner Party: Tragedy of the Sierra,* (San Francisco: A. Carlisle, 1922), ch. 4; also George R. Stewart, *Ordeal by Hunger: The Story of the Donner Party* (Boston: Houghton Mifflin, 1988), 16–18.

3. *Butler v. Reed,* March 1846, LLP.

4. *Burkhardt v. Reed,* November 1842, LLP; *Doyle v. Reed,* November 1843, LLP; *Butler v. Reed,* November and March 1843, LLP; *Reed and Radford v. Phillips et al.,* July 1840, LLP.

5. Alexis de Tocqueville, *Democracy in America* (New York: Signet Books, 2001), 28–42.

6. *Ibid.,* 87.

7. Manuscript records, Sangamon County, 1840 and 1850; Allen information in John Power, *History of the Early Settlers of Sangamon County, Illinois* (Springfield: E. A. Wilson, 1876), 79; Cutler and Bunn information from their obituaries in the *Illinois State Journal,* January 5, 1880, and October 17, 1897; additional Bunn information from Bruce Campbell, *The Sangamon Saga: 200 Years: An Illustrated Bicentennial History of Sangamon County* (Springfield: Phillips Brothers, 1976), 81; Spear information from *Illinois Daily Journal,* October 30, 1852; in addition, I found very useful reference information for this individuals in the "biographies" section of the LLP.

8. *Allen v. Allen,* September 1855, LLP; other information based on search parameters of Lincoln appearing as attorney of record in cases involving one the individuals named here; Arbitration Award in Dispute, December 6, 1851, *CW* 2: 114; see also www.alincoln-library.com/Apps/learn/Articles-1833–October .asp?Month=October&Year=1833.

9. Arbitration Award in Dispute, December 6, 1851, *CW* 2: 114; *VanBergen v. Singleton,* February 1860, LLP.

10. *Taylor and Arnold v. Robinson et al.,* November 1854, LLP.

11. *Hawks v. Lands,* September 1841 (McLean circuit court case) and December 1846 (Illinois Supreme Court case), LLP; biographical information on Hawks at http://www.rootsweb.com/ilmclean/2002/Data/Biographies/gtm-pages /314–318.htm.

12. *Knight v. Carter et al.,* May 1855, LLP.

13. Blackstone, *Commentaries,* 2: 442–43.

14. *Hildreth v. Gill,* September 1858, LLP; *Hood v. Gray,* March 1840, LLP; *Phelps v. McGee,* May 1856 and May 1858, LLP; also *Phelps v. McGee* (Illinois Supreme Court case), December 1856, LLP.

15. *Buckner et al. v. Hamilton,* May 1855, LLP; also *Buckner et al. v. Hamilton,* June 1855 (appeal), LLP.

16. *Hamilton v. Pekin, Illinois,* May 1853, LLP; *O. B. Tweedy and Co. v. Hamilton and Dugger,* June 1858, LLP; *Hamilton v. Haines et al.,* October 1854, LLP.

17. "Penniless" quote in Lincoln to Martin S. Morris, March 26, 1843, *CW* 1: 320.

18. Lincoln, Communication to the People of Sangamon County, March 9, 1832, *CW* 1: 5.

19. Herndon, *Herndon's Lincoln,* 140; Gabor Boritt, *Lincoln and the Economics of the American Dream,* 2nd ed. (Urbana: University of Illinois Press, 1994), 11.

20. Lincoln to John T. Stuart, January 20, 1840, *CW* 1: 185; and Boritt, *Lincoln and the Economics of the American Dream,* ch. 3 and passim.

21. See generally John Launtz Larson, *Internal Improvement: National Public Works and the Promise of Popular Government in the Early United States* (Chapel Hill: University of North Carolina Press, 2001); Sellers, *Market Revolution,* esp.

ch. 5–6; Harry Watson, *Liberty and Power: Jacksonian America* (New York: Hill and Wang, 1990); Stanley I. Kutler, *Privilege and Creative Destruction: The Charles River Bridge Case,* 2nd ed. (Baltimore: Johns Hopkins University Press, 1990); and Davis, *Frontier Illinois,* 229–35.

22. Act of the Illinois State Legislature, January 12, 1835, *CW* 1: 32.

23. *Adams v. Woodford County, Illinois,* June 1853, LLP.

24. *Cullom et al. v. Hawley,* November 1850, LLP; *Gibson et al. v. Hawley,* October 1850, LLP; *Mather, Lamb and Co. v. Hawley et al.,* September 1845, LLP; biographical information on Hawley found at http://www.ci.pekin.il.us /Administration/compplan/2001COMPPLANFIN AL.PDF; for similar lawsuits, see *Jennings v. Woodford County, Illinois,* September 1852 and April 1853, LLP.

25. *Beam and Skinner v. Buckles,* March 1858, LLP.

26. *People v. Young,* November 1846, LLP; *People v. Abel,* December 1846, LLP; *People v. Atterberry,* December 1846, LLP.

27. *In re Killion et al.,* March 1846, and *Judson v. Killion et al.,* March 1846, LLP.

28. Speech on Internal Improvements, June 20, 1848, *CW* 1: 488–89 (emphasis in original).

29. Lincoln to the Commissioner of Patents, March 10, 1849, *CW* 2: 32–35; also Herndon, *Herndon's Lincoln,* 239.

30. Lincoln, Second Lecture on Discoveries and Inventions, February 11, 1859, *CW* 3: 363 (emphases in original).

31. The earliest case in the files of the LLP is *Lewis v. Moffett and Johnson,* August 1849; and *Tunison v. Lewis et al.,* August 1849; the rest occurred in the 1850s.

32. Blackstone, *Commentaries,* 4: 159. William Seward, for example, began litigating patent cases after his practice matured; see Goodwin, *Team of Rivals,* 85.

33. *McCormick v. Talcott et al.,* December 1855, LLP; Herndon, *Herndon's Lincoln,* 285–87; also Duff, *A. Lincoln, Prairie Lawyer,* 323.

34. *Moffett v. Lewis and Johnson,* August 1849 and December 1849 (appeal), LLP; also Susan Krause, "Churning Up Business," *Lincoln Legal Briefs* 65 (January–March 2003): 2.

35. *Hildreth et al. v. Edmunds,* September 1854, LLP, and *Edmunds v. Hildreth et al.* (appeal), December 1854, LLP; Duff, *A. Lincoln,* 260–61.

36. *Bloomington Gas Light and Coke Co. and Charles Herrick v. Robert McCart and Sons and Charles Herrick,* January 1858, LLP; count based on search of LLP, subject "banks and banking" and "insurance," in which Lincoln appeared as one of the attorneys of record.

37. *Illinois Daily Journal,* January 9, 1850.

38. Davis, *Frontier Illinois,* 18–19.

39. See generally John W. Starr, Jr., *Lincoln and the Railroads: A Biographi-*

cal Study (New York: Dodd, 1927); Communication to the People of Sangamon County, March 9, 1832, *CW* 1: 5; Notice of Meeting of Commissioners of the Springfield and Terre Haute Railroad, July 9, 1852, *CW* 2: 133.

40. By way of comparison, Texas attorney William Pitt Ballinger saw a similar evolution in his practice, from early debt and probate cases, to later involvement in more lucrative railroad cases; see John A. Moretta, *William Pitt Ballinger: Texas Lawyer, Southern Statesman, 1825–1888* (Austin: Texas State Historical Association, 2000), esp. 231–45.

41. Report on Alton and Springfield Railroad, August 5, 1847, *CW* 1: 398–405.

42. Lincoln to William Martin, February 19, 1851, *CW* 2: 98–99; February 24, 1851, *CW* 2: 100; March 6, 1851, *CW* 2: 102–3.

43. Lincoln to Isaac Gibson, February 26, 1851, *CW* 2: 101 (emphasis in original); for an excellent overview of this case and the legal issues involved, see William D. Beard, "'I Have Labored Hard to Find the Law': Abraham Lincoln and the Alton and Sangamon Railroad," *Illinois Historical Journal* 85 (Winter 1992), 209–20; *Barret v. Alton and Sangamon Railroad,* November 1851, LLP.

44. *Allen v. Illinois Central Railroad,* October 1855, LLP.

45. *Allen v. Illinois Central Railroad,* March 1859, LLP; *Allen v. Illinois Central Railroad,* July 1864, LLP.

46. See order for change of venue, *Allen v. Illinois Central Railroad,* July 1862, LLP.

47. See Allen's obituary, reproduced at http://www.rootsweb.com/ildewitt /id191.htm.

48. Quote in *Chicago Tribune,* February 12, 1857; *Rock Island Morning Argus,* February 25, 1857, in LLP; "jubilee" quote is from Lincoln's jury charge; see speech to jury in Rock Island Bridge Case, September 22, 1857, *CW* 2: 416.

49. Lincoln, speech to jury in Rock Island Bridge Case, September 22, 1857, *CW* 2: 415–22.

50. *Illinois Daily Register,* September 28, 1857; *Daily Islander and Argus,* March 26, 1858; *Chicago Daily Tribune,* September 26, 1857; *Chicago Daily Democrat,* September 26, 1857.

51. Based on statistical portrait of Lincoln's clients, "peers and clients," reference database, LLP.

52. Herndon, *Herndon's Lincoln,* 284; also *Illinois Central Railroad v. McLean County, Illinois,* September 1853 and December 1855 (appeal), LLP.

53. *Friedlander v. Great Western Railroad,* October 1857, LLP; see also *Bishop v. Illinois Central Railroad,* April 1854, LLP; *Frazier v. Great Western Railroad,* November 1854, LLP; *Gatling et al. v. Great Western Railroad,* November 1857, LLP.

54. I am referring here of course to the "Horwitz thesis"; see Horwitz, *Transformation of American Law*; see also Wythe Holt, "Morton Horwitz and the Transformation of American Legal History," *William and Mary Law Review* 23 (1982): 23–50.

55. Mark Steiner, "Lawyers and Legal Change in Antebellum America: Learning from Lincoln," *University of Detroit Mercy Law Review* 74 (Spring 1997): 427–64, takes Horwitz to task on a variety of points, using Lincoln's law practice as a springboard.

Chapter 5: The Show

1. Quotes from Eliza Poor Donner Houghton, *The Expedition of the Donner Party and Its Tragic Fate,* ch. 5 (e-book text version, www.gutenberg.net); also Stewart, *Ordeal by Hunger,* 17–18, 63–66.

2. Napoleon Murat, *The United States of America,* 1820; quoted in Davis, *Frontier Illinois,* 331; see also John Philip Reid, *Law for the Elephant: Property and Social Behavior on the Overland Trail* (Los Angeles: Huntington Library Press, 1980).

3. See, for example, Tucker, *Trial and Error,* 47–48.

4. Frances Lea McCurdy, *Stump, Bar, and Pulpit: Speechmaking on the Missouri Frontier* (Columbia: University of Missouri Press, 1969), 134–37.

5. Herndon, *Herndon's Lincoln,* 287.

6. *Ibid.,* 331–32.

7. *Ibid.,* 471.

8. *Ibid.,* 282.

9. Lincoln, Address to the Young Men's Lyceum, January 27, 1838, *CW* 1: 115.

10. Herndon in *Herndon's Lincoln,* 275–76.

11. *Thomas v. Wright,* November 1846, LLP. Recent scholarship by Mark Steiner and others at the LLP suggest that Herndon's account was flawed in several respects, most notably the amount of the judgment recovered in the case; see Paul Verduin, "*Rebecca Thomas v. Erastus Wright,*" *Lincoln Legal Briefs* 33 (January–March 1995).

12. *Fleming v. Rogers and Crothers,* March 1858, LLP.

13. Herndon, *Herndon's Lincoln,* 273; Isaac N. Arnold, *Life of Abraham Lincoln,* 84. On Lincoln's general skill with juries, see Woldman, *Lawyer Lincoln,* 46, 128–29; Frank, *Lincoln as a Lawyer,* 23–24; Duff, *A. Lincoln,* 60; also Sandburg, *Lincoln: The Prairie Years,* 43.

14. *Selby v. Dunlap,* March 1854, LLP.

15. David Davis to wife, October 20, 1851, and October 27, 1851, in LLP.

16. Francis Fisher Browne, *The Every-Day Life of Abraham Lincoln* (Lincoln: University of Nebraska Press, 1995), 116; *Fithian v. Casseday,* October 1851, LLP.

17. Lincoln; fragment of Notes for a Law Lecture, [July 1850], *CW* 2: 81.

18. Lawrence M. Friedman, *Crime and Punishment in American History* (New York: Basic Books, 1993), 25–27.

19. *Bench and Bar of South Carolina,* 537; Foote, *Bench and Bar,* 111, 154; Linder, *Early Bench and Bar of Illinois,* 257.

20. Joseph G. Baldwin, *The Flush Times of Alabama and Mississippi: A Series of Sketches* (1854; repr. Baton Rouge: Louisiana State University Press, 1980), 24.

21. Davis, *Frontier Illinois,* 331, cites statistics for Knox County that put the percentage of criminal cases to civil cases at around 20 percent.

22. See generally Davis, *Frontier Illinois,* 335–43.

23. William F. English, "The Pioneer Jurist and Lawyer in Missouri," *University of Missouri Studies* 21 (1947): 10.

24. Kilbourn, *Bench and Bar of Litchfield County, Connecticut,* 328; note the social price William Seward paid in his community when he defended a black man against a murder charge in 1844; see Goodwin, *Team of Rivals,* 85.

25. Relatively few of Lincoln's criminal litigation clients seem to have been granted bail; a conclusion based on database search query, LLP, criminal offenses in which Lincoln was an attorney of record that involved an extant record of bail proceedings; the database indicated thirty-six such cases.

26. See generally David J. Rothman, *The Discovery of the Asylum: Social Order and Disorder in the New Republic* (Boston: Little, Brown, 1971); Norval Norris and David J. Rothman, *The Oxford History of the Prison: The Practice of Punishment in Western Society* (Cambridge: Oxford University Press, 1997); and Friedman, *Crime and Punishment,* 65–68.

27. With regard to the Schuyler county jail, see www.rootsweb.com/ilschuyl/SchuylerCountyHistoricalJail; other jails were similarly situated; see, for example, various descriptions of New York jails in Alderson, *Courts and Lawyers of New York,* 3: 1116–17, and passim.

28. People v. Bosley, May 1855, LLP; *People v. Loe,* August 1852, LLP; *People v. Weaver,* May 1845, LLP.

29. Roy B. Fleming, "Client Games: Defense Attorney's Perspectives on Their Criminal Law Clients," *American Bar Foundation Research Journal* (1986): 263–65.

30. See generally Tucker, *Trial and Error,* 170; Kenneth Mann, *Defending White-Collar Crime: A Portrait of Attorneys at Work* (New Haven, Conn.: Yale University Press, 1985), 39; Fleming, "Client Games," 253–59; Joel Moldovsky and Rose DeWolf, *The Best Defense* (New York: MacMillan, 1975). Abraham S. Blumberg, "The Practice of Law as a Confidence Game: Organization Co-Optation of a Profession," in George F. Cole, ed. *Criminal Justice: Law and Politics* (Belmont, Calif.: Wadsworth, 1993), 214–24, argues that defense attorneys seek this client control as a "double agent," acting in the court system's interests.

31. Blackstone, *Commentaries,* 4:2; Walt Backman, *Law v. Life* (Rhineback, N.Y.: Four Directions, 1995), 115–21.

32. Fleming, "Client Games," 258–61, and passim; see also William F. McDonald, ed., *The Defense Counsel* (Beverly Hills, Calif.: Sage, 1983); and Carl Hossicks, "We Don't Care What Happened, We Only Care about What Is Going to Happen," *Social Problems* 26 (1979).

33. *People v. Bailey,* May 1853, LLP; *People v. Capps,* October 1837, LLP; *Peo-*

ple v. Hollingworth, May 1854, LLP; People v. Allen et al., April 1854, LLP; People v. Camp et al., March 1838, LLP; People v. Brewer, May 1854 and March 1856, LLP; People v. Davis, November 1852, LLP; People v. Brown, November 1852, LLP; People v. Charles, June 1842, LLP.

34. People v. Preston, November 1844, LLP; People v. Spurgeon et al., October 1843, LLP; People v. Shurtliff et al., May 1854 LLP. Woldman, Lawyer Lincoln, 120, has a somewhat different account of this case, based on a recollection in the Herndon-Weik Collection; see Andrew H. Goodpasture, statement to William H. Herndon, March 31, 1869, HI, 572–73; Goodpasture's account, however, seems at odds with the court records concerning the matter of the fine, and his general description seems fanciful enough that I have chosen to disregard this account.

35. Blackstone, Commentaries, 3: 121.

36. Johnson v. Lester, May 1847, LLP; Burt v. Jennings, October 1852, LLP; O'Neal v. Gatten, November 1839, LLP.

37. People v. Thompson, April 1856, LLP.

38. Alderson v. Noland et al., November 1852, LLP; Edmunds v. Simpson et al., July 1841, LLP; Hawthorn v. Wooldridge, October 1836, LLP; Bryan v. Jones, November 1856, LLP; Burt v. Jennings, October 1852, LLP; People v. Patterson, October 1842, LLP; Selby v. Dunlap, March 1854, LLP; Lahr v. Blair, October 1857, LLP; People v. Cordell, May 1838, LLP.

39. See, for example, People v. Beal, October 1855, LLP; People v. Black, April 1859, LLP; People v. Brown, November 1852, LLP; People v. Center, June 1854, LLP; People v. Hollingsworth, April 1859, LLP; People v. Tunison, March 1846, LLP; People v. Williams, November 1853, LLP; Ritchie v. Goodacre, July 1839, LLP; Saunders v. Bell et al., May 1844, LLP; Shipley v. Thomas, May 1847, LLP; Tinker v. Vandeveer et al., June 1841, LLP; Woods v. Ketchum et al., June 1851, LLP; Wooldridge v. Hawthorn, March 1837, LLP.

40. Of the twelve criminal assault cases that went before a jury, Lincoln lost eight (based on LLP database search, heading "assault," in which Lincoln appeared as an attorney of record).

41. People v. Barrett, October 1856, LLP.

42. People v. Patterson, October 1842, LLP.

43. People v. Atkin, October 1839, LLP; People v. McCardle et al., May 1853, LLP; People v. Lane et al., May 1847, LLP.

44. People v. Bohen et al., March 1857, LLP. Friedman, Crime and Punishment, 2, points out that stealing and drinking are the two most common criminal offenses in American history.

45. Mark E. Steiner, "The Lawyer as Peacemaker: Law and Community in Abraham Lincoln's Slander Cases," Journal of the Abraham Lincoln Association 16 (1995): 5.

46. Frost v. Gillenwaters, October 1845, LLP.

47. Boggs v. Overton, April 1844, LLP.

48. Lincoln to Thomas Lincoln and Thomas Johnson, December 24, 1848, *CW* 2: 16; *People v. Johnson,* September 1856, LLP; Henry C. Whitney to William H. Herndon, June 23, 1887, *HI,* 636.

49. On occasion, Lincoln (and/or one of his partners) assisted the state attorney's office in a murder prosecution; see *People v. Denton and Denton,* October 1847, LLP; *People v. Littler,* April 1857, LLP; *People v. Wyant,* April 1857, LLP.

50. *Sangamon Journal,* February 9, 1831; see also Davis, *Frontier Illinois,* 7–8.

51. *Sangamon Journal,* August 11, 1832; *Illinois State Journal,* January 4, 1850, February 7, 8, 9, and 15, 1850, February 28, 1850, March 27, 1850, and April 4, 9, 1850; see also description of murder trial in English, "Pioneer Lawyer and Jurist in Missouri," 79. It is interesting to note how often lawyers themselves liked to highlight their murder trials by way of dramatizing their profession; see, for example, the various descriptions of murder trials in Chester, *Courts and Lawyers of New York,* esp. vol. 3.

52. See James Gourley, interview with William H. Herndon, [1865–66], *HI,* 451.

53. *People v. Truett,* October 1838, LLP. Duff, *A. Lincoln,* ch. 4, gives a somewhat overwrought description of the trial. Lincoln believed there was some political fallout from his and Stuart's participation in the case; see Lincoln to John T. Stuart, March 1, 1840, *CW* 1: 206–7 fn.

54. For a general description of the incident, see Duff, *A. Lincoln,* 352; and Walsh, *Moonlight,* 14–17; court records themselves are found in *People v. Armstrong,* May 1858, LLP.

55. William Wallace to William H. Herndon, June 3, 1865, *HI,* 22.

56. Hannah Armstrong, interview with William H. Herndon, [c. 1866], *HI,* 326; my conclusions here differ from Duff, *A. Lincoln,* 353, who argues that Lincoln "readily consented to lend his efforts toward getting him off"; Woldman, *Lawyer Lincoln,* 121, agrees, citing the lost letter he supposedly sent to Hannah; but the letter is erroneously dated, and its language and characteristics do not look at all like Lincoln's normal correspondence.

57. William Walker to William H. Herndon, June 3, 1865, *HI,* 22; also J. Henry Shaw to William H. Herndon, September 5, 1866, *HI,* 332–33.

58. J. Henry Shaw to William H. Herndon, August 22, 1866, *HI,* 316; a rumor later circulated that Lincoln had practiced a choice bit of courtroom deception by using an almanac from the wrong year, but this was flatly denied by Shaw (who was part of the prosecution's team) and Walker; see Walker to William H. Herndon, August 27, 1866, *HI,* 325; see also Duff, *A. Lincoln,* 358–59, who I think correctly discards the story as an unfounded rumor.

59. William Walker to William H. Herndon, June 3, 1865, *HI,* 23; also J. Henry Shaw to William H. Herndon, September 5, 1866, *HI,* 333.

60. Hannah Armstrong, interview with William H. Herndon, [c. 1866], *HI,* 527; Lincoln to Hannah Armstrong, September 18, 1863, *CW* 6: 462;

61. I refer here of course to John Evangelist Walsh, *Moonlight: Abraham Lin-*

coln and the Almanac Trial (New York: St. Martin's Press, 2000), 2, who argues that the case caused Lincoln to do something "wholly out of character, manipulate the truth," and accuses Lincoln of "witness tampering," "suppression of evidence," and "suborning perjury." Leaving aside the flimsy evidence Walsh marshals for all these assertions, he does not try to establish an antebellum professional context for any of these charges.

62. Swett to William H. Herndon, January 17, 1866, *HI,* 168.

Chapter 6: Death and the Maidens

1. Leonard Swett to William H. Herndon, January 17, 1866, *HI,* 162–69; also Michael Burlingame and John R. Turner Ettlinger, eds., *Inside Lincoln's White House: The Complete Civil War Diary of John Hay* (Carbondale: Southern Illinois University Press, 1997), 128, 193, 247; Lamon, *Recollections of Abraham Lincoln,* ch. 2–3 and passim; and Donald, *"We Are Lincoln Men,"* 65–66.

2. Leonard Swett to William H. Herndon, January 17, 1866, *HI,* 166 (emphasis in original).

3. *Ibid.,* 64.

4. Thomas P. Lowry, *Don't Shoot That Boy! Abraham Lincoln and Military Justice* (New York: Da Capo Press, 1999), 94, 112–13, 142, 180, and passim.

5. Leonard Swett to William H. Herndon, January 17, 1866, *HI,* 166 (emphasis in original); Lamon, *Recollections,* 103.

6. Anonymous to Abraham Lincoln, [December 30, 1861], in Harold Holzer, ed., *Dear Mr. Lincoln: Letters to the President* (Reading, Mass.: Addison Wesley, 1993), 155; Michael Burlingame, ed., *Lincoln Observed: Civil War Dispatches of Noah Brooks* (Baltimore: Johns Hopkins University Press, 1998), 215.

7. Burlingame and Ettlinger, *Inside Lincoln's White House,* 222; Lincoln to Ulysses S. Grant, August 17, 1864, *CW* 7: 499; Lincoln to Thomas H. Clay, October 8, 1862, *CW* 5: 453.

8. Gary Laderman, *The Sacred Remains: American Attitudes toward Death, 1779–1883* (New Haven, Conn.: Yale University Press, 1996), 22–30; quote at 26; also James S. Curl, *The Victorian Celebration of Death* (Detroit: Partridge Press, 1972), ch. 9.

9. Burlingame, *Lincoln Observed,* 215; Lincoln to Phoebe Ellsworth, May 25, 1861, *CW* 4: 385; also Donald, *Lincoln,* 254, 306. On the circumstances surrounding these deaths, see generally Burlingame, *Inner World of Abraham Lincoln,* 94–96.

10. Nathaniel Grigsby to William H. Herndon, September 4, 1865, *HI,* 94; see also his interview with Herndon, September 12, 1865, *HI;* N. W. Branson to William H. Herndon, August 3, 1865, *HI,* 90–91; William G. Greene to William H. Herndon, May 30, 1865, *HI,* 19; see also Sarah Bush Lincoln to William H. Herndon, September 8, 1865, *HI,* 108; Browne, *Everyday Life of Abraham Lincoln,* 159–60.

11. Lincoln, Lyceum Address, January 27, 1838, *CW* 1: 115 (emphasis in original); on his religious fatalism, see generally Allen C. Guelzo, *Abraham Lincoln, Redeemer President* (Grand Rapids, Mich.: William B. Eerdman's, 1999), 325–42 and passim; on his ambition and the role it played in his psychological makeup, see Burlingame, *Inner World of Abraham Lincoln,* ch. 8.

12. *People v. Fraim,* April 1839, LLP.

13. *Connelly and Way v. Van de Velde et al.,* June 1854, LLP.

14. There are 509 extant cases that generally fit this description (based on database search, LLP, subject heading "inheritance," with Lincoln as an attorney of record).

15. *Knapp v. Loutzenhiser,* November 1845, LLP; the Mexican War veterans case is *Ellis et al. v. Trent et al.,* October 1853, LLP; *Lewis v. Breckenridge,* October 1857, LLP.

16. *Peter v. Martin et al.,* October 1841, LLP.

17. See, for example, *Preston et ux. v. Hussey and Hussey,* November 1842, LLP; *Prettyman v. Carlisle et al.,* April 1857, LLP.

18. Number based on database search, LLP, "inheritance-dower," with Lincoln as an attorney of record; *Alexander et al. v. Danielle et al.,* March 1855, LLP; for typical guardianship case, see *Banta v. Banta et al.,* September 1856, LLP.

19. *Babcock v. Black et al.,* October 1860, LLP; *Irwin v. Stevens,* April 1857, LLP; *Marsh v. Wernwag,* November 1839, LLP.

20. See generally Laderman, *Sacred Remains,* 9, 22–30, 69–76; also Robert W. Haberstein and William M. Lamers, *The History of American Funeral Directing,* 2nd ed. (Milwaukee: Bulfin Press, 1962), 245–50.

21. Based on database search, LLP, for cases occurring in the year 1850 for which Lincoln was an attorney of record; on Enos's background, see the brief biographical sketch at www.rootsweb.com/ilsangam/1876/enosp.htm; Enos actually died in 1832, but a case involving his estate came to court in 1850; the Trailor murder case was *People v. Trailor and Trailor,* June 1841, LLP, an interesting case during which, as it turned out, the supposed victim was actually alive; see also Lincoln to Joshua Speed, June 19, 1841, *CW* 1: 254–58.

22. Lincoln to T. J. Turner, February 8, 1850, *CW* 2: 72 (emphasis in original); the editor of the *Collected Works,* Roy P. Basler, states in the footnote that the case that was the subject of this letter could not be identified, but the Lincoln Legal Papers project has subsequently done so; it was *Kemper v. Adams and Bovey,* March 1858, LLP.

23. *People v. Anderson and Anderson,* November 1856, LLP.

24. Baker, *Mary Todd Lincoln,* 126, 210–12; Elizabeth Keckley, *Behind the Scenes, Or, Thirty Years a Slave, and Four Years in the White House,* reprint ed. (New York: Oxford University Press, 1989), 145.

25. See, for example, Laderman, *Sacred Remains,* 76.

26. Lamon, *Recollections,* 87.

27. Dennis Hanks, interview with William H. Herndon, September 8, 1865, *HI,* 105; Jason Duncan to William H. Herndon, [1866–67], *HI,* 541. There are numerous recollections of Lincoln's aversion to women in general; see, for example, Abner Y. Ellis, interview with William H. Herndon, [date unknown], *HI,* 170; John Hanks, interview with William H. Herndon, [1865–66], *HI,* 455; David Turnham to William H. Herndon, December 17, 1866, *HI,* 518; see also Burlingame's very thorough chapter on the subject in his *Inner World of Abraham Lincoln,* ch. 6; and Douglas Wilson's equally excellent discussion in *Honor's Voice,* 109–14.

28. Lincoln to C. U. Schlater, January 5, 1849, *CW* 2: 19; Anna Caroline Gentry, September 17, 1865, *HI,* 131.

29. Whitney, *Life on the Circuit with Lincoln,* 36.

30. Numbers based on a database search, LLP, subject heading "women as litigants," in which Lincoln appeared as an attorney of record.

31. See, for example, *Graves v. Penny and Campbell,* August 1851, LLP; *Hickox v. Waller,* October 1852, LLP; *Hampton v. Hall,* November 1846, LLP; *Barret v. Sanders and Beck,* March 1845, LLP; *Bishop v. Bishop et al.,* April 1856, LLP.

32. *Beam and Skinner v. Buckles,* March 1858, LLP; *Beerup et al. v. Britton,* March 1851, LLP; *Benedict v. Pearson,* October 1855, LLP.

33. *Barret v. McDonald et al.,* April 1859, LLP; this case was also part of the litigation involving the Columbus Machine Manufacturing Company discussed in chapter 4.

34. *Bishop v. Bishop et al.,* April 1856, LLP.

35. Of the twenty-three extant slander cases involving women as plaintiff litigants, only two cases (in which the type of slander was identifiable from extant records) involved accusations that had no overt sexual dimension; see *Allen et ux. v. Blue* (perjury), September 1843, LLP; and *Chase v. Blakely and Blakely,* November 1841 (theft), LLP; for perceptive general comments on these cases, see also Steiner, "Lawyer as Peacemaker," 6–8.

36. *Jacobus v. Kitchell et ux.,* September 1851, LLP.

37. See *Albin v. Bodine,* May 1850, LLP; and Steiner, "Lawyer as Peacemaker," 8–9.

38. Lamon, *Recollections,* 83.

39. Steiner, "Lawyer as Peacemaker," 6.

40. *Fancher v. Gollogher,* May 1850, LLP.

41. *Martin v. Underwood,* April 1858, LLP.

42. *Edwards et ux. v. Patterson et ux.,* June 1844, LLP.

43. *Patterson et ux. v. Edwards et ux.,* December 1845, LLP (emphasis added); a somewhat similar case may be found in *Sanders et ux. v. Dunham,* November 1851, LLP.

44. *Ryan v. Anderson,* May 1845, LLP. Blackstone, *Commentaries,* 4: 209–10, defined this in large part in terms of a young woman's forfeiture of lands to her next of kin.

45. *Anderson v. Ryan,* December 1846, LLP.

46. A point made effectively by Daniel W. Stowell, "Femmes *Un*Covert: Women's Encounters with the Law," and Dennis E. Suttles, "'For the Well-Being of the Child': The Law and Childhood," in Stowell, ed., *In Tender Consideration,* 17–46.

47. *Beerup v. Beerup,* June 1853, LLP; see also the brief discussion of the case in Stowell, "Femmes *Un*Covert: Women's Encounters with the Law," in Stowell, *In Tender Consideration,* 23.

48. See generally Nancy Wollock, *Women and the American Experience,* 3rd ed. (Boston: McGraw-Hill, 2000), 127; also John D'Emilio and Estelle B. Freedman, *Intimate Matters: A History of Sexuality in America* (Chicago: University of Chicago Press, 1988), 73–84; and Sara M. Evans, *Born for Liberty: A History of Women in America* (New York: Free Press, 1985), 63–69.

49. *Clarkson v. Clarkson,* August 1860, LLP; *Duhamel v. Duhamel,* October 1860, LLP; *Hook v. Denton,* August 1859, LLP; *Beard v. Beard,* May 1853, LLP; *Sinclair v. Sinclair and Francis, Conservator,* March 1853, LLP.

50. Based on database search, LLP, subject heading "divorce," with Lincoln as attorney of record; the search yielded 107 cases.

51. *Hill v. Hill,* November 1852, LLP; *Goodman v. Goodman,* March 1842, LLP; *Enslow v. Enslow,* October 1853, LLP.

52. *Caldwell v. Caldwell,* August 1858, LLP.

53. *Graham v. Graham,* October 1859, LLP; *Waddell v. Waddell,* November 1853, LLP. Jesse W. Weik, *The Real Lincoln: A Portrait,* 148–49, observes that Lincoln hated divorce cases, an observation Weik attributes to Billy Herndon.

54. *Jackson v. Jackson,* August 1858, LLP; *Howey v. Howey,* October 1858, LLP; *Kyle v. Kyle,* March 1846, LLP.

55. *Philbrick v. Philbrick,* May 1847, LLP.

56. Caleb Carman, interview with William H. Herndon, October 12, 1866, *HI,* 373; this idea of Lincoln's legal culture as essentially paternalistic when related to family and gender matters has been recently advanced by Daniel W. Stowell and the various contributors to his edited collection of essays, *In Tender Consideration,* esp. 5–6.

57. Elizabeth Todd Edwards, interview with William H. Herndon, [1865–66], *HI,* 443; and Ninian Edwards, interview with William H. Herndon, [1865–66], *HI,* 446.

Chapter 7: Storytelling

1. On Elizabeth's background, see generally Wilson, *Honor's Voice,* 180; Baker, *Mary Todd Lincoln,* 49–51, 74–78; and Winkle, *Young Eagle,* 162–63.

2. Elizabeth Todd Edwards, interview with William H. Herndon, [c. 1865–66], *HI,* 443–44.

3. Elizabeth and Ninian W. Edwards, interview with Jesse W. Weik, December

20, 1883, *HI,* 592; on Weik's background, see Michael Burlingame's introduction to Weik's *The Real Lincoln: A Portrait* (Lincoln: University of Nebraska Press, 2002; originally published in 1922), xxii–xxiii; and Donald, *Lincoln's Herndon,* 296–98.

4. Elizabeth and Ninian W. Edwards, interview with Jesse W. Weik, December 20, 1883, *HI,* 592.

5. Isaac N. Arnold, *The Life of Abraham Lincoln* (Lincoln: University of Nebraska Press, 1994; originally published in 1884), vii; David Davis, interview with William H. Herndon, September 19, 1866, *HI,* 346–47.

6. Joseph B. Oakleaf, *Abraham Lincoln as a Criminal Lawyer* (Rock Island, Ill.: Augustana Book Concern, 1923); Hand's speech is available in Illinois Supreme Court, *Proceedings Commemorative of the One Hundredth Anniversary of the Death of Abraham Lincoln* (Bloomington, Ill.: The Court, 1909).

7. Charles W. Moores, "Abraham Lincoln: Lawyer," *Indiana Historical Society Publications* 7 (1922): 520; Woldman, *Lawyer Lincoln,* 128; also Herndon, *Herndon's Lincoln,* 290; and Curtis, *True Life of Abraham Lincoln,* 83; Arnold, *The Life of Abraham Lincoln* (Chicago: Jansen, McClury, 1885), 59; Anthony Gross, *Lincoln's Own Stories* (New York: Harper, 1912), 22–23; John T. Richards, *Abraham Lincoln, the Lawyer-Statesman* (Boston: Houghton Mifflin, 1916), 21; Henry B. Kranz, *Abraham Lincoln: A New Portrait* (New York: Putnam, 1959), 50; see also Herbert Agar, *Abraham Lincoln* (Hamden, Conn.: Archeon Books, 1965), 46; Henry Bryan Binns, *The Life of Abraham Lincoln* (London and New York: J. M. Dent and Sons, 1927), 89; Josiah Gilbert Holland, *Life of Abraham Lincoln,* (Springfield, Ill.: Gurdon Bill, 1866), 77; John A. Sharp, *Abraham Lincoln* (London: Epuorth Press, 1919), 39; "Lincoln's Decision to Study Law," *Lincoln Lore* 276 (July 23, 1934): 1; J. T. Hobson, *Footprints of Abraham Lincoln* (Dayton, Ohio: Otterbein Press, 1909), 39; R. M. Benjamin, "Lincoln the Lawyer," *Central Law Journal* 68 (March 1909): 218; and Hertz, *New Life of Lincoln,* 48.

8. Noah Brooks, *Abraham Lincoln and the Downfall of American Slavery* (New York: G. P. Putnam and Sons, 1894), 83. There are many other examples of this perspective; see, for example, Curtis, *True Abraham Lincoln,* 79; Arnold, *Life of Abraham Lincoln,* 84; Henry Oliver Evans, *Abraham Lincoln as a Lawyer* (Pittsburgh: Smith Brothers, 1927), 8–9; Tarbell, *Life of Abraham Lincoln* 2: 63, Joseph H. Cooper, "Abraham Lincoln Wasn't a Yuppie," *National Law Journal* 9 (February 23, 1987): 13.

9. Joseph Gillespie to William H. Herndon, January 31, 1866, *HI,* 182; Woldman, *Lawyer Lincoln,* 68, 94, 190–93.

10. "Close insight" quote is Hill, *Emancipator,* 91; Woldman, *Lawyer Lincoln,* 3; Duff, *A. Lincoln, Prairie Lawyer,* 366, 368.

11. James Baldwin, *Abraham Lincoln: A True Life* (New York: American Book, 1904), 129. Again, there are many examples of this perspective in the Lincoln literature; see, for example, Tarbell, *Life of Abraham Lincoln,* 2: 42, 44–45; Brooks, *Abraham Lincoln and the Downfall of American Slavery,* 83; Sandburg, *The Prairie*

Years, 60–61; William O. Stoddard, *Abraham Lincoln: The True Story of a Great Life* (New York: Fords, Howard, and Hulbert, 1885), 127–28; and Kranz, *New Portrait,* 26.

12. Duff, *A. Lincoln,* 355; see also Gross, *Stories,* 18–45.

13. Kilbourn, *The Bench and Bar of Litchfield County, Connecticut,* 114; *Bench and Bar of Tennessee,* 115; Foote, *Bench and Bar,* 46, description of Webber at 109; *Bench and Bar of South Carolina,* 142, 150, 179, 199, 253.

14. Seward's quote in Carl Schurz, *Reminiscences,* 3 vols. (New York: McClure, 1907–8), 2: 222; on the origins of the term "pettifogger," see "A Fog Named Sue," *Word Detective* (December 16, 2003), at www.word-detective.com/121603.html. Herndon himself disparaged Lincoln for his "pettifogging" in Bowling Green's courtroom in New Salem; see Herndon, *Herndon's Lincoln,* 93.

15. Conclusions based on data search for cases in which Lincoln is listed as an attorney of record, 1837, LLP; the rock case is *Bryan v. Smith,* October 1837, LLP; the probate case was *Carrico v. Carrico et al.,* March 1837, LLP.

16. Conclusions based on numbers in reference section, "cases by jurisdiction," LLP.

17. My sentiments here are echoed by Steiner, "Learning from Lincoln," 431.

18. Linder, *Early Bench and Bar,* 37, 40.

19. I'm thinking here in particular of his palpable irritation at his inability to influence the course of the Taylor administration, despite the fact he had actively campaigned for the Whig presidential candidate; see, for example, Lincoln to Walter Smith, January 5, 1849, *CW* 2: 18; Lincoln to James M. McLean, January 11, 1849, *CW* 2: 22; Lincoln to William M. Meredith, March 9, 1849, *CW* 2: 32; Lincoln to Josiah M. Lucas, April 25, 1849, *CW* 2: 43–44; Lincoln to Thomas Ewing, April 26, 1849, *CW* 2: 44–45.

20. *Abrams v. Abrams,* June 1856, LLP.

21. *Fithian v. Walker,* April 1839 and May 1842 (appeal), LLP; *James v. Redmon et al.,* October 1853, LLP.

22. *Fithian v. Casseday,* October 1851, LLP; *Fithian v. Cunningham,* May 1841, LLP; *Fithian v. Cunningham et al.,* May 1847 and May 1846, LLP; *Fithian v. Mobley et al.,* August 1849, LLP.

23. *Foster v. Cassidy,* October 1838, LLP; *Foster v. Cosby,* April 1861, LLP; *Foster v. Richmond,* April 1859, LLP.

24. Henry Whitney, interview with Jesse W. Weik, [1887–89], *HI,* 732; for examples, see *Caldwell v. Caldwell,* October 1857, LLP; *Fox v. Johnson,* January 1860, LLP; *Mark v. Bailey et al.,* October 1855, LLP; *Dryden et al. v. Warfield and Martin,* July 1843, LLP; *People for the Use of Burr et al. v. Austin,* May 1845, LLP; and Duff, *A. Lincoln,* 125.

25. Sandburg, *Prairie Years,* 2: 66.

26. Samuel C. Parks to William H. Herndon, March 25, 1866, *HI,* 238; Herndon, *Herndon's Lincoln,* 262–64, 278; David Davis, interview with William H. Herndon,

September 19, 1866, *HI,* 347; and Henry C. Whitney to William H. Herndon, August 27, 1887, *HI,* 633.

27. *Bench and Bar of South Carolina,* 248. Duff, *A. Lincoln,* 58 also dismissed as "poppycock" the idea that Lincoln could "put forth his best effort when convinced of the justice of the cause"; Spiegel, *A. Lincoln, Esquire,* 46, likewise expresses skepticism on this point.

28. See *People v. Patterson,* April 1859, LLP.

29. *Cromwell and McNaghton v. Bailey,* September 1839, LLP, and *Bailey v. Cromwell and McNaghton,* July 1841 (appeal), LLP; for examples of how Lincoln's admirers have used this case, see Hobson, *Footprints,* 39; Tarbell, *Lincoln,* 2: 51–52.

30. *Matson v. Bryant et al.,* August 1847, LLP.

31. *People v. Kern,* April 1847, LLP; *People v. Pond,* November 1845, LLP; *People v. Scott,* April 1847, LLP; Thomas J. DiLorenzo, *The Real Lincoln: A New Look at Abraham Lincoln, His Agenda, and an Unnecessary War* (Roseville, Calif.: Prima, 2002), 15; Lerone Bennett, Jr., *Forced Into Glory: Abraham Lincoln's White Dream* (Chicago: J. P. Johnson, 2000), 280.

32. Woldman, *Lawyer Lincoln,* 64.

33. Number based on search category "African-Americans," with Lincoln as an attorney of record, LLP.

34. The divorce case was *Shelby v. Shelby,* July 1841, LLP; the Florville cases are *Florville v. Allin et al.,* August 1849, LLP; *Florville v. Stockdale et al.,* August 1849, LLP; *Unknown v. Unknown,* c. June 1847 (case no. L05636), LLP. On Lincoln's relationship with Florville, see Lincoln to Charles R. Welles, September 27, 1852, *CW* 2: 159.

35. Lincoln, speech in Chicago, Illinois, July 10, 1858, *CW* 2: 492.

36. Herndon, *Herndon's Lincoln,* 390–91.

37. See, for example, Robert V. Bruce, "The Riddle of Death," in Boritt, *Lincoln Enigma,* 138.

38. Lincoln, Fragment of Notes for Speeches, [c. August 21, 1858], *CW* 2: 549; Fragment on slavery, [c. July 1854], *CW* 2: 222.

39. See, for example, Frank, *Lincoln as a Lawyer,* esp. ch. 5.

40. Lincoln, Message to Congress, July 17, 1862, *CW* 5: 328–31; Richard Hofstadter, "Abraham Lincoln and the Self-Made Myth," in *The American Political Tradition and the Men Who Made It,* 2nd ed. (New York: Alfred Knopf, 1973), 117.

Chapter 8: Grease

1. Based on data search, LLP, cases between June and December 1850, in which Lincoln appeared as an attorney of record; the mechanic's lien case was *Allsup v. Argo,* October 1850; a typical cash debt case was *Lyons v. Hill et al.,* November 1850.

2. See, for example, Lincoln's speech at Springfield, Illinois, July 11, 1836, *CW*

1: 50; his remarks in the Illinois legislature related to public lands, January 17, 1839, *CW* 1: 132–34; his speech on the subtreasury, December 26, 1839, *CW* 1: 159–80; and his speech on the state bank, January 21, 1840, *CW* 1: 185–95.

3. Lincoln to Norman P. Judd, November 16, 1858, *CW* 1: 338.

4. Lincoln told this joke during a cabinet meeting; see Howard K. Beale, ed., *Diary of Gideon Welles,* 3 vols. (New York: W. W. Norton, 1960), 1: 370.

5. Lincoln to William A. Crafts, February 6, 1849, *CW,* 2: 25; Lincoln to John W. Vance, July 7, 1844, *CW* 1: 340.

6. *Ricketts v. Goings,* October 1855, LLP; *Hamilton v. Maloney,* January 1859, LLP; *Andrews v. House,* November 1851, LLP.

7. *Ricketts v. Goings,* October 1855, LLP; *Hamilton v. Maloney,* January 1859, LLP; *Andrews v. House,* November 1851, LLP.

8. *Owen v. Ferrin,* March 1842, LLP.

9. See *B. C. Webster and Co. for Use of Matheny and Roberts v. Hickox,* March 1852, LLP; *B. C. Webster and Co. for Use of Matheny and Roberts v. Wells,* November 1854, LLP; *B. C. Webster and Co. v. Archer,* November 1843, LLP; *B. C. Webster and Co. v. Dresser,* March 1850, LLP; *B. C. Webster and Co. v. Kilbourn and Archer,* November 1843, LLP; *B.C. Webster and Co. v. Snelson,* November 1843, LLP.

10. See, for example, Woldman, *Lawyer Lincoln,* 172.

11. *Browning v. Springfield, Illinois,* November 1853, LLP.

12. I am thinking here of course of Horwitz, *Transformation of American Law*; see also William E. Nelson, *The Americanization of the Common Law: The Impact of Legal Change on Massachusetts Society, 1760–1830* (Cambridge: Harvard University Press, 1975), 117–20; Lawrence M. Friedman, *A History of American Law,* 2nd ed. (New York: Touchstone, 1986); Charles Sellers, *The Market Revolution: Jacksonian America, 1815–1846* (New York: Oxford University Press, 1991), 47. For a cogent critique of these arguments, see Steiner, "Lawyers and Legal Change in Antebellum America: Learning from Lincoln," *University of Detroit Mercy Law Review* 74 (Spring 1997): 427–29 and passim.

13. I use the qualifier "might be inclined" because I have not seen an example of anyone making this exact argument, but only because Lincoln's debt and business litigation was so badly neglected by those early historians who want to portray Lincoln as champion of the poor and oppressed. In other contexts, early Lincoln biographers are quite inclined toward this approach; see, for example, Woldman, *Lawyer Lincoln,* 115–35; Isaac Arnold's treatment of *Case v. Snow* in his *The Life of Abraham Lincoln,* 4th ed. (Lincoln: University of Nebraska Press, 1994), 85–87; and Godfrey (Lord) Charnwood, *Lincoln* (Lincoln: University of Nebraska Press, 1995), 82.

14. *Friedlander v. Great Western Railroad,* October 1857, LLP.

15. Notes for a Law Lecture, c. July 1850, *CW* 2: 81.

16. For a rare exception (that proves the rule), see Lincoln to Lewis M. Hays, April 23, 1851, and October 27, 1852, *CW* 2: 105, 160.

17. Lincoln to Garland B. Shelledy, February 16, 1842, *CW* 1: 270 (emphases in original); there are numerous other examples of his businesslike legal correspondence in the *Collected Works;* see, for example, Lincoln to Onslow Peters, June 25, 1852, *CW* 2: 120–21; Lincoln to Solon Cumins, February 14, 1853, *CW* 2: 190; Lincoln to Jonathan Haines, November 24, 1856, *CW* 2: 382–83.

18. *Abrams v. Abrams,* June 1856, LLP; *People v. Williams,* June 1845, LLP.

19. *Madux v. VanBrunt and Watrons,* December 1859, LLP; *Colbern v. Wallace,* March 1838, LLP.

20. *Plummer v. Plummer,* November 1856, LLP; *Clark v. Jones,* June 1859, LLP; *Clifton v. Mayall,* July 1855, LLP; *Enslow v. Enslow,* October 1855, LLP.

21. Tucker, *Trial and Error,* 73.

22. Mann, *Defending White-Collar Crime,* 122.

23. Blackstone, *Commentaries,* 1: 120.

24. Lincoln to Usher F. Linder, February 20, 1848, *CW* 1: 453 (emphases in original).

25. My reading of the Lincoln marriage has been heavily influenced here by Michael Burlingame's excellent essay, "The Lincolns' Marriage: 'A Fountain of Misery, of a Quality Absolutely Infernal,'" in his *The Inner World of Abraham Lincoln,* 268–56; others, most notably Jean H. Baker, have a far different opinion concerning the overall happiness or unhappiness of the Lincoln marriage; see Baker, *Mary Todd Lincoln,* 97–100, 228–40, and passim; and "The Lincoln Marriage: Beyond the Battle of Quotations," 38th Annual Fortenbaugh Memorial Lecture, Gettysburg College (1999), esp. 26–27; even Baker concedes the existence of "bad moments" in the Lincoln marriage, a perspective not at great variance with my overall point here.

26. James A. Garfield to Burke Hinsdale, January 6, 1863; Theodore C. Smith, ed., *The Life and Letters of James A. Garfield,* 2 vols. (New Haven, Conn.: Yale University Press, 1925), 1: 266.

27. Lincoln, Message to Senate and House of Representatives, July 17, 1862, *CW* 5: 331.

28. Lincoln, Response to a Serenade, February 1, 1865, *CW* 8: 254.

29. Edwin M. Stanton to John A. Dix, April 15, 1865, in *Official Records of the War of the Rebellion,* Series 1, Vol. 46, 780; John Hay, November 11, 1864, in Burlingame and Ettlinger, *Inside Lincoln's White House,* 249.

30. John Hay, November 11, 1864, in Burlingame and Ettlinger, *Inside Lincoln's White House,* 243.

31. Lincoln, First Inaugural Address, March 4, 1861, *CW* 4: 271; speech at Chicago, Illinois, July 10, 1858, *CW* 2: 492.

32. His chief critic here, of course, is Lerone Bennett; see his *Forced Into Glory: Abraham Lincoln's White Dream*; he is joined in his criticism, to a much less shrill degree, by Vincent Harding, *There Is a River: The Black Struggle for Freedom in America* (New York: Harcourt, Brace and Jovanovich, 1981); and

George M. Frederickson, "A Man but Not a Brother: Abraham Lincoln and Racial Equality," *Journal of Southern History* 51 (February 1975): 39–58. Oates, *Abraham Lincoln: The Man behind the Myths,* 21–30, offers a useful overview of the literature that is critical of Lincoln's race policies.

33. John Hay, December 18, 1864, in Burlingame and Ettlinger, *Inside Lincoln's White House,* 254.

34. Lincoln, Message to Congress, December 1, 1862, *CW* 5: 537.

35. Goodwin, *Team of Rivals,* 703.

Conclusion

1. Mary Todd Lincoln, interview with William H. Herndon, c. September 1866, *HI,* 359.

2. Mary quoted in Isaac N. Arnold, *The Life of Abraham Lincoln* (Lincoln: University of Nebraska Press, 1994; originally published in 1884), 429–30.

3. *Ibid.,* 430.

4. See generally Lawrence M. Friedman, *American Law: An Introduction,* 2nd ed. (New York: W. W. Norton, 1998) 282; Robert Stevens, *Law School: Legal Education in America from the 1850s to the 1980s* (Chapel Hill: University of North Carolina Press, 1983); James Willard Hurst, *The Growth of American Law: The Lawmakers* (Boston: Little, Brown, 1950).

5. New York *Herald Tribune,* July 27, 1926.

Bibliography and Sources

Primary Sources

Alverstone, Right Hon. Viscount. *Recollections of Bar and Bench*. 4th ed. London: Edward Arnold, 1915.

Baldwin, James G. *The Flush Times of Alabama and Mississippi*. Baton Rouge: Louisiana State University Press, 1980; originally published in 1853.

Basler, Roy P., ed. *The Collected Works of Abraham Lincoln*. 9 vols. Urbana: University of Illinois Press, 1955.

Beale, Howard K., ed. *Diary of Gideon Welles*. 3 vols. New York: W. W. Norton, 1960.

Blackstone, William. *Commentaries on the Laws of England*. 4 vols. Chicago: University of Chicago Press, 1979; originally published in 1765.

Browne, Francis Fisher. *The Everyday Life of Abraham Lincoln*. Lincoln: University Press of Nebraska, 1994; originally published in 1887.

Chester, Alden. *Courts and Lawyers of New York: A History, 1609–1925*. 3 vols. New York: American Historical Society, 1925.

Chitty, Joseph. *A Treatise on Pleading, and Parties to Actions, with Second and Third Volumes, Containing Precedents of Pleadings, and an Appendix of Forms*. 3rd American ed. from the 2nd English ed. Philadelphia: I. Riley, 1819.

Foote, Henry S. *The Bench and Bar of the South and Southwest*. St. Louis: Soule, Thomas, and Wentworth, 1876.

Harris, Gibson W. "My Recollections of Abraham Lincoln." *Farm and Fireside*, December 1, 1904. Lincoln Library and Museum, Fort Wayne, Ind.

Hay-Stuart Papers. Lincoln Library Manuscripts Collection, Springfield, Ill.

Herndon, William H. *Herndon's Life of Lincoln: The History and Personal Recollections of Abraham Lincoln*. New York: Da Capo Press, 1983; originally published in 1888.

Higgins, Jesse, and William Sampson. *Sampson against the Philistines, or the Reformation of Lawsuits; and Justice Made Cheap, Speedy, and Brought to Every Man's Door*. Philadelphia: B. Graves, 1805.

Illinois Daily Journal. Illinois State Historical Library, Springfield, Ill.

Illinois State Journal. Illinois State Historical Library, Springfield, Ill.

Illustrated Atlas Map of Menard County, Illinois. Chicago: W. R. Brink, 1874.

Kilbourn, Dwight C. *The Bench and Bar of Litchfield, Connecticut, 1709–1909*. Union, N.J.: Lawbook Exchange, 2002; originally published in 1909.

Knapp, Samuel L. *Biographical Sketches of Eminent Lawyers, Statesmen, and Men of Letters.* Boston: Richardson and Lord, 1821.

Konefsky, Alfred S., and Andrew J. King, eds. *The Papers of Daniel Webster: Legal Papers, the Boston Practice.* Hanover, N.H.: University Press of New England, 1983.

Lamon, Ward Hill. *Recollections of Abraham Lincoln.* Lincoln: University of Nebraska Press, 1994; originally published in 1895.

Linder, Usher. *Reminiscences of the Early Bench and Bar of Illinois.* Chicago: Chicago Legal News, 1879.

Lincoln Legal Papers. DVD-ROM database. Urbana: University of Illinois Press, 2000.

Memorials of the Life and Character of Stephen T. Logan. Springfield, Ill.: H. W. Rokker, 1882.

O'Neall, John B. *Biographical Sketches of the Bench and Bar of South Carolina.* 2 vols. Charleston, S.C.: S. G. Courtenay, 1859.

Palmer, John M. *Bench and Bar of Illinois.* Chicago: Lewis, 1899.

———. *Personal Recollections of John M. Palmer: The Story of an Earnest Life.* Cincinnati: R. Clark, 1901.

Power, John. *History of the Early Settlers of Sangamon County, Illinois.* Springfield, Ill.: E. A. Wilson, 1876.

Sangamon Journal. Illinois State Historical Library, Springfield, Ill.

Schurz, Carl. *Reminiscences.* 3 vols. New York: McClure, 1907–8.

Smith, O. H. *Early Indiana Trials and Sketches.* Cincinnati: Moore, Wilstach, Keys, 1858.

Smith, Theodore C., ed. *The Life and Letters of James A. Garfield.* 2 vols. New Haven, Conn.: Yale University Press, 1925.

"Stephen Logan Talks about Abraham Lincoln." *Bulletin of the Abraham Lincoln Centennial Association* 12 (September 1928): 1–5.

Story, Joseph. *Commentaries on Equity Jurisprudence, as Administered in England and America.* 2 vols. New York: Arno Press, 1972; originally published in 1835.

Stuart, John Todd Papers. Illinois State Historical Library, Springfield, Ill.

Tocqueville, Alexis de. *Democracy in America.* 2 vols. New York: Alfred A. Knopf, 1945; original English translation in 1835.

United States War Department. *The War of the Rebellion: A Compilation of the Official Records of the Union and Confederate Armies.* 128 vols. Washington, D.C.: Government Printing Office, 1880–1901.

Ward, W. H. "The Legal Profession." *Southwestern Quarterly* 1 (March 1852): 158–60.

Weik, Jesse W. *The Real Lincoln: A Portrait.* Lincoln: University of Nebraska Press, 2003; originally published in 1923.

Whitney, Henry C. *Life on the Circuit with Lincoln.* Boston: Estes and Lauriat, 1892.

Williams, Charles Richard, ed. *The Diary and Letters of Rutherford Birchard Hayes.* 5 vols. Columbus: Ohio State Archaeological and Historical Society, 1922.

Wilson, Douglas L., and William O. Stoddard, eds. *Herndon's Informants: Letters, Interviews, and Statements about Abraham Lincoln.* Urbana: University of Illinois Press, 1997.

Winnick, R. H., ed. *The Letters of Archibald MacLeish.* Boston: Houghton Mifflin, 1983.

Secondary Sources

Agar, Herbert. *Abraham Lincoln.* Hamden, Conn.: Archeon Books, 1965.

Angle, Paul M. *"Here I Have Lived": A History of Lincoln's Springfield, 1821–1865.* New Brunswick: Rutgers University Press, 1950.

———. *One Hundred Years of Law.* Springfield, Ill.; Brown, Hay and Stephens, 1928.

———. "Where Lincoln Practiced Law." *Lincoln Centennial Association Papers* (1927): 22–28.

Arnold, Isaac N. *The Life of Abraham Lincoln.* Lincoln: University Press of Nebraska, 1994; originally published in 1869.

Backman, Walt. *Law v. Life.* Rhineback, N.Y.: Four Directions, 1995.

Baker, Jean H. "The Lincoln Marriage: Beyond the Battle of Quotations." Thirty-eighth Annual Fortenbaugh Memorial Lecture, Gettysburg College, 1999.

———. *Mary Todd Lincoln: A Biography.* New York: W. W. Norton, 1987.

Balleisen, Edward J. *Navigating Failure: Bankruptcy and Commercial Society in Antebellum America.* Chapel Hill: University of North Carolina Press, 2000.

Beard, William D. "'I Have Labored Hard to Find the Law': Abraham Lincoln and the Alton and Sangamon Railroad." *Illinois Historical Journal* 85 (Winter 1992): 209–20.

Bennett, Lerone, Jr. *Forced Into Glory: Abraham Lincoln's White Dream.* Chicago: J. P. Johnson, 2000.

Benjamin, R. M. "Lincoln the Lawyer." *Central Law Journal* 68 (March 1909): 218–25.

Bergen, A. "Lincoln as a Lawyer." *Journal of the American Bar Association* 5 (June 1926): 390–91.

Binns, Henry Bryan. *The Life of Abraham Lincoln.* London and New York: J. M. Dent and Sons, 1927.

Bissett, Clark B. *Abraham Lincoln: A Universal Man.* San Francisco: John Hall, 1928.

Bloomfield, Maxwell. "Lawyers and Public Criticism: Challenge and Response in Nineteenth-Century America." *American Journal of Legal History* 15 (1971): 269–87.

———. "The Texas Bar in the Nineteenth Century." *Vanderbilt University Law Review* 32 (1979): 261–76.

Boorstin, Daniel J. *The Mysterious Science of the Law: An Essay on Blackstone Commentaries.* 2nd ed. Chicago: University of Chicago Press, 1996.

Boritt, Gabor. *Lincoln and the Economics of the American Dream.* 2nd ed. Urbana: University of Illinois Press, 1994.

———, ed. *The Lincoln Enigma: The Changing Faces of an American Icon.* Cambridge: Oxford University Press, 2002.

Brent, James Allen. "The Arkansas Bar in the Age of Sectionalism, 1819–1861." Ph.D. diss., Auburn University, 1996.

Brocket, Linus P. *The Life and Times of Abraham Lincoln, Sixteenth President of the United States, Including His Speeches, Messages, Inaugurals, Proclamations, etc. etc.* Philadelphia: Bradley, 1865.

Brooks, Noah. *Abraham Lincoln and the Downfall of American Slavery.* New York: G. P. Putnam and Sons, 1894.

Burlingame, Michael. *The Inner World of Abraham Lincoln.* Urbana: University of Illinois Press, 1994.

———, and John R. T. Ettlinger, ed. *Inside Lincoln's White House: The Complete Civil War Diary of John Hay.* Carbondale: Southern Illinois University Press, 1999.

———, ed. *Lincoln Observed: Civil War Dispatches of Noah Brooks.* Baltimore: Johns Hopkins University Press, 1998.

Campbell, Bruce. *The Sangamon Saga: 200 Years: An Illustrated Bicentennial History of Sangamon County.* Springfield, Ill.: Phillips Brothers, 1976.

Charnwood, Godfrey (Lord). *Lincoln.* Lincoln: University of Nebraska Press, 1995; originally published in 1916.

Clark, Christopher. *The Roots of Western Capitalism: Western Massachusetts, 1780–1860.* Ithaca: Cornell University Press, 1992.

Cole, George F., ed. *Criminal Justice: Law and Politics.* Belmont, Calif.: Wadsworth, 1993.

Coleman, Peter. *Debtors and Creditors in America: Insolvency, Imprisonment for Debt, and Bankruptcy, 1607–1900.* New York: Beard Books, 1999.

Cook, Charles M. *The American Codification Movement: A Study of Antebellum Legal Reform.* Westport, Conn.: Greenwood Press, 1981.

Cooper, Joseph H. "Abraham Lincoln Wasn't a Yuppie." *National Law Journal* 9 (February 23, 1987): 13–17.

Cullen, Charles T. "New Light on John Marshall's Legal Education and Admission to the Bar." *American Journal of Legal History* 16 (1972): 345–62.

Curl, James S. *The Victorian Celebration of Death.* Detroit: Partridge Press, 1972.

Curtis, William Elroy. *The True Abraham Lincoln.* Philadelphia: J. B. Lippincott, 1903.

D'Emilio, John, and Estelle B. Freedman. *Intimate Matters: A History of Sexuality in America.* Chicago: University of Chicago Press, 1988.

Darrow, Clarence. *The Story of My Life*. New York: Da Capo Press, 1996; originally published in 1932.

Davis, James Edward. *Frontier Illinois*. Bloomington: Indiana University Press, 2000.

DiLorenzo, Thomas J. *The Real Lincoln: A New Look at Abraham Lincoln, His Agenda, and an Unnecessary War*. Roseville, Calif.: Prima, 2002.

Dirck, Brian R. "Labors of the Profession: The Law Practice of Nathaniel Hart Davis, a Texas Attorney, 1850–1861." *East Texas Historical Journal* 31 (1993): 24–40.

———. *Lincoln and Davis: Imagining America, 1809–1865*. Lawrence: University Press of Kansas, 2001.

Donald, David. *Lincoln's Herndon: A Biography*. 2nd ed. New York: Da Capo, 1989.

———. *Lincoln*. New York: Simon and Schuster, 1995.

———. *We Are Lincoln Men: Abraham Lincoln and His Men*. New York: Simon and Schuster, 2003.

Duff, John J. *A. Lincoln, Prairie Lawyer*. New York: Rinehart, 1960.

English, William F. "The Pioneer Lawyer and Jurist in Missouri." *University of Missouri Studies* 21 (1947): 7–23.

Evans, Henry Oliver. *Abraham Lincoln as a Lawyer*. Pittsburgh: Smith Brothers, 1927.

Evans, Sara M. *Born for Liberty: A History of Women in America*. New York: Free Press, 1985.

Fleming, Roy B. "Client Games: Defense Attorney Perspectives on Their Relations with Criminal Clients." *American Bar Association Research Journal* (1986): 253–70.

Frank, John P. *Lincoln as a Lawyer*. Urbana: University of Illinois Press, 1961.

Frederickson, George M. "A Man but Not a Brother: Abraham Lincoln and Racial Equality." *Journal of Southern History* 51 (February 1975): 39–58.

Friedman, Lawrence M. *A History of American Law*. 2nd ed. New York: Touchstone, 1986.

———. *American Law: An Introduction*. 2nd ed. New York: W. W. Norton, 1998.

———. *Crime and Punishment in American History*. New York: Basic Books, 1993.

Gawalt, Gerard W. "Massachusetts Lawyers: A Historical Analysis of the Process of Professionalization, 1760–1840." Ph.D. diss., Clark University, 1977.

Goodrich, Chris. *Anarchy and Elegance: Confessions of a Journalist at Yale Law School*. Boston: Little, Brown, 1991.

Goodwin, Doris Kearns. *Team of Rivals: The Political Genius of Abraham Lincoln*. New York: Simon and Schuster, 2005.

Gross, Anthony. *Lincoln's Own Stories*. New York: Harper, 1912.

Guelzo, Allen C. *Abraham Lincoln, Redeemer President*. Grand Rapids, Mich.: William B. Eerdman's, 1999.

Harding, Vincent. *There Is a River: The Black Struggle for Freedom in America.* New York: Harcourt, Brace and Jovanovich, 1981.

Harris, Michael H. "The Frontier Lawyer's Library: Southern Indiana, 1800–1850, as a Test Case." *American Journal of Legal History* 16 (1972): 239–51.

Hay, John, and John Nicolay. *Abraham Lincoln: A History.* 10 vols. New York: Century, 1890.

Hertz, Emanuel. *Abraham Lincoln: A New Portrait.* 2 vols. New York: Horace Liveright, 1931.

Hill, Frederick Trevor. *Lincoln, Emancipator of the Nation.* New York: D. Appleton, 1923.

———. *Lincoln the Lawyer.* Littleton, Colo.: Fred B. Rothman, 1986; originally published in 1906.

History of Sangamon County, Illinois, 1881. Chicago: Inter-State, 1881.

Hofstadter, Richard. *The American Political Tradition and the Men Who Made It.* 2nd ed. New York: Alfred Knopf, 1973.

Holland, Josiah Gilbert. *The Life of Abraham Lincoln.* Springfield, Ill.: Gurdon Bill, 1866.

Holt, Wythe. "Morton Horwitz and the Transformation of American Legal History." *William and Mary Law Review* 23 (1982): 23–50.

Holzer, Harold, ed. *Dear Mr. Lincoln: Letters to the President.* Reading, Mass.: Addison-Wesley, 1993.

Horwitz, Morton. *The Transformation of American Law, 1780–1860.* Cambridge: Oxford University Press, 1994.

Hossicks, Carl. "We Don't Care What Happened, We Only Care about What Is Going to Happen." *Social Problems* 26 (1979): 1–29.

Hurst, James Willard. *The Growth of American Law: The Lawmakers.* Boston: Little, Brown, 1950.

Illinois Supreme Court. *Proceedings Commemorative of the One Hundredth Anniversary of the Death of Abraham Lincoln.* Bloomington, Ill.: Court, 1909.

Jarvis, Robert M. "An Anecdotal History of the Bar Exam." *Georgetown Journal of Legal Ethics* 9 (1996): 374–91.

Johannsen, Robert W. *Stephen A. Douglas.* 2nd ed. Urbana: University of Illinois Press, 1997.

Kaufman, Kenneth C. *Dred Scott's Advocate: A Biography of Roswell M. Field.* Columbia: University of Missouri Press, 1996.

Keckley, Elizabeth. *Behind the Scenes, or, Thirty Years a Slave, and Four Years in the White House.* Reprint ed. New York: Oxford University Press, 1989.

King, Willard L. *David Davis, Lincoln's Campaign Manager.* Chicago: University of Chicago Press, 1974.

Kranz, Henry B., ed. *Abraham Lincoln: A New Portrait.* New York: G. P. Putnam's Sons, 1959.

Krause, Susan. "Churning Up Business." *Lincoln Legal Briefs* 65 (January–March 2003): 2.

Kutler, Stanley I. *Privilege and Creative Destruction: The Charles River Bridge Case.* 2nd ed. Baltimore: Johns Hopkins University Press, 1990.

Laderman, Gary. *The Sacred Remains: American Attitudes toward Death, 1779–1883.* New Haven, Conn.: Yale University Press, 1996.

Lamers, William C. *The History of American Funeral Directing.* 2nd ed. Milwaukee, Wis.: Bulfin Press, 1962.

Larson, John Launtz. *Internal Improvement: National Public Works and the Promise of Popular Government in the Early United States.* Chapel Hill: University of North Carolina Press, 2001.

"Lincoln's Contacts with Law Students." *Lincoln Lore* 280 (August 20, 1934): 1.

"Lincoln's Decision to Become a Lawyer." *Lincoln Lore* 226 (January 5, 1948): 1.

"Lincoln's Law Library." *Lincoln Lore* 219 (February 17, 1941): 1.

Long, T. B. *Forty Years of Oratory.* 2 vols. Indianapolis: Bowen-Merrill, 1898.

Lowry, Thomas P. *Don't Shoot That Boy! Abraham Lincoln and Military Justice.* New York: Da Capo Press, 1999.

Luthin, Reinhard H. *The Real Abraham Lincoln: A Complete One Volume History of His Life and Times.* Englewood Cliffs: Prentice-Hall, 1960.

Mann, Bruce H. *Republic of Debtors: Bankruptcy in the Age of American Independence.* Cambridge, Mass.: Harvard University Press, 2002.

Mann, Kenneth. *Defending White-Collar Crime: A Portrait of Attorneys at Work.* New Haven, Conn.: Yale University Press, 1985.

Masters, Edgar Lee. *Lincoln the Man.* New York: Dodd, Meade, 1931.

McCurdy, Frances Lea. *Stump, Bar, and Pulpit: Speechmaking on the Missouri Frontier.* Columbia: University of Missouri Press, 1969.

McDonald, William F., ed. *The Defense Counsel.* Beverly Hills, Calif.: Sage, 1983.

McGlashan, C. F. *History of the Donner Party: A Tragedy of the Sierra.* San Francisco: A. Carlisle, 1922.

McNamara, Martha J. "Disciplining Justice: Massachusetts Courthouses and the Legal Profession, 1750–1850." Ph.D. diss., 1995.

Miers, Earl S., and William E. Baringer. *Lincoln Day by Day: A Chronology, 1809–1865.* Dayton, Ohio: Morningside, 1991.

Moldovsky, Joe, and Rose DeWolf. *The Best Defense.* New York: MacMillan, 1975.

Moll, Richard W. *The Lure of the Law: Why People Become Lawyers and What the Profession Does to Them.* New York: Penguin Books, 1990.

Moore, Charles Washington. "Abraham Lincoln: Lawyer." *Indiana Historical Society Publications* 7 (1922): 485–535.

Moretta, John A. *William Pitt Ballinger: Texas Lawyer, Southern Statesman, 1825–1888.* Austin: Texas State Historical Association, 2000.

Neely, Mark E., Jr. *The Last Best Hope of Earth.* Cambridge, Mass.: Harvard University Press, 1993.

Nelson, William E. *The Americanization of the Common Law: The Impact of Legal Change on Massachusetts Society, 1760–1830.* Cambridge, Mass.: Harvard University Press, 1975.

Nolan, Dennis R., ed. *Readings in the History of the American Legal Profession.* Indianapolis: Michie, 1980.

Norris, Norval, and David J. Rothman. *The Oxford History of the Prison: The Practice of Punishment in Western Society.* Cambridge: Oxford University Press, 1997.

Oakleaf, Joseph B. *Abraham Lincoln as a Criminal Lawyer.* Rock Island, Ill.: Augustana Book Concern, 1923.

Oates, Stephen. *Abraham Lincoln: The Man behind the Myths.* New York: HarperCollins, 1984.

Reid, John Philip. *Law for the Elephant: Property and Social Behavior on the Overland Trail.* Los Angeles: Huntington Library Press, 1980.

Richards, John T. *Lincoln, the Lawyer-Statesman.* Boston: Houghton Mifflin, 1916.

Rothman, David J. *The Discovery of the Asylum: Social Order and Disorder in the New Republic.* Boston: Little, Brown, 1971.

Rotundo, E. Anthony. *American Manhood: Transformations in Masculinity from the Revolution to the Modern Era.* New York: Basic Books, 1993.

Sandburg, Carl. *Abraham Lincoln: The Prairie Years.* 2 vols. New York: Harcourt, Brace, 1926.

Sarat, Austin, and William L. F. Felstiner. "Law and Social Relations: Vocabularies of Motive in the Lawyer-Client Interaction." *Law and Society Review* 22 (1988): 737–54.

———. "Lawyers and Legal Consciousness: Law Talk in the Divorce Lawyer's Office." *Yale Law Review* 98 (1989): 1663–87.

Sellers, Charles. *The Market Revolution: Jacksonian America, 1815–1846.* Cambridge: Oxford University Press, 1991.

Sharp, John A. *Abraham Lincoln.* London: Epuorth Press, 1919.

Shenk, Joshua L. *Lincoln's Melancholy: How Depression Challenged a President and Fueled His Greatness.* Boston: Houghton Mifflin, 2005.

Simenhoff, Mark, ed. *My First Year as a Lawyer.* New York: Walker, 1994.

Simpson, A. W. B. *A History of the Common Law of Contract: The Rise of the Action of Assumpsit.* Oxford: Clarendon Press, 1973.

Skeel, David A. *Debt's Dominion: A History of Bankruptcy Law in America.* Princeton, N.J.: Princeton University Press, 2001.

Smith, Alan M. "Virginia Lawyers, 1690–1776: The Birth of an American Profession." Ph.D. diss., Johns Hopkins University, 1967.

Spiegel, Allen T. *A. Lincoln, Esquire: A Shrewd, Sophisticated Lawyer in His Time.* Macon, Ga.: Mercer University Press, 2002.

Starr, John W., Jr. *Lincoln and the Railroads: A Biographical Study.* New York: Dodd, 1927.

Steiner, Mark. "The Lawyer as Peacemaker: Law and Community in Abraham Lincoln's Slander Cases." *Journal of the Abraham Lincoln Association* 16 (1995): 1–22.

———. "Lawyers and Legal Change in Antebellum America: Learning from Lincoln." *University of Detroit Mercy Law Review* 74 (Spring 1997): 427–64.

Stevens, Robert. *Law School: Legal Education in America from the 1850s to the 1980s.* Chapel Hill: University of North Carolina Press, 1983.

Stewart, George R. *Ordeal by Hunger: The Story of the Donner Party.* Boston: Houghton Mifflin, 1988.

Stephenson, Nathaniel W. *Lincoln: An Account of His Personal Life.* Indianapolis: Bobbs-Merrill, 1922.

Stoddard, William O. *Abraham Lincoln: The True Story of a Great Life.* New York: Fords, Howard, and Hulbert, 1885.

Stowell, Daniel W., ed. *In Tender Consideration: Women, Families, and the Law in Abraham Lincoln's Illinois.* Reprint ed. Urbana: University of Illinois Press, 2006.

Tarbell, Ida M. *The Life of Abraham Lincoln.* 2 vols. New York: Lincoln Historical Society, 1924.

Temple, Wayne C. "Lincoln's First Step to Becoming a Lawyer." *Lincoln Herald* 70 (Winter 1968): 207–11.

Tilton, Henry Clay. "Lincoln and Lamon: Partners and Friends." *Transactions of the Illinois State Historical Association* (1931): 180–86.

Townsend, William H. "Lincoln's Law Books." *American Bar Association Journal* 15 (March 1929): 125–26.

———. "Stuart and Lincoln." *American Bar Association Journal* 17 (February 1931): 82–86.

Tucker, John C. *Trial and Error: The Education of a Courtroom Lawyer.* New York: Carroll and Graf, 2003.

Verduin, Paul. "*Rebecca Thomas v. Erastus Wright.*" *Lincoln Legal Briefs* 33 (January–March 1995): 2.

Walsh, John Evangelist. *Moonlight: Abraham Lincoln and the Almanac Trial.* New York: St. Martin's Press, 2000.

Warren, Charles. *A History of the American Bar.* 3rd ed. New York: Howard Fertig, 1966.

Warren, Louis A. *Lincoln's Youth: Indiana Years, Seven to Twenty-One, 1816–1830.* Indianapolis: Indiana Historical Society, 2000.

Watson, Harry. *Liberty and Power: Jacksonian America.* New York: Hill and Wang, 1990.

Wilson, Douglas. *Honor's Voice: The Transformation of Abraham Lincoln.* New York: Vintage, 1999.

Winkle, Kenneth J. *The Young Eagle: The Rise of Abraham Lincoln.* New York: Taylor, 2001.

Woldman, Alfred A. *Lawyer Lincoln.* Boston: Little, Brown, 1937.

Wollock, Nancy. *Women and the American Experience.* 3rd ed. Boston: McGraw-Hill, 2000.

Wyatt-Brown, Bertram. *Southern Honor: Ethics and Behavior in the Old South.* Cambridge: Oxford University Press, 1982.

Index

Abell, Bennet, 84–85
Abrams, Jane, 145, 162
Abrams, William, 145, 162
Ackley, Alvin, 150
Adams, Robert H., 20, 98, 158
Adams, William T., 84
Adkin, David, 113
Alexander, Milton, 63
Allen, Charles, 118
Allen, Robert, 78
Allen, William J., 65
Allen, Wilson, 94–95
Almanac case, 115–19, 123, 142, 150
Alton and Sangamon Railroad, 92–93
Ambos, Peter, 67–68
Amory, Thomas Coffin, 14
Anderson, Elias, 132
Anderson, George, 126–27
Anderson, Theodore, 37, 127
Andrews, John, 158
Armstrong, Hannah, 116–19, 121
Armstrong, Jack, 116
Armstrong, William ("Duff"), 116–19, 123
Arnold, Isaac, 140
Arnold, Robert C., 79
assault, 104, 145
assumpsit, writ of, 62, 66, 74
attachment, writ of, 62
Atterberry, Bluford, 84–85
Atwood, Cole, and Crane, 66
Ayers, John, 65
Ayers, Josiah, 65

Bailey, David, 147–48
Bainbridge, Thomas, 71

Baker, Christina, 19
Baker, Edward, 27, 28, 122
Baker, Jesse, 19
Baldwin, James, 142
Baldwin, Joseph G., 107
Ballinger, William Pitt, 20
bankruptcy, 63–64
banks, 91, 156
bar associations, 35–36, 139–40, 175
bar examinations, 21–22
Barnett, Egbart, 109
Barrett, Edward, 113
Barrett, James A., 67–68, 92–93, 129
Barrett, William D., 66
Barton, Roger
Basler, Roy P., ix, 1
B. C. Webster and Company, 158
Beam, Samuel, 128
Beard, Martin, 134
Beard, Mary, 134
Beard, William, 134
Beecher, Henry Ward, 57
Beerup, Caroline, 133
Beerup, Sinai Ann, 128
Beerup, Stephen, 133
Beerup, Thomas, 128
Bell, James, 60–62
Benedict, Anna, 128
Bennett, Lerone, 148
Berry, William, 54–55, 59
Billington, John, 61
Birch, Jonathan, 51
Black, John, 125
Black Hawk War, 20, 24, 49, 76
Blackstone, Sir William, 16–17, 20, 26,

30, 34, 37, 44, 58–59, 75, 81, 87, 106, 110, 112, 164, 175
Blair, Montgomery, 170
Blane, George, 71
Bledsoe, Albert, 49
Boggs, Henry, 114
Bohen, Larry, 113
Boorstin, Daniel, 16
Booth, John Wilkes, 173
Bosley, Walter, 109
Bradford, Reuben, 77
Brewer, Thomas, 111
Brown, Sam, 111
Brown, Welcome P., 6
Browning, Andrew, 159
Bryan, Nicholas, 62
Buckles, John, 84, 128
Buckner, Aylett, 81
Bullock, Maria, 150
Bunn, Jacob, 78
Burr, Nancy, 150
Burr, Saban, 150
Butler, Gold, 79
Butler, William, 21, 77, 99

Cabiness, Ethan T., 33
Caldwell, George, 135
Caldwell, Laura, 135
Caldwell, John, 124
Campbell, David B., 49, 150
Cannon, Henry, 61–62
Capole, R. T., 6
Carothers, William, 71
Carter, Washington, 80
"case law" method, 175
cases: *Abrams v. Abrams* (1856), 145; *Alexander v. Parrish* (1851), 63; *Blankenship v. McGenty* (1836), 21; *Boggs v. Overton* (1844), 114; *Dred Scott v. Sanford* (1856), 148; *Hamilton v. Buckner* (1855), 81–82; *Hawks v. Lands* (1846), 80; *Hawthorn v. Wooldridge* (1837), 25; *People v. Barrett* (1842), 113; *People v. Kern* (1847), 148; *People v. Patterson* (1858), 147; *People v. Pond* (1845), 148; *People v. Scott* (1847), 148; *People v. Truett* (1838), 28; *Thomas v. Wright* (1846), 103; *Thompson v. Crane* (1858), 71–72; *Tuthill v. Tuthill* (1850), 6
Cassedy, George, 105
Charles, Andrew, 111
Chase, Salmon, 20
"Chicken Bone" case, 104, 142
Chitty, Joseph, 17
Church, Leman, 42
Clark, Charles J., 19
Clarkson, John, 134
Clarkson, Nancy, 134
Clay, Henry, 156, 165
Clinton, DeWitt, 84, 89
Close, John, Jr., 19
Colson, Isaac, 19
Colson, Jane, 19
Colton, Wells, 114
Columbus Machine Manufacturing Co., 67
Combs, Allen, 60
Connelly, John, 123
contract cases, 80–81, 83, 148, 159
Cosby, Aaron, 66
Courtney, Edward S., 106
Cox, James, 19
Cox, Jesse, 60
Cox, Nancy, 19
Crafts, William, 157
Crane, Elisha, 71–72
Craw, Henry A., 64
criminal law, 36, 106–19
Crittenden, John J., 20
Crittenden, Robert, 20
Cutler, Amos, 78

Dane, Nathan, 19
Danielle, John, 125
Danielle, Margaret, 125

Darrow, Clarence, 10

Davis, David, 47, 49–52, 105, 112, 114, 140, 142, 163, 165, 174

Davis, Jefferson, xii, 14

Davis, Joseph, 14

Davis, Levi, 26

Davis, Nathaniel Hart, 175

Davis, Oliver L., 43

Dean, William, 62

debt: Blackstone and, 58–59; collection and Lincoln's practice, 17, 59–75, 78, 79–80, 124, 155–59, 174; "confessing judgment," 61, 66, 77; and creditors, 61–63, 70, 128, 145, 156–57; and debtors, 61, 70–71, 76–77, 128, 144, 156–57; Lincoln's private life and, 54–56, 162; "set off," 63, 80; social context of, 56–58; and women, 128–29; writ of, 62

Democratic Party, 9, 28, 63–64, 84, 90, 116, 169, 170

Dennis, Rachel, 150

Denton, Richard, 134

Dickey, Theophilus Lyle, 49

DiLorenzo, Thomas, 148

divorce, 6, 61, 89, 133–36, 145, 162, 163

Donner Party, 99–100, 106

Douglas, Stephen, 5, 11, 12, 26, 72–73, 97, 147, 152

dower cases, 124–25

Doyle, Maurice, 77

Duff, John, 141–42

Dugger, Jefferson, 82

Duhamel, Desiree, 134

Duhamel, Edmund, 134

Dummer, Henry, 24–26

Dunlap, James, 104

Early, Jacob, 28, 115–16

Eastep, James, 19

Eastham, Marvelous, 126

Eddy, Jabish, 81–82

Eddy, Joseph, 81–82

Edmunds, Alexander, 89–90, 112

Edwards, Ambrose, 130–31

Edwards, Elizabeth, 137–39, 140

Edwards, Ninian, 120, 137–39, 140

Edwards, Tabitha, 130–31

Edwards, Thomas, 19

Effie Afton (Rock Island Bridge) case, 95–97, 142, 144, 151

Eighth Judicial Circuit (Illinois), 45–52, 84, 140, 142, 174

Elkin, Garrett, 61

Ellett, Henry T., 42

Ellsworth, Elmer, 122

Emancipation Proclamation, 152, 167, 169

Enos, Pascal, 126

Enslow, David, 135, 163

Enslow, Hetty, 135

Fancher, Emily, 129–30

Ferguson, Alexander, 19

Ferrin, Samuel, 158

Ficklin, Orlando, 105

Field, Roswell, 14

Finn, William, 124

Fithian, William, 105, 145

Fletcher, Nathan, 150

Florville, William ("Billy the Barber"), 149

Fogg, Godfrey, Sr., 68

Fonda, Henry, 3

Foote, Henry S., 41, 69, 143

Ford, Timothy, 143

Foster, Joseph, 146

Fourteenth Judicial Circuit (Illinois), 45, 46

Fraim, William, 123

Friedlander, Lewis, 98, 160

Friedman, Lawrence M., 106

Frost, William, 113–14

Gaillard, Theodore, 143

Gambrell, James, 64

Gardner, Littleton, 60
Garfield, James, 166
Gibson, Isaac, 93
Gilbert, John, 60, 67
Gill, Thomas, 81
Gillenwaters, Wesley, 113–14
Gillespie, Joseph, 141
Glynn, Michael, 126
Godbey, Russell, 9–10, 12, 14, 16, 22, 32
Goddin, Archibald, 62, 66
Goings, Josephus, 158
gold rush, California, 79, 124, 135
Gollogher, Daniel, 130
Goodman, Solomon, 135
Goodrich, Chris, 10
Goodwin, Doris Kearns, 171
Graham, Amanda, 135
Graham, John, 135
Grant, John N., 60
Grant, Ulysses S., 30, 121, 168
Gray, John W., 81
Gray, Moses, 109
Great Western Railroad, 160
Green, Bowling, 15, 19
Greene, William, 54–55, 59
Greer, William, 71
Gridley, Asahel, 49, 50, 114, 142
Gridley, Jeremiah, 13
Griffin, Jesse, 65
Grundy, Felix, 106

Hagood, Johnson, 14
Hamilton, Lorenzo, 81–82, 93–94, 98
Hamilton, Mark, 158
Hand, John P., 140
Hanks, Dennis, 15
Hannegan, Edward, 105
Hardin, Henry, 60
Harding, George, 88
Harrison, Asa, 71
Hart, John, 62
Harvard law school, 175
Hassen, William, 81

Hatch, Edward, 13
Hawks, Matthew, 79–80
Hawley, Gideon, 84
Hawthorn, James P., 25
Hay, John, 1, 168, 170
Hayes, Rutherford B., 11, 17
Henning, Fanny, 73
Henry, James D., 21
Henry, James Edward, 20
Herndon, William Henry, 29–31, 37, 38, 39, 40, 46, 47, 68, 72, 74, 75, 76, 79, 88, 98, 101–3, 111, 123, 133, 134, 138–40, 147, 150, 151, 163, 173, 174
Hildreth, Thomas, 81
Hill, William, 134–35
Hiltibran, David, 109
Hitchcock, Roland, 143
Hoar, Ebenezer, 14
Hoffman's Row, 21, 26, 36
Hofstadter, Richard, 152
Holley, John, 14
Holt, Joseph, 121
Hood, Archibald, 81
Hook, Sarah, 134
Hooker, John, 147
House, Fielding, 158
Howey, James, 135
Howey, Susan, 135

Illinois Central Railroad, 94–98, 140, 146
insurance companies, 91
Irwin, Hugh, 125

Jackson, Andrew, 135
Jackson, Harriet, 135
Jacobus, Mary Ann, 129
James, Levi, 145
Jefferson, Thomas, 17
Johns, Edmund, 162
Johnson, David, 143
Johnson, Reverdy, 88
Johnson, Thomas, 114

Johnson, Willis, 89
Jones, Nathan, 163

Keeling, Hayden, 79
Keeling, Lewis, 79
Keeling, Singleton, 124
Kent, James, 17, 18–19
Kirk, William, 126
Kitchell, Elizabeth, 129
Kitchell, Milden, 129
Knight, Eliphalet, 80
Kyle, Joseph, 135

Lamon, Ward Hill, 48–49, 120–21, 140, 150, 163, 165, 174
land speculation, 75, 76, 78, 79, 80
Lands, Samuel, 79
Langdell, Christopher, 175
law books: *A Treatise on Pleading and Parties to Action* (Chitty), 17–18, 36, 44, 62, 93; *Commentaries on American Law* (Kent), 19; *Commentaries on the Laws of England* (Blackstone), 16–17, 34, 37, 44, 58–59, 81, 87, 110, 112, 164, 175; *Digest of the Laws of Evidence in Civil and Criminal Cases* (Swift), 19; *Equity Jurisprudence* (Story), 18, 37; *General Abridgment and Digest of American Laws* (Dane), 19; *Revised Statutes of Illinois,* 18, 37; *Treatise on Bills of Exchange and Promissory Notes* (Swift), 19
Lawrence, George, 49
Lawson, Hugh, 143
lawyers: circuit system, and, 44, 45; criminal clients and, 109–10; law school, 10, 175; legal education, 15–19, 175; and "legal self," 71, 109–10; and the Market Revolution, 61; professionalism, 34–36, 41–42, 69, 143–44, 161, 162; in Springfield, Illinois, 33 and trials, 101–2
Lewis, Thomas, 89

Lincoln, Abraham: ambition, 12–13, 123, 145, 165; appearance in court, 104–6; circuit riding, 44–53, 163, 165, 174–75; competitiveness, 12, 145; courtroom, behavior in, 40–43, 101–6, 118; and criminal law, 106–19, 123, 126–27; and death, 121–27; distance from clients and other lawyers, 7, 51–53, 69–70, 72–74, 83, 110–11, 125–26, 137, 161–65, 170–72; economic beliefs, 83–84, 86, 156; education, 13–14; humor of, 39–40, 49–50, 104, 128, 129, 157; and internal improvements, 83–87, 156; as judge, 51, 174; and juries, 66, 72, 84, 88, 96–97, 101–6, 116–19, 145, 147, 150; law offices of, 26, 36–40, 47, 70, 108, 133, 150, 163, 165, 173; lawyer's ethics, 2, 12; legal education of, 9–10, 16–20; legal fees, 5, 61, 64, 98; and the Market Revolution, 61, 98, 155–60; myths about law practice of, 2–3, 43, 52, 139–42, 147–54; "Notes for a Law Lecture," 1–2, 4, 160–61; partners, law, 23–32; as president, 120–21, 166–72; professionalism, 43–45, 146; and race, 130–31, 147–49, 152, 167, 169, 171; and railroads, 91–98, 159–61; reasons for becoming a lawyer, 11–20; relationships with other lawyers, 21, 43–44; settlements out of court, 67, 145, 158, 160–61; speaking skills and the law, 4–5, 15, 101–5; and women, 121, 124–25, 128–39, 165
Lincoln, Edward (son), 122, 126–27
Lincoln, Mary Todd, 27, 30, 38–39, 47, 73, 102, 127–28, 138–39, 165, 173–74
Lincoln, Robert (son), 173, 175
Lincoln, Tad (son), 173
Lincoln, Thomas (father), 12, 14
Lincoln, Willie (son), 127
Linder, Usher, 29, 42, 45, 46, 145
Lockwood, Samuel D., 42

Loe, Moses, 109
Logan, Stephen T., 20, 25–29, 31, 36, 46, 60, 65, 135, 142, 150, 163
Lomax, William, 42
Louthan, James, 126
Loutzenhiser, Charles, 124
Loutzenhiser, Henry, 124
Lowery, Lamb and Company, 33
Lukins, Peter, 19

MacLeish, Archibald, 11
Madux, John, 162
Maloney, Thomas, 158
malpractice, medical, 104
Manny, John H., 88
Market Revolution, 56–58, 71, 74, 77, 155–60
Marsh, Matthew, 19
Marshall, John, 12, 141, 144
Marshall, Sally, 19
Martin, Matthew, 124
Martin, Nancy, 130
Martin, William D., 41, 93
masculinity, 11, 38, 40–41, 45, 51–53, 165
Matson, Robert, 148
Matson slave case, 148–49
Mattlen, James, 61
Mayall, Napoleon, 163
Mayer, Daniel, 143
McCollom, George W., 65
McCormick, Cyrus, 88
McCormick Reaper case, 88–89, 168
McDonald, Nancy, 129
McDonald, William, 129
McGee, Joseph, 81
McHenry, H. T., 67
McNutt, Alexander G., 68
McRady, John, 143
mechanic's liens, 67, 156
Metzker, James, 116–19
Miller, Stephen D., 41
Moffett, John, 89
Moore, Isaac, 111

Morgan, John, 127
Morgan, Patrick, 112
Morris, Chester, 111
murder, 61, 115–19, 123, 126–27

Nance, Thomas, 19
Neely, Mark E., Jr., ix
New Salem, Illinois, 9, 13, 15, 16, 19, 26, 51, 54, 59, 96, 117, 136
Nibs, William, 45
Nicolay, John, 1
Norris, James, 116–17
Northwest Ordnance (1787), 148, 149

Oakleaf, Joseph Benjamin, 140
Oliver B. Tweedy and Co., 82
O'Neal, John Belton, 13–14
Overton, Henry, 114
Owen, Wilson, 158

Packard, Major, 150
Pantier, John, 126
Parks, Samuel, 147
partnerships, business, 78–83, 124, 159
partnerships, law, 24–27
patent cases, 87–91
Patterson, Allen, 113
Patterson, Angus, 13, 16
Patterson, Maria, 130
Peter, Zachariah, 124
Petigru, James L., 41
Phelps, C. C., 33
Phelps, Dick H., 81
Philbrick, Laura, 136
Philbrick, Samuel, 136
Pigeon Creek, Indiana, 15
Pike, Albert, 17
Plumer, William, 16
Plummer, Nancy, 163
Plummer, William, 163
Pope, Rufus, 126
Potts, Thomas D., 65–66
Pratt, Augustus, 150

Prettyman, Benjamin S., 49
probate cases, 80, 123–24
Purvance, Robert, 71

Radford, Reuben, 55
Rague, John F., 33
railroads, 78, 91–98, 146, 159–61, 174–75
Ralston, Alexander, 60, 67
"Reaper" Case, 88
Reed, James Frazier, 76–77, 93–94, 98, 99–100, 106
Republican Party, 47, 90, 151, 156, 165–66, 169, 170
Richardson, John Smith, 143
Richmond, Braddock, 62, 66
Ricketts, William, 158
Ritter, John, 19
riverboats, 95–98
Robert McCart and Sons, 91
Robinson, John, 79
Rockhill and Co., 79
Rockwell, Norman, 3
Rowan, John, 42
Ryan, Michael, 131

Sandburg, Carl, xi, 146
Sargeant, John, 57
Schaack, Peter van, 23
scire facias proceeding, 62
Scott, Dred, 14
Second Confiscation Act (1862), 152, 166–67
seduction, 132
Selby, Paul, 104
Sellers, Charles, 160
Seward, William, 13, 30, 143
Shakespeare, William, 37, 171, 175
Shelledy, Garland B., 161
Sherman, William Tecumseh, 168
Sherwood, Thomas, 42
Shields, James, 72
Simon, Keating Lewis, 42

Sinclair, John, 134
Sinclair, Lucy, 134
Singleton, William, 79
Skinner, Permelia, 128
slander, 105, 113–14, 129–31
Smith, Lyle, 13
Smith, Thomas P., 62
Snyder, John, 100
Spear, David, 66, 78
Spear, Isaac, 78
Speed, Joshua, 30, 73
Springfield, Illinois, 1, 15, 21, 24, 26, 30, 33, 36–37, 46, 70, 72, 76, 78, 99, 117, 126–27, 128, 135, 138, 139, 156, 157, 158, 159, 173
Stanton, Edwin M., 30, 88, 168
Stapp. Milton, 150
St. Clair, H. C., 79
Steiner, Mark, 113, 129
Story, Joseph, 18
Strother, Ann, 81
Strother, R. T., 82
Stuart, John T., 23–29, 31, 36, 46, 48, 49, 81, 84, 92, 111
Supreme Court (Illinois state), 60, 81, 82, 89, 90, 98, 117, 131, 132, 144, 148
Supreme Court (United States), 84, 120, 144, 167, 174
Swett, Leonard, 43, 48, 49, 52, 119–21, 139, 147, 163, 165, 174
Swift, Zepheniah, 19

Tarbell, Ida, 3, 5
Taylor, Zachary, 1, 165
Thayer, Asahel, 157
Thayer, Joseph, 157
Thayer, Martin, 157
Thomas, James, 103
Thomas, Rebecca, 103
Thompson, David, 112
Thompson, Frank, 71–72
Tinsley Building, 36, 76, 77
Tocqueville, Alexis de, 16, 77, 83, 94

Trailor, Archibald, 126
Trent, Alexander, 19
Trotter, George, 126
Truett, Henry, 28, 115–16
Turner, Thomas J., 126
Turney, Benjamin, 150
Tuthill, Gershom, 6
Tuthill, Sophia, 6

Underwood, William, 130

VanBergen, Peter, 55–56, 59, 79
Van de Velde, James Oliver (Bishop), 123
vi et armis, writ of, 112
Voorhees, Daniel Wolsey, 49, 106

Waddell, Rebecca, 135
Waddell, Squire, 135
Walker, Isaac, 145
Walker, William, 117–18
Ward, W. H., 22
Watkins, William, 55

Watson, Peter, 88
Way, John, 123
Weaver, Bill, 109
Webber, Richard H., 143
Webster, Daniel, 10–11, 13, 42
Weik, Jesse, 31, 139
Wernwang, William, 125
Whig Party, 1, 9–10, 25, 26, 30, 47, 63, 71, 84, 87, 88, 90, 156, 166, 175
Whitney, Henry C., 43, 46, 48–49, 52, 114–15, 128, 139, 140, 146, 150, 165, 174
Wilbourn, John, 60
Williams, Jacob, 162
Wilmet, William H., 36
Woldman, Alfred, 141, 149
Woodworth, Asahel, 60
Wooldridge, David, 25
Wright, Erastus, 103
writs, legal, 62–63, 66

Young, Matthew, 19
Young, William P., 84–85

BRIAN DIRCK is associate professor of history at Anderson University in Anderson, Indiana. He is the author of *Lincoln and Davis: Imagining America, 1809–1865,* and numerous other books and articles on Abraham Lincoln and the Civil War.

The University of Illinois Press
is a founding member of the
Association of American University Presses.

Composed in 10/13.25 ITC Cheltenham
with Parkinson Condensed display
by Type One, LLC
for the University of Illinois Press
Designed by Dennis Roberts
Manufactured by Thomson-Shore, Inc.

University of Illinois Press
1325 South Oak Street
Champaign, IL 61820-6903
www.press.uillinois.edu